ROULTEDGE LIBRARY EDITIONS: CHRISTIANITY

Volume 13

CHRISTIANS AND CHRISTIANITY IN INDIA AND PAKISTAN

CHRISTIANS AND CHRISTIANITY IN INDIA AND PAKISTAN

A General Survey of the Progress of Christianity in India from Apostolic Times to the Present Day

P. THOMAS

Taylor & Francis Group

LONDON AND NEW YORK

This edition first published in 2021
by Routledge
4 Park Square, Milton Park, Abingdon, Oxon OX14 4RN
605 Third Avenue, New York, NY 10017

Routledge is an imprint of the Taylor & Francis Group, an informa business

First published 1954 Allen & Unwin. Copyright 1954 P. Thomas

All rights reserved. No part of this book may be reprinted or reproduced or utilised in any form or by any electronic, mechanical, or other means, now known or hereafter invented, including photocopying and recording, or in any information storage or retrieval system, without permission in writing from the publishers.

Trademark notice: Product or corporate names may be trademarks or registered trademarks, and are used only for identification and explanation without intent to infringe.

British Library Cataloguing in Publication Data
A catalogue record for this book is available from the British Library

ISBN: 978-0-367-62307-4 (Set)
ISBN: 978-1-003-10879-5 (Set) (ebk)
ISBN: 978-0-367-63136-9 (Volume 13) (hbk)
ISBN: 978-1-003-11231-0 (Volume 13) (ebk)

Publisher's Note
The publisher has gone to great lengths to ensure the quality of this reprint but points out that some imperfections in the original copies may be apparent.

Disclaimer
The publisher has made every effort to trace copyright holders and would welcome correspondence from those they have been unable to trace.

I ANGEL

Christian influence is clearly discernible in this fourth-century terracotta work.

(*Peshawar Museum*)

CHRISTIANS
AND CHRISTIANITY
IN INDIA
AND PAKISTAN

A GENERAL SURVEY OF THE PROGRESS
OF CHRISTIANITY IN INDIA
FROM APOSTOLIC TIMES TO THE PRESENT DAY

BY

P. THOMAS

LONDON
GEORGE ALLEN & UNWIN LTD
RUSKIN HOUSE · MUSEUM STREET

First published in 1954

This book is copyright under the Berne Convention. Apart from any fair dealing for the purposes of private study, research, criticism or review, as permitted under the Copyright Act, 1911, no portion may be reproduced by any process without written permission. Enquiry should be made to the publisher.

*Printed in Great Britain
in 12pt. Bembo type
by C. Tinling & Co., Ltd.,
Liverpool, London and Prescot*

TO MY WIFE

PREFACE

Many friends, both Christian and non-Christian, have pointed out to me the need for a book giving a connected account of Christianity in India from the time of the Apostle Thomas, who preached the Gospel in India, to the present day. Existing books, written by Europeans or Americans mainly, are inclined to treat the subject from a denominational point of view and usually skip over the fourteen centuries that intervened between the advent of the Apostle in India and the arrival of the Portuguese; wherever efforts had been made by them to touch upon this period of Indian Christian history, the authors had shown marked antipathy towards Indian traditions, especially of Kerala, where the Church the Apostle founded has flourished to the present day. This is probably due to the authors' want of familiarity with the traditions of the South.

Born and brought up in a family of Syrian Christians in Malabar tracing their origin to the Apostle Thomas, I have had opportunities of studying the vital traditions of South India which many others had not. Hence in this work my main effort has been to put the history of Indian Christianity in its correct perspective.

The emphasis, again, is on the greater Church of Christ. The House of Many Mansions has been built by a large number of workers, and the labour of none is decried.

The friends who have encouraged me to write this book are too many to be mentioned here individually. I must, however, record my gratitude to Dr. John Matthai who, amidst his multifarious preoccupations, was kind enough to go through the manuscript and offer valuable suggestions.

THE AUTHOR

CONTENTS

CHAPTER		PAGE
I	India in the First Century of the Christian Era	1
II	The Apostles of India	12
III	The early Malabar Church	29
IV	The coming of the Portuguese and the Mission of St. Francis Xavier	44
V	Robert de Nobili, the Roman Brahmin and the Madura Mission	63
VI	The Syrians and the Portuguese	76
VII	Christianity in Mogul India	105
VIII	Begum Zebunissa Joanna Samru, the Christian Princess of Sardhana	126
IX	Early Protestant Missions	150
X	Crusade on the Naboabs	168
XI	Progress of Christianity under the British	185
XII	The Influence of Christianity on Hinduism	204
XIII	Some Christian Communities of the West Coast	224
XIV	Christianity in Modern India	240
	Bibliography	245
	Index	246

ILLUSTRATIONS

1. Angel — *frontispiece*
2. Thomas Clears His Doubt — *facing page* 52
3. St. Francis Xavier — 53
4. Akbar Meeting the First Jesuit Mission — 116
5. De Nobili and a Disciple — 116
6. A Mogul Painting of the Assault on Hugli — 117
7. St. Thomas Mount, Mylapore — 180
8. St. John's College, Sardhana — 180
9. St. Thomas Cathedral, Mylapore — 181
10. Christian Medical College Hospital, Vellore — 181

CHAPTER I

INDIA IN THE FIRST CENTURY OF THE CHRISTIAN ERA

THE first century of the Christian era is one of those periods in Indian history of which little is known. Events of importance, to be sure, did happen during this period also, but we have no record of them due to the general indifference of ancient Indian writers to historical subjects. Ancient Indians had taken a lively interest in practically every field of human activity and have left us voluminous works on various subjects but not one book of pure history. The merely mundane did not interest them, and till the time of the Muslim conquest the history of India is largely a matter of conjecture, the main sources of information being stray accounts left by foreigners and indigenous religious literature.

Before the beginning of the Christian era, the vast Mauryan empire, built by Chandragupta and expanded and consolidated by his grandson Asoka, had shown signs of disintegration. Asoka's successors did not possess the wisdom and strength of mind that distinguished this emperor or probably they took the doctrines of Buddhism too seriously to be good rulers; whatever the cause, the central authority weakened and the numerous potentates who owed reluctant allegiance to Magadha threw off the yoke and declared their independence. The Central Asian hordes ever on the prowl for weak spots in the Indian empire burst in through the Khyber and Bolan to plunder, pillage and carve out kingdoms for themselves. They overran the Greek kingdom of Bactria, entered the Punjab and fanned out north and south. The influence of these Scythian nomads, known in Hindu legend as the Sakas, extended from Kashmir to Western India. The Kushans, the northern branch of the Sakas, settled down in Kashmir and the Punjab, accepted Buddhism and built a flourishing empire.

Central India too claimed the attention of the Sakas. Here the powerful kingdom of Ujjain successfully resisted their expansion for some time, but in the first century of the Christian era the kingdom fell. The Saka era which begins in 78 A.D. in all probability marks the overthrow of Ujjain by the Sakas and the coronation of their emperor.

In the fourth and fifth decades of the first century of the Christian era, Gundaphoros was the most important king in North-Western India. The extent of his dominion is not known but his influence was felt in Parthia and Western India. His name was well known in Syria and the Mediterranean regions of Asia and Africa, and it was to his kingdom that Apostle Thomas came to preach Christ.

Amidst all the wars and turmoil of continuous Saka invasions, there was tremendous religious activity in India, especially among the Buddhists. They preached the Law to the oppressed and oppressors alike and converted many Saka chiefs and kings to Buddhism. Their conversion paved the way for missionary activities in their homeland in Central Asia, and the barbarous nomads of these regions were brought under the softening influence of Buddhism.

The Sakas had no great culture of their own to boast of and generally accepted the religion and culture of the peoples they conquered. The Northerners accepted the Hellenized form of Buddhism prevalent in Gandhara and the Land of the Five Rivers, and the Southerners Jainism and Hinduism. They were incorporated in the social scheme of India and soon lost their individuality as a separate nation.

While North India was thus subject to invasions by barbarous nomads from Central Asia, conflicts of the South were of a less severe nature. In the Deccan ruled the powerful Andhras who stood as a barrier between the Sakas and kingdoms of South India. There were certainly wars between the monarchs of South Indian kingdoms, but these wars were between nations that followed the same religion and code of ethics and recognized the need for protecting the civil population whether of their own kingdom or of the enemy. Nor are we correct in saying that the wars were between nations; the wars were between kings and their soldiers and the duty of the civil population was merely to watch the progress of battle and pay their homage to the victor. These ancient notions, religiously followed in South India, made wars in these regions more of a diversion for kings and soldiers than a misfortune to the people. Till Tippu Sultan, late in the eighteenth century, in imitation of the northern vandals indulged in wholesale massacre and enslavement of civil population and destruction of shrines, conflicts among South Indian Hindu kings had not seriously disrupted the economy of village life, the mainstay of every kingdom in ancient India. South India never had a Mihiragula or Mahmud of Ghazni. Protected by the Vindhyas on the north and the sea on the other sides, the country had enjoyed practical immunity from the marauding hordes of Central Asia who spent themselves up on the plains of the Punjab or Hindustan. It was due to this freedom from fear of foreign invasion that South Indians were able to remain in the ancient world an industrious, peace-loving, prosperous race who had cultivated extensive commercial relations with the outside world. The swarthy sons of the South were excellent traders and seamen and they carried the civilisation and wares of their land to the islands of the Southern Ocean and to the ports of distant lands.

In the beginning of the Christian era, South India was divided into three principal kingdoms: The Chera, the Pandyan and the Chola. The Chera kingdom corresponded to present Kerala excluding the extreme south, the Chola territory lay on the east coast from the mouth of the Krishna to the present Ramnad district, and between the two was the powerful Pandyan kingdom with its capital at Madura. These were the kingdoms of the three crowned kings, but owing nominal allegiance to one or other of these were a number of chieftains whose loyalty depended upon the strength of the suzerain to enforce it.

The country was fairly well governed though the kings were perpetually watching one another, and petty jealousies and lust for power often made war inevitable. The highways of internal trade were kept safe, as the interest of trade was a sacred trust to kings. Impaling was the common form of punishment for highway robbery. Justice was fairly well administered according to the standards of the time. In India, it is well to remember, despotism never degenerated into the depths it did in the Roman world where the emperor recognized no power above him either in heaven or on earth. The Roman Emperor was himself a god. Indian kings were only deputies or 'portions' of gods and there were fearless Brahmins who told recalcitrant despots in open assemblies what they should and should not do.

In the ancient world commercial and cultural intercourse between nations was more free than in the middle ages. The religious fanaticism that marred history in the dark ages had not yet made nations exclusive and arrogant. The ancients kept an open mind in religious matters and were willing to learn and to teach. The obstacles that stood in the way of cultural contact between nations in those days were mainly those of nature and not of man: great distances, impassable mountains, wild deserts and stormy seas. But the profits of trade made men brave these dangers and commercial enterprise was in no small measure responsible for the advancement of civilization.

Alexander's conquests opened up contact between North India and the Mediterranean region. Many of the myths Herodotus had woven round the fabulous India from hearsay were exploded by the scribes of Alexander who wrote from observation. Alexander, during his lifetime, gave a semblance of unity to his vast and unwieldy conquests, but on his death the loosely held structure tottered and tumbled down. The ideals of cultural and commercial contacts, however, continued. Greek and Indian artists worked side by side in the Hellenized kingdom of Gandhara. Regular envoys were sent by Greek kings to Indian courts, matrimonial alliances between Eastern and Western princes became common, and caravans laden with merchandise passed up and down the Khyber for trading centres from the Bay of Bengal to the Black Sea.

More important than the overland route was the sea route by which trade was carried on between India and the West. In the beginning of the Christian era navigation between India and the Red Sea was difficult and dilatory; vessels usually sailed from the ports of Malabar hugging the coast up the Indian Ocean, round Arabia to the Red Sea and discharged the cargo at Bernice the Egyptian port from where it was transported by caravan to Alexandria and other Mediterranean centres. The cargo meant for Syria and Asia Minor was discharged at the ports of the Persian Gulf.

This was a long and tedious voyage fraught with many dangers and interminable delays, but still the profits were good and the risks worth taking. And then the Egyptian mariner Hippaulus revolutionized maritime trade by his discovery of the regularity of the monsoon. By patient observation and study he found out that the wind blew in a westerly direction in the Indian Ocean for half the year and in an easterly direction during the other half. He wished to put his theories to the test, and trusting to the west wind the bold mariner plunged into the unknown sea and made straight for India (a voyage in its daring comparable to that of Columbus) and in the surprisingly short period of forty days reached India. Here he waited for the change in the direction of wind and when the wind started blowing from the east he sailed back to Bernice.

This epoch making voyage opened up unforeseen possibilities for trade. Fleets laden with costly cargo began to sail regularly between Bernice and Indian ports, and the price of Indian luxuries was considerably reduced in the Mediterranean cities where even the common folk could afford them. Rome was the most important market for Indian goods at the time and the fashionable ladies of the Imperial City vied with one another for the possession of pearls and other precious goods from India. The craze for Indian luxuries brought forth some bitter comments from the watchdogs of the Empire. Pliny complained that India drained

Rome annually to the extent of 55,000,000 sesterces* (about £500,000) and the feminine fashions were in no small measure responsible for this huge drain. Petronius expressed horror at the immodesty of ladies of fashion who went about clad in 'webs of woven wind' as he termed the muslin imported from India.

The principal ports of India at the time were Barygaza (Broach) at the mouth of the Narbadda, Kalyana in Northern Konkan, Tindis near modern Mangalore, Musiris (Muyiri Kotta, Malayalam, Musiri, Tamil; modern Cranganoor) and Nelcynda or Nirkunram farther south in the Pandyan kingdom. The main port of the Cholas on the east coast was Puhar or Kaveripatanam on the mouth of the Kaveri. The Cholas were a maritime people and they were mainly responsible for carrying Indian religion, culture and art to Indonesia.

Of the ports on the west coast, the most important was Musiris. The Chera king had his capital at Tiruvanchikkulam not far from the harbour. The main exports of Musiris were pearls, precious stones of all kinds, ivory, silk in the web, Malabathrum, spices and the far famed pepper of Malabar.†

* "Our ladies glory in having pearls suspended from their fingers, or two or three of them dangling from their ears, delighted even with the rattling of pearls as they knock against each other; and now, at the present day, the poorer classes are even affecting them as people are in the habit of saying that 'a pearl worn by a woman in public is as good as a lictor walking before her'. Nay even more than this, they put them on their feet, and that not only on the laces of their sandals but all over the shoes; it is not enough to wear pearls, but they must tread upon them, and walk with them under foot as well." Again, "I once saw Lollia Paulina, the wife of the Emperor Caius—it was not any public festival or any solemn ceremonial, but only at an ordinary betrothal entertainment—covered with emeralds and pearls, which shone in alternate layers upon her head, in her hair, in her wreaths, in her ears, upon her neck, in her bracelets and on her fingers, and the value of which amounted in all to 40,000,000 sesterces; indeed she was prepared at once to prove the fact by showing the receipts and acquaintances." Pliny. "This," moralizes the ancient, "is the price we pay for our luxuries and our women."

† It is interesting to speculate on the part the humble pepper creeper of Malabar has played in shaping world history. As is well known Columbus was on the look out for pepper when he stumbled on America. It was pepper that brought Vasco da Gama to Malabar; the subsequent interest the nations

The flourishing trade between Rome and South India could not be carried on without close contact between the countries and regular diplomatic relations. Indian kings had trade agents in Bernice, Alexandria and Rome, and Roman Emperors in Indian ports and in Madura. On the occasion of the ascension of Augustus Caesar to the throne, the Pandyan king is known to have sent an embassy to congratulate the emperor. Two Roman cohorts were stationed in Musiris to look after the interests of Roman nationals and to keep the coast clear of the pirates that infested the Malabar coast at the time. Musiris had a Roman temple. The Pandyan kings, to add to their pomp, often kept Roman mercenaries as bodyguards and Tamil literature speaks of these strange soldiers as 'dumb Mlecchhas, with their long coats and armours, and their murderous souls, who might be seen acting as sentries at the palace gates.' Roman coins were legal tender in the ports and in Madura.

Egyptians had no monopoly of the Indian trade. Side by side with the Egyptians traded Arabs, Syrians and Persians whose fleets too came to Indian ports. Nor did Indians always wait for the foreigners to come to them. The medieval taboo prohibiting sea voyages was not yet in force; if it already existed it was mainly confined to the Aryans, and Dravidians did not attach much importance to it. South Indians were good shipbuilders and seamen and wealthy traders outfitted sizable fleets of merchantmen and traded with the East and West. In Alexandria, the great emporium of the Roman Empire, Dravidian traders were a familiar sight. A strange story is related of a lone Indian sailor found in a ship by the guards of the coast of the Red Sea and produced in the court of the Egyptian monarch Euergetes (2nd century B.C.). He had sailed from India, and in the voyage his shipmates had perished.

The Baveru Jataka bears further testimony to the fact that ancient Indians did not fight shy of navigating the ocean.

---

of Western Europe took in Indian affairs and its far reaching effect on world civilisation are too well known to deserve mention here.

The Chera kingdom is of particular interest to us. It was here that Apostle Thomas founded a Church which has survived the vicissitudes of centuries and has come down to us with increased strength and vitality.

In the rich mythology of the Hindus the origin of Chera or Kerala is attributed to a miracle performed by the Brahmin warrior Parasurama. Parasurama is fabled to have destroyed the whole race of Kshatriyas because of the arrogance of this race and the cold-bloodedmurder of his father by one of them. After, the genocide Parasurama repented of his rashness that led to country-wide misery and in expiation wished to bestow a suitable gift on Brahmins. With this in view he ascended a peak at the northern extremity of the Western Ghats and threw his powerful battle-axe southwards into the ocean. The axe fell at Cape Comorin and a strip of land emerged from the sea which he named Chera and gave to Brahmins as a gift.

Shorn of its mythical embellishments, the account indicates that Parasurama conquered the land and divided it among his Brahmin followers. The rulers of Kerala at that time were Nayars who were subjected to the Nambudiris as the Brahmin followers of Parasurama were called. The Nayars were treated well and they formed the martial class of Malabar while the Nambudiris remained the virtual rulers and sacerdotal hierarchy. Both the communities lived on cordial terms. While the Nambudiris lived on rent, the Nayars constituted the body of regular fighters and generals, and civil servants. The rest of the population were farmers, artisans and aborigines who lived in subjection to the Nambudiris and Nayars. The latter, though nominally Sudras, had, for all practical purposes the status of Kshatriyas, the soldier caste, second only to Brahmins. This social system has existed in Malabar from the very dawn of its history to the present day.

In the beginning of the Christian era the Chera kingdom was an independent entity ruled by a king whose titular name was Perumal (literally the Great One). His powers were considerably limited by the assemblies of Nambudiris and Nayar nobles without whose concurrence he could do little. The state religion was Hinduism and Vedic ritual was strictly followed by the Nambudiris. Buddhism had been preached in the Chera kingdom and Asoka in his edicts claimed that Keralaputra was conversant with the Sacred Law and hospitals for the sick had been established in his kingdom on Buddhist models. But it is doubtful if the Law had any influence on the king or his people. There is, however, a legend which indicates that a Perumal became apostate to a 'Bauddha* faith' and had to abdicate. The date of this Perumal is unknown and the authenticity of the legend is still to be proved, the Muslims claiming that he was apostate to Islam and died in Mecca whereas the Christians maintain that he embraced Christianity and died at Mylapore to which place he repaired after his abdication.

Anyway, at the time of the visit of St. Thomas the Nambudiris were the religious dictators of Malabar and the final authorities on social codes. Notions of caste were stretched to the extreme and Malabar, till recently, was the most caste-ridden country in India. Distance between man and man was rigidly measured; the plan of houses members of each caste were entitled to construct was laid down with meticulous care; the way of dressing hair, wearing clothes etc. were given in detail; the manner of speech and gestures during conversation and right of way when members of different castes met were all dealt with in the elaborate caste code of Malabar; and any lapse was punished with exemplary severity and even death.

The distance a Nayar had to keep from a Nambudiri was arm's length. The artisan castes were untouchable to the Nayars and unapproachable by twenty-five paces to the Nambudiris. The Panchamas or aborigines were unapproachable by ten paces to the artisans, by twenty to the Nayars and by sixty to the Nambudiris. Some of the outcastes had to keep away from the Nayars and Nambudiris as far as individual notions of pollution dictated. And then there were the unlookables whose sight was pollution;

* On the rise of Buddhism the word 'Bauddha' became synonymous with 'heretical' among the Hindus and does not indicate merely Buddhism.

these naturally lived in the jungles feeding on edible roots and hunting lizards, and seldom ventured into villages.

This social system which appears so iniquitous to the moderns was accepted as heaven-ordained in Malabar and had worked quite smoothly in spite of obvious defects. No castes seemed to mind their own humiliation as long as there were some other castes for them to humiliate. The 'unlookables' had the birds and beasts of the jungle.

As the landed gentry of the land and keepers of the Vedas, the Nambudiris enjoyed powers and privileges which no other community on earth had enjoyed for so long in continuity. By a curious social system which permitted legal marriage only to the eldest son, the property of a Nambudiri family remained undivided from generation to generation, and from the time of Parasurama right down to the twentieth century the Nambudiri families and their property have come down practically intact.

The country was well governed by the Perumal. From the volume of trade that passed through Musiris it is clear that the waterways and roads by which the pepper and spices of the hinterland were transported to the port were kept clear of highway men. The lowlands of Malabar produce nothing of worth except coconuts; the pepper and spices are grown in the interior. The farmers enjoyed considerable security of person and property. Once his social superiority was conceded, the Brahmin could be exceptionally generous and well-meaning, and he often cashiered the king if the well-being of farmers and tradesmen suffered through oppression or neglect.

Musiris was a cosmopolitan port. Merchants of all nations were found there: Egyptians, Syrians, Arabs and Persians who came in their trading vessels with gold and implements of war for exchange with the produce of India; Chinese in their uncouth junks laden with bales of silk for exchange with Indian goods and the gold of the Westerners. Musiris was at that time the main transit emporium of trade between the West and Far East. Traders of all important nations had their settlements and factories at Musiris, as shipping was not regular and the cargo had to be stored awaiting the arrival of trading fleets. The ubiquitous Jew was already there, no one could say when and whence he came; but he had extensive trade connections and a high standing in the Perumal's court. It was, in fact, the Jewish settlement in Musiris that attracted St. Thomas to the port. Romans, as already mentioned, had a temple and two cohorts stationed in Musiris.

The Perumal was a liberal in religious matters. All his subjects had freedom of worship. Though officially a Hindu, Buddhists and Jains had full liberty to preach their doctrines. So long as caste rules were not violated, Hinduism did not care much what a man believed or which god he worshipped.

CHAPTER II

THE APOSTLES OF INDIA

THE origin of Christianity in India is traced to Thomas Didymus, the Apostle. While most of Jesus' disciples confined their activities to the Mediterranean region, Thomas chose as his field of labour the distant and little known East with its strange people and stranger gods. He first preached the Gospel in Parthia, then in North-Western India and came by sea to Malabar. According to the traditions of Malabar he landed in Musiris in the year A.D. 52.

The Apostle first addressed his message to the Jews of Malabar. The advent of the long awaited Messiah must have been welcome news to the sons of Israel living in Malabar in practical isolation. But it was not his own small community that interested the Apostle. Having got most of the Jews to accept his momentous message, Thomas boldly preached the Gospel to the people of Malabar, and the response was astonishing.

Compared to the Apostles who had converted the Roman world, Thomas had an extremely difficult task before him. The Romans and Greeks were, no doubt, highly civilized races far in advance of the nations of the time in those sciences that lead to material prosperity. The Roman Empire was the wonder of the ancients and Greek culture was the wonder of the Romans themselves. But below the glittering surface of wondrous Rome was an abysmal void which all the art and ingenuity of Greece could not fill. The spirit of man grew sick of the eternal round of pleasures, both of the flesh and of the intellect, and yearned for something more substantial than gladiatorial shows, pleasure baths, theatres, fashion parades, art galleries filled with superb sculptures and exciting news of victories over Goths and Parthians. Greek philosophy did not meet the needs of the soul. It provided intellectual diversion to the idle and the inquisitive, but those who looked for light in a world of shadows found in the hair-splitting quibblings of the Greeks but futility and weariness of spirit. The gods of Romans and Greeks were the playthings of humans. And when Roman Emperors and their mistresses, some of whom notorious for their scandalous lives, claimed divine honours for themselves and had temples built in their honour, the people in general could not help feeling that they were better beings than their gods. The Roman world was crying for a religion that appealed to the soul of man and Christianity came to its aid.

But in India things were quite different. Hinduism in its comprehensive synthesis catered to the needs of all. It had a hereditary sacerdotal hierarchy, well distributed throughout the length and breadth of the country, whose one occupation was the study, practice and preaching of religion. Things that did not have some relation with soul or life after death did not interest this hierarchy. Buddha's message of Ahimsa and forbearance had, under the able leadership of Asoka, permeated all Indian thought, and Buddhist missionaries were at work building the Aryan Path from Alexandria to Peking.

Thus the Apostle of the East was not preaching to a world seeking spiritual guidance, but to a people intent on teaching others a spiritual way of life. Besides, far removed from the main centres of early Christianity he had to work in practical isolation. Hence the wonder is not that he did not meet with the phenomenal success that attended the labours of some of his compeers in the West, but rather that he achieved so much; for within a period of twenty years he claimed for his Master a large percentage of the population of South India including many high born Brahmins and ruling chiefs.

The personality of the Apostle and his exemplary life must have been in no small measure responsible for his success. We know very little about Thomas's personality. He was not an intellectual of the calibre of St. Paul who had studied at the feet of Gamaliel, but a Galilean fisherman and as such no match for the Brahmins in the subtleties of polemics. Thomas was, however, a zealot as is evident from the Gospel account of his eagerness to go and die with the Master when the other disciples wavered. He was a staunch believer in the triumph of Christ, but the crucifixion and the Day of Disgrace stunned him. We know, on the authority of the Gospel, that the dismayed disciple flatly refused to believe in the Resurrection till he digged his finger in the wound of the Risen Christ. A legend says that the finger remained red ever afterwards. But once convinced, Thomas plunged into the Master's work with his old zeal and laid down his life for the Master. It was probably as an expiation for his original unbelief in the Resurrection that Thomas decided to court the hazards of evangelizing the East while his comrades remained to work on familiar ground.

The traditions of Malabar Christians attribute the Apostle's success not to his polemic ability but to his saintly life and the miracles he performed. It may be mentioned here that arguments never won even Jesus Christ any adherents. Jesus was an adept in arguments and silenced many quibbling Scribes and Pharisees by His ready wit and knowledge of scriptures; but the defeated disputant did not remain to pray but went away to plot. This had probably a profound influence on Thomas; for we have few accounts of his discussions with the learned but a rich lore of the saintly life he lived and the miracles he performed in the Land of the Perumals.

It is not clear if the Perumal himself was converted, but many of his near relatives were. The greatest success of the Apostle was in a city called Palur (the modern Chowghat in the Ponnani Taluk of the Malabar District) a busy centre of inland trade at the time. Palur was an important stronghold of Brahminism and most of the blueblooded Nambudiris of the Perumal's kingdom lived here. Pratically the whole Brahmin community of Palur was converted by the Apostle.

This notable conversion of the most influential Brahmin community of Chera is attributed to a miracle. The Brahmins, so goes the story, were having their morning ablutions in the temple tank, when the Apostle passed that way. As is customary in ritual bathing, the Brahmins were repeating Vedic incantations and sprinkling water upwards by the cup of the palm. The Apostle wished to know of them why the Brahmins were doing this and was told that the water was thrown upwards as an offering to the gods.

"In that case," said the Apostle, "your offerings do not seem to be acceptable to the Power Above. Otherwise the water would not have fallen back to the tank."

This naturally elicited a retort and the Brahmins asked if the Sadhu from the West, as he was known among the Brahmins, could make the water drops stand in mid air. Thomas said he could, but he would do so only if the Brahmins promised to accept his Master as the Saviour. The Brahmins agreed and the Apostle sprinkled water upwards and made the drops remain suspended in mid air glistening in the rays of the morning sun.

Most of the leading Brahmins of Palur were baptized. A few did not accept the new faith and they cursed and abandoned Palur; ever since the place has been known as Chowghat (a corruption of the Malayalam Sapakkad, meaning Accursed Forest).

The better classes of Malabar Christians of the present day trace their descent from the Palur Brahmins converted by the Apostle. Four families namely, Kalli, Kaliankavu, Sankarapuri and Pakalomattam were the most important among the Palur community, and sacerdotal classes in Malabar were drawn from these families from the time of the Apostle till the arrival of the Portuguese. The office of the Archdeacon was hereditary in the Pakalomattam family, and Malabar Christians trace the continuity of the family tradition from remote antiquity to the present day. It was to the Pakalomattam family that the Malabar Christians turned for Bishops after the historic Coonen Cross revolt of 1653 against Portuguese domination. The last of the male lineal descendants died in 1813 without leaving a male issue, but the main stock has left a prolific progeny through female and junior male descendants.

St. Thomas preached throughout the length and breadth of the

Chera kingdom, and the converts were many. He had seven churches built for the congregation: Cranganoor, Quilon, Parur, Niranam, Chayil and Palur. The original churches fell into ruins and had to be rebuilt; but the Apostolic origin of the present churches is strongly held by all Malabar Christians.

After consecrating a near relative of the Perumal as the Bishop of Chera, St. Thomas left for China. We have very little knowledge of his activities in this country, but he returned to Malabar. He then crossed the Ghats to the kingdoms of Pandyan and Cholas and embarked on a strenuous course of Gospel work. Having by now obtained a thorough knowledge of the language and people of South India, and with a strongly established reputation for saintliness and well-organized church as a background in the Chera kingdom, the Apostle's labours in the Tamil kingdom produced remarkable results. People flocked to see him and to hear him preach. His saintliness became a byword in South India. Even those kings and nobles who did not accept the new faith evinced great regard for the Sadhu from the West, and he was revered all over the country as a teacher and messenger of God. He founded several Bishoprics in the Tamil country, and his following and influence became so great that the established religions of the land stood in danger of disintegration.

This naturally roused the animosity of a great many Brahmins. We hear of false accusations and great miracles. One of these is particularly interesting as it shows the extent the Apostle's enemies were prepared to go to bring about his ruin.

A widow belonging to a respectable family was found with child, and the infant, on birth, was killed. The crime came to the knowledge of the authorities and the woman was apprehended and asked to name her paramour. Persuaded by the enemies of the Apostle, the woman gave out the name of the man as the Sadhu from the West. The saint was summoned before the magistrate and on hearing of the false accusation the Apostle commanded the dead child to revive and give out the name of its father; which the child is said to have done exonerating the saint.

False accusations and more open form of opposition to the saint and his teachings became more common and began to gain momentum as these were engineered by vested interests that stood to lose heavily if the old religion and its rich temples were abandoned by the people and the princes. Subtle and indirect forms of opposition proving of no avail, the enemies of the Apostle decided to remove him by the old, old method, and awaited an opportunity which soon presented itself.

A Malayalam poem compiled by one Maliakkel Thomas towards the close of the 16th century from older works and the oral traditions of Malabar gives a graphic account of the martyrdom of the Apostle at Mylapore. The subject matter of the poem is the advent of St. Thomas and his activities in Malabar and elsewhere; the author says that it is the summary of an ancient work written by a disciple of the Apostle whom he claims as his 48th ancestor. The following is a free rendering of that portion of the quaint poem which deals with the martyrdom of the saint:

"Mar Thoma, who had established the Way in several countries and regions of the earth, and whose laws were faithfully followed by the leaders and followers of the communities he had founded, was, in the early hours of the 3rd day of July 72, going on a journey and happened to pass by the Mount in Mylapore. Here stood a temple of Kali, and the priests of the temple, the bitter enemies of the Apostle, furiously issued forth from the temple and stopped the saint.

" 'No man,' said they, 'shall pass this way without worshipping at the shrine; hence come with us and worship the goddess. If you do this, not only shall we let you pass this way unmolested but shall feed you sumptuously on delicacies.'

" 'What?' replied Mar Thoma, 'Am I to sell my soul for a morsel of rice, and worship the devil? But if you insist I shall do your bidding and you shall see how your goddess will run away from her shrine and the temple itself be destroyed by fire.'

" 'Do not utter blasphemy,' cried the priests, and they forced him to go to the temple.

"As the saint approached the temple, a splendrous light shone forth and Kali ran out of the temple and the temple itself was consumed by fire. Thereupon, the infuriated priests fell upon Mar Thoma like mad animals. And one of them taking a long spear thrust it cruelly into the heart of the Apostle. After doing this evil deed, they ran away from the place for fear of the people.

"Mar Thoma then knelt on a stone and prayed. Angels on wings carried news of the tragedy to the king and to the worthy Bishop Poulose. The king and the Bishop with a great following immediately reached the spot and saw the Apostle in a pool of blood with the fatal wound still fresh and the spear stuck to his side. Bishop Mar Poulose removed the spear, and as they were about to take the Apostle in their car for treatment, Mar Thoma spoke to them in a faint voice: 'No treatment is necessary for me now. The day of my great happiness is come.' He then spoke to the people who stood near him weeping, and three Nalikas* before sunset, the great Mar Thoma, alas! passed away."

The body was buried in a nearby church and Mylapore ever since became a centre of pilgrimage for Christians in general and Asian Christians in particular.

In Malabar the advent, labours and martyrdom of the Apostle constitute a living tradition, and the rich folklore, songs and dances of Malabar Christians describe in vivid detail the work of the Apostle in South India. Many a spot in the interior and coastal regions of Kerala is pointed out as hallowed by the footsteps of the First Messenger of Christ, and in the mountain fastness of Malayattoor, in the Union of Cochin and Travancore, is a church built on a spot where the saint used to retreat for spiritual communion with God. Here a feast is celebrated on the first Sunday after Easter and people from all over Malabar and distant Tamil districts flock to the place in pilgrimage. For the Christians of Malabar the belief in the Apostolic origin of their religion is almost an article of faith, and no serious student of Christianity in Malabar can doubt the validity of the tradition.

Independent evidence also supports the authenticity of the

* A Nalika is a time division of Malabar equivalent to 24 minutes.

Indian tradition. All early Christian writers are agreed that Thomas is the Apostle of India. Jerome who wrote in the fourth century of the Christian era observes: "The Son of God was present to all places, with Thomas in India, with Peter in Rome, with Paul in Illyria, with Titus in Crete, with Andrew in Achaia, and with every preacher of the gospel in all the regions they traversed."

Yes, 'Thomas in India' was an accepted fact.

Some detailed account of the Apostle Thomas and his mission is found in the *Acts of the Holy Apostle Thomas*, an apocryphal work believed to be of Eastern origin. There is an interesting but miraculous account of how St. Thomas happened to undertake the mission to India. After the Ascension of Christ, Thomas was spending his anxious days in Jerusalem not knowing where and how to begin his mission. One day while he was wandering by the Market Place he happened to meet Abbanes, the trade agent of king Gundaphoros, and fell into conversation with him. Abbanes told the Apostle that he was on the look out for a good architect to build a palace for Gundaphoros who was interested in foreign styles and was willing to pay handsome remuneration for a really good architect. Well, Thomas was a fisherman and knew little about architecture. But as the two were conversing, Jesus miraculously appeared on the scene dressed as a citizen of the place and joined the conversation. Jesus recommended Thomas to Abbanes as a good architect, and Thomas who recognized the Master took the hint and agreed to accompany Abbanes to India.

Reaching India, the architect was introduced to Gundaphoros who questioned him on the art and science of architecture. Thomas's knowledge of architecture seemed profound and the king engaged him immediately and asked him to submit a plan. The plan was duly submitted and it was even better than the king expected. So the king entrusted the architect with the necessary funds for building the palace, and on receiving an assurance that the palace would be ready within six months, went on a long journey so that he could, on return, gaze on the wondrous structure in its virgin freshness.

After six months Gundaphoros returned but found no palace. In the king's absence the architect had given away the money to the poor and the needy and spent his time in preaching the Gospel. The enraged monarch summoned the Apostle to his presence and asked him where the promised palace was.

"I have built the palace," was the calm reply, "but you cannot see it just now. It is in heaven and you shall repair to it after death."

Well, the king had no patience to wait and the evasive architect was thrown into prison. But that night a strange thing happened. The king's brother Gad died suddenly and in the early hours of the morning the shades of the departed one appeared before Gundaphoros and reported the existence of a beautiful palace in heaven built by angels and kept reserved for Gundaphoros. Gundaphoros immediately repented, released the Apostle, and embraced Christianity.

The story in a slightly different form is current among Malabar Christians too.

The account of the apocryphal writer, though no doubt inspired by a love of the miraculous, has an element of truth in it. For though long rejected as a figment of the imagination, the discovery in India of coins bearing the bust and name of king Gundaphoros lent considerable support to the story. The discovery was made in the nineteenth century, but unfortunately we know very little about Gundaphoros except that he was an Indo-Scythian who ruled in North-Western India.

It is quite probable that the Apostle travelled by the overland route to the domains of Gundaphoros and preached the gospel in his kingdom before South India claimed him. It may be mentioned in this connection that Parthia was also associated with the Apostle's activities. There were in Persia and Afganistan, at that time under the Parthians, considerable numbers of Jews of the Dispersion and the anxiety of the Apostle to communicate to his countrymen the Glad Tidings of the advent of the Messiah must have led him to these regions first. To this day many tribesmen of the Indo-Afghan border claim their descent from Israel.

After preaching the gospel in Gundaphoros' kingdom, other countries claimed the Apostle's attention. A zealot of Thomas's energy could not find peace as long as a single country remained ignorant of the life and teachings of the Master. The anarchical conditions then prevailing in Hindustan proper and news of the existence of numerous Jewish communities on the ports of the West Coast must have influenced the Apostle's decision to proceed to the Malabar Coast from the kingdom of Gundaphoros.

By whichever route the Apostle reached Musiris, it is fairly certain that he preached the gospel in Afghanistan, the Punjab and Sind. Mysterious rumours of the existence of isolated Christian communities persisted through ages down to medieval times and a Jesuit Mission working in Mogul India actually undertook a perilous journey to the mountains of Hindu Kush to locate these communities. They did not, it is true, find these Christian communities. The probabilities are that St. Thomas founded several Christian communities in the North-West, the Punjab and Sind and through centuries of political turmoil, isolation and neglect these communities dwindled into insignificance.

An Eastern tradition, while supporting the Indian belief of the martyrdom and burial of the Apostle in Mylapore, mentions that the body was transferred from its original resting place to Edessa (Urfah) on the Euphrates valley, then an important centre of Eastern Christianity. In this city was celebrated annually on the 3rd July a great festival to commemorate the translation of the relics. Of the hymns sung on the occasion, the following, believed to have been composed by Ephraem, a famous doctor of the Eastern Church who lived in the fourth century of the Christian era, would be of interest:

> Blessed art Thou, Thomas the Twin, in thy deeds! twin is thy spiritual power: not one thy power, not one thy name;
> But many and signal are they; renowned is thy name among the Apostles.
> From my lowly state, thee I haste to sing.

Blessed art thou, like unto the solar ray from the great orb;
    thy grateful dawn India's painful darkness doth dispel.
Thou the great lamp, one among the Twelve, with oil from
    thy cross replenished, India's night floodest with light.
Blessed art thou, whom the Great King hath sent; that India
    to His One-Begotten thou shouldst espouse; above snow
    and linen white, thou the dark bride didst make fair.
Blessed art thou, whom the unkempt hast adorned, that
    having become beautiful and radiant, to her spouse she
    might advance.
Blessed art thou, who hast faith in the bride, whom from
    heathenism from demon's errors and from enslavement to
    sacrifices thou didst rescue.
Her with saving hath thou cleanest, the sunburnt thou
    hast made fair, the Cross of Light her darkened shades
    effacing.
Blessed art thou, O thrice-blessed city! that hast acquired
    this pearl, none greater doth India yield:
Blessed art thou, worthy to possess the priceless gem! Praise
    to thee, O gracious Son, who thus thy adorers dost
    enrich!*

Of the translation of the Apostle's body to Edessa Bishop Gregory of Tours who lived in the sixth century of the Christian era writes:

"Thomas the Apostle, according to the history of his passion, is declared to have suffered in India. After a long time his blessed body was taken into the city which they called Edessa, in Syria and there buried. Therefore in that Indian place where he first rested there is a monastery and a church of wonderful size, and carefully adorned and arranged. And in this temple God exhibits a great miracle. For a lamp which is placed in it and lighted before the place of his burial, burns by the Divine Will by night and by day, receiving from no one a supply of oil or wick; neither is it extinguished by the wind nor overset by accident, nor is it ex-

* Medlycot.

hausted by its burning. And it has its supply through the merit of the Apostle."

It is remarkable that local tradition knows nothing about the translation of the body to Edessa, but has always held that the body of the Apostle remains to this day at its original resting place in Mylapore. Further, the Portuguese who took possession of the site claim to have discovered in 1523 some bones of the skull and of the spine in the grave. It is probable that some relics were removed to Edessa but not the whole body. And it is but reasonable to assume that the translation of the relics and the celebration of the feast were calendared to fall on the date of the Apostle's martyrdom.

The fame of the miraculous powers of the relics of St. Thomas spread throughout Christendom. Before the ninth century it had definitely reached England. For in the *Anglo-Saxon Chronicle* we find reference to the fulfilment of a vow made by King Alfred by the power of which he overcame the Danes. According to this document, in the year 883 "Sighlem, Bishop of Shireburn, and Aethalstan conveyed to Rome the alms which the king had vowed to send hither, and also to India to St. Thomas and St. Bartholomew, when they sat down against the army at London; and there, God be thanked, their prayer was very successful after that vow." It is related that the worthy Bishop with his company visited the tomb of St. Thomas and returned to England with spices and other cargo from India.

The reference to St. Bartholomew is significant. Though St. Thomas is generally believed to be the Apostle of India and there is no Indian tradition about Bartholomew's visit, there are references to his mission to India in early Christian writings. Pantaenus, the famous Alexandrian philosopher, is believed to have visited India in the second century of the Christian era and found a community of Christians who traced their origin to St. Bartholomew. Eusebius of Caesarea writing in the fourth century observes: "About the same time (A.D. 180) the school of the faithful at Alexandria was governed by a man most distinguished for his learning, whose name was Pantaenus: as there had been a school of sacred learning established there from ancient times, which has continued down to our own times and which we have understood was held by men able in eloquence and the study of divine things. For the tradition is that this philosopher was then in great eminence as he hàd been first disciplined in the philosophical principles of those called Stoics. But he is said to have displayed such ardour, and so zealous a disposition respecting the divine word that he was constituted a herald of the gospel of Christ to the nations of the East; and advanced as far as India. For there were still many evangelists of the word, who were ardently striving to employ their inspired zeal after the apostolic example, to increase and build up the divine word. Of these Pantaenus is said to have come as far as the Indies. And the report is that he there found his arrival anticipated by some who were there acquainted with the gospel of Matthew to whom Bartholomew, one of the apostles, had preached and had left them the Gospel of Matthew in the Hebrew characters, which was also preserved until this time. Pantaenus, after many praiseworthy deeds, was finally at the head of the Alexandrian school commenting on the treasure of divine truth, both orally and in his writings."*

Jerome has also a reference to Pantaenus: "Pantaenus, a philosopher of the Stoic sect . . . was a man of so great prudence and of so great erudition, as well in the divine scripture as in secular literature, that he was also sent to India by Demetrius, Bishop of Alexandria, at the request of the ambassadors of that nation. There he found that Bartholomew, one of the twelve apostles had preached the coming of our Lord Jesus Christ according to the Gospel of Matthew, which written in Hebrew characters, he brought with him on his return to Alexandria."†

It may appear strange that the Christian tradition of Malabar and South India knows nothing of the visit of St. Bartholomew to India, and stranger still that Pantaenus has nothing to say of St. Thomas and the Christian communities he had founded. This

* Quoted in *Apostles of India*.
† Ibid.

has led some historians to suppose that the country Pantaenus visited was not India but some region then confused with India. It is true that some ancient writers had but an inadequate conception of the geographical position of India and often confused Arabia and Central Asia with India; but others like Pliny had a fairly accurate idea of the geography of India. Jerome at least knew what he was talking about. For he mentions that "Pantaenus, on account of the rumour of his excellent learning was sent by Demetrius into India that he might preach Christ among the Brahmins and philosophers of that nation." Brahmins certainly did not exist anywhere except India.

Rufinus, a contemporary of Jerome, also bears testimony to the fact that India was the portion allotted to Bartholomew when the Apostles divided the world for mission work. "In that division of the world made by the Apostles for the preaching of the word of God, by drawing lots, while different provinces fell to different Apostles, Parthia fell to Thomas, to Matthew fell Ethiopia, and the 'Citerior India' adherent to it is said to have fallen to Bartholomew. Placed between this Citerior India and Parthia but far to the interior, lies 'Ulterior India' inhabited by peoples of many and diverse tongues."

To the Romans and Greeks 'Citerior India' was the coastal region of Western India and Konkan and Fr. Perumalil and following him Fr. Heras are of opinion that North Konkan was the scene of Bartholomew's activities.* We must remember that in the 2nd century of the Christian era it was possible for one Christian community to exist in some part of India without knowing of the existence of their brethren elsewhere in the Peninsula. It is definitely known that there were Christians in India in regions other than the South and the Malabar Coast. The celebrated Cosmas of Alexandria, called the Indian Voyager because of his extensive trade relations with India, found the Church "very widely diffused, and the whole world filled with the doctrine of Christ which is being day by day propagated and the Gospel preached over the whole earth. This, as I have seen

* The *Two Apostles of India* by the Rev. Henry Heras S.J.

with my own eyes in many places and have heard narrated by others, I, as a witness of the truth relate. In the island of Taprobane (Ceylon) in further India, where the Indian Sea is, there a church of Christians where clergy and faithful are to be found; whether also further beyond, I am not aware. Such also is the case in the land called Male where the pepper grows. And in the place called Kalliana there a Bishop usually ordained in Persia, as well as in the isle called the Isle of Dioscroris (Socotra) in the same Indian Sea." There were Christians also in the Maldive Islands. According to Philostorgius who lived in the fourth century of the Christian era, one Theophilus the Indian visited his native land as the head of an embassy of Christians sent by Constantius. This Theophilus was a native of Divus, the ancient name of the Maldive Islands. Theophilus is said to have introduced certain reforms in the Divus Church, but little else is known about him.

Both Father Perumalil and Heras are of opinion that modern Kalyan, in North Konkan, (now a suburb of Bombay, but a port of considerable importance in ancient India and probably Kalliana of Cosmas) was the centre of Bartholomew's activities. According to St. Bede he arrived at the place dressed as a Sadhu and started preaching in the chief temple of the city and performed many miracles. He has also left us a pen portrait of the Apostle. "He has black hair, his complexion is white, his eyes are large, his nostrils equal and straight, his ears are covered with the locks of hair from his head, he has a long beard with very few grey hairs. His body is of a proportionate size, neither very tall nor very short. He goes dressed in a white garment. He prays a hundred times during the day and as many times during the night; his voice is like the sound of a bugle. The angels of God accompany him nor do they allow him to undergo fatigue or thirst. He is always in the joy of God, day and night; he foresees everything and speaks and understands all tongues."

The Apostle preached in the country and converted Polymius the king who gave orders for the removal of the idol of 'Astaruth' from the chief temple of the city. This enraged the enemies of the Apostle and they prevailed upon 'Astreges' brother of Polymius to persecute and behead the Apostle.

Fr. Perumalil identifies Astaruth with Ashtamurti, a name of Shiva, and Astreges with Arishtakarman and Polymius with Pulomavi of the Puranas.

The Church Bartholomew founded did not have the same good fortune as that attended the labours of his compeer farther south. The existence of the Christians of Bartholomew was known to early Christian writers but in India itself no tradition is left of this community. In the year 1321, the Dominican Missionary Jordanus and four Franciscans visited Thana, where the Franciscans were martyred, but Jordanus' account is not quite clear whether he had found any Christians of Bartholomew in the region. But we know for a fact that when the Portuguese arrived at the site two centuries later they found no Christians there and heard no traditions concerning St. Bartholomew.

Now to revert to St. Thomas. The first European to visit the shrine of St. Thomas and leave an authentic account was the famous Venetian traveller Marco Polo. During his extensive travels in the East, he visited the Coromandel Coast, then known to Europeans as Ma'bar, in the 13th century and has recorded the following:

"The body of Messer Saint Thomas the Apostle lies in the province of Ma'bar at a certain town having no great population. 'tis a place where few traders go because there is very little merchandise to be got there and it is a place not very accessible. Both Christians and Saracens, however, greatly frequent it in pilgrimage. For the Saracens also do hold the saint in great reverence and say that he was one of their own Saracens and a great prophet, giving him the title of 'Avarian' which is as much to say 'Holy Man'. The Christians who go thither in pilgrimage take of the earth from the place where the saint was killed and give a portion thereof to any one who is sick of a quarton or tertian fever; and by the power of God and of St. Thomas the sick man is continently cured. . . . The Christians who have charge of the Church have a great number of Indian nut trees, whereby they get their living: and they pay to one of those brother kings six groats for each tree every month."*

Marco Polo also mentions an interesting local tradition that St. Thomas was accidentally killed by a hunter who was shooting peacocks in a wood where the saint was meditating. Because of this accidental offence, "none of the poor man's tribe could ever enter the place where the saint lay buried. Nor could twenty men force them in nor ten hold them there on account of the virtue of that sacred body."

The story was probably invented by local Brahmins who did not wish to be known as the descendants of the murderers of a man held in great esteem throughout the land.

The Christian community of whom Marco Polo speaks died away soon after his visit. For when the Portuguese took over the shrine they found few Christians there and the lamp at the shrine itself was tended by a Muslim watchman, which, however, testifies to Marco Polo's observation that the saint was held in great veneration by the Muslims.

* Yule's edition.

CHAPTER III

THE EARLY MALABAR CHURCH

THE communities St. Thomas founded in the Chola and Pandyan kingdoms did not long survive the zeal of his enemies. But in the Chera kingdom the Church flourished. The cause of the practical annihilation of the Christian communities in the Pandyan and Chola kingdoms is said to be persecution. But persecution alone does not explain the facts fully. Hindu kings have always been known to be tolerant towards religious persuasions other than their own, and ancient South Indian monarchs were remarkably so. Hence the probabilities are that political motives rather than religious persecution were responsible for the disappearance of the Christian communities in the Chola and Pandyan kingdoms.

The Cheras, Cholas and Pandyans were at constant war with one another and the fortunes of war varied. All accounts show that the Chera king had a powerful ally in the Christian merchants of Musiris who had extensive trade relations with the West and the island of Ceylon. They were in a position to advance the Chera king large sums of money and supply him with arms in his campaigns against the Pandyans, and his independence and prestige were in no small measure dependent on the friendship of the Christians. The needs of the times also imbued warlike qualities in the Malabar Christians and they became well known as a military class able to give solid support to the Perumal in his campaigns against his enemies.

Thus the Christians as a community began to be considered as the allies of the Cheras. Among newly formed communities, as is well known, communal feelings are exceptionally strong and the Pandyans and Cholas distrusted the Christians of their own kingdom. This was probably the real cause of the hostility of Pandyans and Cholas towards Christians who enjoyed the patronage of the Cheras.

Whether the Apostle gave the South Indian Church a Dravidian or Syrian liturgy is not known. From all accounts it is clear that the Apostle did not interfere with the time honoured customs of the Indian congregation. Notions of social distinctions as embodied in caste were not discarded. In the manner of dress, usages and language Indian Christians were allowed to follow their own traditions. The only innovation was in the name: the Christians were known as Nazranis, or followers of the Nazarene, a term still used in all government documents in the Union of Travancore and Cochin. The Apostle's main emphasis was on his followers accepting Christ as the Saviour and the Cross as the mark of the Nazrani. Hence the probabilities are that St. Thomas gave the primitive Indian church a simple Dravidian liturgy which they could understand and appreciate.

From the time of the Apostle's martyrdom till the fourth century of the Christian era very little is known about the state of Christianity in India. But in the fourth century an epoch making event which put Christianity on a firm footing in India took place. This was the immigration into Malabar of a large colony of Syrians under the leadership of a merchant prince called Canai Thoma or Thomas of Canaan. According to the traditions of Malabar the Bishop of Uraha (Edessa) had a vision of St. Thomas who commanded him to send someone to tend his flock in Malabar. Historians are of opinion that the immediate cause of the emigration of the Syrians was persecution at home. Whatever the motive of the exodus, the arrival of the powerful colonists raised the strength and prestige of the Malabar Church.

Canai Thoma is revered as the Father of the Nation by the Christians of Malabar who follow the Syrian rite. The merchant was a remarkable man. His personality and wealthy following impressed the Perumal. The Perumal also realized the advantage of having in his country a colony of able foreigners well known for their commercial acumen and whose name commanded respect in the markets of the world. Thoma had extensive trade connections with the great ports of the Mediterranean, Persian Gulf and the Indian Sea. It is more than probable that Thoma's agents were important personages in Musiris and he himself had visited the port and the Perumal. Anyway, he received a royal welcome from the Perumal and the colonists were treated with the greatest deference. For their residence was allotted a suburb of Musiris which they named Mahadevar Patanam or the City of the Great God. In course of time Mahadevar Patanam became second in importance only to Tiruvanchikkulam where the Perumal himself had his residence.

The exodus of the Syrians took place in the year A.D. 345. Thoma brought with him seventy-two families consisting of about 400 members including a Bishop named Joseph and several priests. These Syrian immigrants were not treated as untouchable foreigners by the high born Malabar Christians (which was their attitude towards the Portuguese when these came to Malabar at a later date) but as the countrymen of Mar Iso (Lord Jesus) and Mar Thoma (Lord Thomas) and as such worthy of the greatest honour and respect. The Syrians and Malabar Christians soon entered into matrimonial relations and merged into a single community. Canai Thoma himself married a Christian lady from Malabar.

The standing of Canai Thoma with the Perumal was very high. His vast resources and personal ability won for him many honours from the Perumal. He was a trusted adviser of the Perumal. In all commercial matters his counsel was supreme and he was the virtual dictator of the commercial policy of the monarch. He was given the monopoly of inland and foreign trade and on this account Thoma and his descendants were given the title of Perum Chetty or Great Merchant; because of the splendour of his princely household Thoma and his heirs were also known as Ravi Kartan (Lord Sun) or in common parlance Iravi Kortan.

Many a Malayalam ballad describes in glowing terms the greatness of Canai Thoma and the prosperity that descended on the Perumal's kingdom because of the alliance between the king and the merchant prince. Thoma's voice was supreme in the councils of the ruler and very often he dined with the Perumal. During the feasts in the court Thoma was served on double leaves, a regal privilege, in memory of which Malabar Christians to this day fold the ends of the leaves from which they eat on ceremonial occasions.

An old song tells us how Thoma and his descendants came to be the lords of the five castes of artisans in Malabar. An intercommunal marriage against the traditional usages of the castes was forced on one of the five castes by the Perumal, and all the five castes made a joint protest. The Perumal took no notice of the grievance and the castes decided to abandon their native land. By a well-organized secret plan, they put out boldly into the sea and almost overnight sailed away to an unknown destination.

Because of the exodus the arts and crafts suffered. A man's occupation was forged to his caste and no other castes would undertake the work of the artisans. No houses could be built or repaired in the Perumal's land and the old song tells us that the lizard and the white ant reigned on the throne of the Perumal himself. His palace was fast falling into ruins. In this predicament the Perumal turned to Thoma, and the merchant undertook the difficult and delicate task of tracing and reclaiming the lost castes.

Thoma was a great sailor and he fitted out a fleet and set sail in search of the deserters. Fortunately he had not to sail far; for he found them in the island of Simhala (Ceylon). Thoma was a well-known figure in the ports of Simhala and had no difficulty in persuading the king of this place to give permission to the castes to return. They were promised pardon and recognition of their traditional usages. They were not, however, satisfied with this but wanted the protection and patronage of the powerful merchant. Thoma agreed to be their leader and spokesman and on this condition the castes returned to Musiris with Thoma.

In recognition of this signal service of Thoma, the Christians were made lords of these castes. It is interesting to note that to this day at the time of wedding in a well-to-do Christian family in Malabar a member of the tailor caste sings an old song dwelling upon the greatness and achievements of the bridegroom's illustrious ancestor and receives a ceremonial present from him.

The Syrians brought a new vigour to the Malabar Church. The Bishop and the clergy organized the church and introduced the Syrian liturgy. From now on the Nazranis began to be known as Syrian Christians. Churches sprang up throughout the length and breadth of the Perumal's kingdom and Canai Thoma and his followers endowed them magnificently. A regular flow of clergy and Bishops was kept up from Syria.

Under the able guidance of the Syrians who were happily free from many of the superstitions regarding dress, diet and occupation, the Malabar Christians while retaining their military traditions also took to business and agriculture. With Thoma and his men controlling the export and import trade of Musiris, the inland trade of Malabar soon passed into the hands of the Syrian Christians. The fashionable imitated some of the Syrian customs such as using carpets and curtains in the houses, and wearing turbans and robes. The Malabar Christians adopted the Syrian usage of shaving their heads clean.

The good relations that existed between the Perumal and Canai Thoma continued among their descendants. Ravi Kartan of Musiris, the heir to the title of Thoma, enjoyed monopoly of trade from generation to generation and his power and prestige waned only after domination of the Indian Sea by the Muslims. There were also fresh immigrants from Syria but none proved so powerful as Thoma and his men.

Several Syrian Christian celebrities, by their signal service to the state secured exceptional privileges for themselves and their community, and the Syrians came to be respected and feared by all. Some of the copper plate grants given to the Syrians have come down to modern times and throw a flood of light on the status of the community which had been incorporated in the social scheme of Malabar. One of the existing plates was granted by the Emperor Vira Raghava Perumal to the reigning Iravi Kortan of Cranganoor in the year A.D. 774 on the occasion of the gift of the principality of Manigramam for some important service he had rendered the Perumal, the exact nature of which is not known. The inscription is thus translated:

"Hari! Prosperity! Adoration to the great Ganapathy! On the day of the Nakshatra Rohini, a Saturday after the expiration of the twenty-first day of the solar month Mina (of the year during which) Jupiter was in the sign of Makara (Pisces) while the glorious Vira Raghava Chakravarti of the race that has been wielding the sceptre for several thousands of years in succession from the glorious king of kings, the glorious Vera Kerala Chakravartin was ruling prosperously:

"While we were pleased to reside in the great palace, we conferred the title of Manigramam on Iravi Kortan alias Cheraman Loka Perum Chetty of Mahadevar Pattanam.

"We also gave him the right of festive clothing, house pillars, the income that accrues, the export trade, monopoly of trade, the right of proclamation, forerunners, the five musical instruments, the conch, the lamp in day time, the carpet, the palanquin, the royal parasol, the drum, the gateway with ornamental arch, and monopoly of trade in the four quarters.

"We also gave the oil mongers and the five classes of artisans as slaves.

"We also gave with the libation of water (caused it to be) written on a copper plate to Iravi Kortan who is the Lord of the City, the brokerage on articles that may be measured with the para, weighed by the balance or measured with the tape, that may be counted or weighed, and on all other articles between the river mouth of Kodungalloor and the gate chiefly between the four temples and the privileges attached to each temple.

"We gave this as property of Cheraman Loka Perum Chetty alias Iravi Kortan, and his children and children's children in due succession.

"The witnesses who know this are:—We gave it with the knowledge of the villagers of Panniyur and the villagers of Soigram. We gave it with the knowledge of the authorities of Venadu and Odunadu. We gave it with the knowledge of the authorities of Eranadu and Valluavanadu. We gave it for the time that the moon and the sun shall exist.

"The handwriting of Cheraman Loka Perum Dattan Nambi

Sadayan, who wrote this copper plate with the knowledge of all these witnesses."

Another plate, still extant, was granted by a Perumal named Sthanu Ravi Gupta to Maruvan Sapor Iso, the Syrian founder of Quilon, who transferred certain privileges conferred on him by the Perumal to a Parish church with due legal formality.

The copper plates and the living traditions of Malabar show that the Christians as a community held a very high social position under the Perumals and their descendants, the rulers of Cochin. At the time of the arrival of the Portuguese their privileges were many:

* "They were numbered among the noble classes of Malabar. 'They were preferred to the Nayars and enjoyed the privileges of being called by no other name than that of the sons of kings. They were permitted to wear gold tresses in the hair locks in marriage feasts, to ride on elephants and to decorate the floor with carpets.' They were entrusted with the protection of the artisan classes. Their servants had charge of the coconut plantations, and if they were molested by any one or if their occupation was otherwise interfered with they appealed to the Christians who protected them and redressed their grievances. The Christians were directly under the king and were not subject to local chiefs. A Hindu doing violence to a Christian had his crime pardoned only in the case of his offering to the church a hand either of gold or silver according to the seriousness of the offence, as otherwise the crime was expiated in blood. They never saluted any one below their own rank, because it was dishonourable to their status. When they walked along the road they saluted others at a distance, and if anybody refused to reciprocate it, he was put to death. The Nayars who were of the military clan regarded them as brethren and loved them exceedingly. All communities had special men-at-arms called Amouchi who were bound on oath to safe-guard the people or places under their protection even at the cost of their lives. They (the Amouchi) respected the Christians before whom they never ventured to sit unless invited

* Anantakrishna Ayyar, *Anthropology o the Syrian Christians.*

to do so. They were very strong and powerful and their Bishops were respected and feared like kings. To erect a playhouse was the privilege of kings and the same privilege was given to the Christians also. They were given seats by the side of kings and their chief officers. Sitting on carpets, a privilege enjoyed by the ambassadors was also conceded to them. In the 16th century when the Rajah of Parur wished to concede the privilege to the Nayars in his dominion, the Syrian Christians resented and immediately declared war against him if he persisted. Conscious of his inability to enforce his will, in opposition to theirs, he was obliged to leave matters on their ancient footing. The immunity and honours above mentioned, rendered the dignity of their Bishop very considerable.

"The Syrian Christians were almost on a par with their sovereigns. They were allowed to have a military force of their own which was composed chiefly of Shanars, the caste that cultivated the palm tree. Besides the Brahmins, they were the only inhabitants of the country who were permitted to have enclosures in front of their houses. 'In front of their girdle they were accustomed to formerly carry a long metal handle; sometimes the handle was made of gold and beautifully worked. From the end of the handle were suspended chains of the same metal to one of which was fastened a steel, with which to sharpen the poniard; to another a small metal box which contained quicklime. This lime was prepared in a peculiar manner to improve the flavour of the betel which they in common with all other natives of India both men and women, were continually chewing.

" 'In former times they seldom appeared abroad without being well armed. Besides the poniard just mentioned, a few carried matchlocks or rude muskets; others would bear lance at the end of which were suspended steel rings, which made an agreeable sound when the lance was in motion. But the greater part of them carried only a naked sword in the right hand and a buckler in the left arm. They were trained in the use of these weapons at the early age of eight years, and continued to exercise them till twenty-five which accounted for their using them with such dexterity. They were very expert huntsmen, soldiers, and they were therefore held in much estimation by the rulers of the country. A native prince was respected or feared by his neighbours according to the number of Syrians in his dominions'."

The patronage of the Perumals was in no small measure responsible for the prosperity and prestige of the Syrian Christians and they have ever been grateful to the Perumals and their descendants. But it is worth our while to remember that the exalted social status and privileges granted to the Syrians and their elevation in the social scale above the Nayars, the traditional military class from whom the chiefs and generals of the Perumal's army were drawn, could not have been a matter of mere charity. The last sentence in the above quotation is particularly significant. The Christians were staunch allies and loyal subjects of the Perumal and were a source of great military and monetary strength to the Perumal. It is doubtful if the Chera kingdom would have existed as an independent entity so near the powerful Pandyans without the help of the Christians and it is quite probable that the fate that befell the Cholas would have overtaken the Cheras too but for the active support of the Syrian Christians.

According to the traditions of Syrian Christians, there existed an independent Christian kingdom in Malabar called Valiar Vattam. Valiar Vattam kings ruled for several centuries till the kingdom was ceded to Diamper as the last Valiar Vattam king died without a male issue. It appears the first Valiar Vattam king was a converted relative of the Rajah of Diamper and according to the laws of succession Valiar Vattam left without a male heir had to merge into Diamper. The Syrians, however, preserved the royal emblems of Valiar Vattam and presented them to Vasco da Gama on his arrival in Cochin as a token of their friendship and regard for the king of Portugal. An Arabian traveller who visited Malabar in the ninth century also mentions a 'Christian Emir living near Cranganoor'.

It is interesting to note in this connection that in the year 1439, Pope Eugene IV despatched envoys to this Christian king of India and the letter of introduction begins as follows:

"To my most beloved son in Christ, Thomas the illustrious Emperor of the Indians, health and Apostolic benediction. There often has reached us a rumour that your serenity and also all who are the subjects of your kingdom are true Christians——"

Travellers appear to have exaggerated the importance of the Valiar Vattam king considerably, but his existence was a fact.

The rise of Islam and the dominance of the Indian Sea by Muslims put the affairs of the Syrian Christians in a bad way. The seaborne trade of Malabar passed from the Christians to the Muslims. There was considerable animosity between the two, and the flow of Bishops from Syria was obstructed by the Muslims. Persecution bewildered the Christian communities of Western Asia and only those Bishops who had the approval of their Muslim rulers were permitted to occupy their sees. The political upheavals in Syria and Persia had their repercussions in Malabar too. Christian fleets disappeared from the trade routes, and Muslims captured the trade of the Malabar ports. Their powerful connections in the ports of India and the Persian Gulf and their influence in the great Muslim courts of the world made the Perumals court their favours. They were also in a position to chastise an unobliging Perumal. Cranganoor was sacked by the Arabs and the centre of trade shifted to the newly risen port of Calicut in the north.

The authority of the Perumal himself waned. Rebellion and insurrection ravaged the hitherto peaceful land of the Perumals. Chieftain warred against chieftain and the Arabs plundered the ports and lowlands. Independent principalities sprang up everywhere. This state of anarchy continued for some time till Malabar settled down to the three large size independent kingdoms of Kozhikkod (Calicut), Cochin and Travancore. Of these Kozhikkod under its titular rulers called Samoothiri (Zamorin) was a staunch ally of the newly risen Muslim power, Cochin an ally of the old but broken Christian power at constant enmity with Kozhikkod, and Travancore an insignificant principality in the south not much in the limelight of contemporary power politics. This was roughly the position when the Portuguese came to India.

It is remarkable that the Syrian Christians during these periods of confusion managed to maintain their high social status and enjoy practical monopoly of the inland trade. Bishops often came from Western Asia, though not regularly. Through Syrian contact a system of Church government was evolved in which Bishops were to be of foreign extraction especially from the then well-known centres of Christianity in Western Asia but internal administration was carried on by the Archdeacons. Pending the arrival of Bishops, the Archdeacons were the virtual rulers of the community. The office of the Archdeacon, as we have already seen, was hereditary in the Pakalomattam family of Apostolic origin. Though dissensions had often threatened the unity of the Church, the system had worked fairly well and the Portuguese when they tried to interfere with it stirred up a veritable hornets' nest, as we shall see presently.

A word may here be said about the vexed question of whether or not the Malabar Church had remained formally subject to Rome before the arrival of the Portuguese. Sectarian prejudices have obscured historical facts and a heated controversy has been raging for years on the subject; from the temper of the disputants the controversy, it appears, will continue till the Second Coming.

It is true that in the Nicene Council held in A.D. 325, India was represented and one of the dignitaries who signed the decrees was 'John, Bishop of Persia and Great India'. Whether he was an Indian or Persian is not known, but it is more likely that he was a Persian. Little else is known about this Bishop. The Catholics are of opinion that the Bishops of Malabar were ordained and sent by the successors of John, and they brought with them the Syro-Chaldean liturgy.

In the fourth century, however, the Nestorian doctrine of the dual nature of Christ's Person gained ground, but a section of Christians refuting Nestorius propounded the monophysite dogma of the single nature and person of Christ while the Catholics held the middle dogma of the singleness of Christ's Person but the duality of His Nature. For the few centuries that succeeded, Christendom was torn asunder by conflicts between the followers of these divergent views. To a non-Christian these differences might appear slight, but the feelings these generated were great. People were hunted, excommunicated and killed; Bishops warred on Bishops; and few showed any Christian charity towards their opponents. Finally the Nestorians and Monophysites broke off with Rome and under the patronage of Muslim rulers who were inimical with the Roman world gained considerable influence in Asia. Persia became a great stronghold of Nestorians. Jacobus Zanzalus who organised the Monosphysites in his capacity as the Patriarch of Antioch had a great following and the Monophysites took the name of Jacobites. There were also Catholics in these regions who were subject to Rome but followed the oriental liturgy.

All the three churches have at present adherents in Malabar and each sect tries to show that the Malabar Church originally belonged to them. From the inadequate historical material available every zealot is in a favourable position to propound his own pet theories. The accounts of ignorant European travellers who dubbed as 'Nestorian heretics' all Christians who did not appear in boots and top hats have added to the confusion, and Archbishop Menezies who destroyed all Syrian records that might have thrown some light on the matter has left the impartial inquirer in complete darkness.

The Malabar Church suffered practical isolation with the rise of Islam and the dominance of the Indian Seas by the Muslims. The Syrians, however, clung tenaciously to their traditions and made desperate attempts to get Bishops from Western Asia. Of the geography of Western Asia they knew little; of the theological niceties that rocked that ancient centre of Christianity perhaps less. What they apparently wanted was a Bishop of Western Asian appearance who did not understand their language Malayalam, and as long as a person of this description came to them by sea they were not interested in his doctrines or his *bona fides*. In fact the Malabar Christians were at times reduced to such desperate straits in the matter of obtaining foreign Bishops that any pirate who managed to capture a Syrian or Persian of respectable appearance with a flowing beard was in a position to palm him off to Malabar Christians as a Bishop at a very good price.

Nor were real Bishops lacking whose zeal for the gospel was not so marked as their love of power and wealth. Many a Bishop who had been deprived of his see in Persia or Asia Minor appeared in Malabar with forged documents supposed to be signed by venerable authorities, and ruled the Malabar Church. Such Bishops have come to Malabar even after the dominance of Indian Seas had passed to the Portuguese, and their number must have been quite considerable during Arab domination.

Under such conditions it is idle to maintain that the Malabar Church had consistently remained faithful to a particular dogma or denomination. All that we can say is that it has remained remarkably Christian during this period of isolation and confusion and this in itself is a great achievement considering the odds it had to contend with.

The early missionaries, as we have seen, were of Western Asian and Alexandrian origin. Once Christianity conquered Rome, the barbarous races of Western and Northern Europe were brought under Christian influence mainly through the activities of the missionaries of the Mediterranean region. India too had contributed her share in this great work. We have already noticed a reference to Theophilus, the Indian, a native of Maldive. In the Roman Martyrology is an entry under date August 8th (452) which reads: "At Vienne (in Dauphine) France, the Feast of S. Severus, Priest and Confessor, who undertook a troublesome pilgrimage from India in order to preach and, coming in the aforesaid city, converted by his preaching and miracles a large multitude of heathen to the faith of Christ." Severus, we are told, was a man of wealth who at a very young age sold away his possessions and distributed the money to the poor. He then became an anchorite but the Master's call came for field work and he travelled to Europe and embarked upon a vigorous missionary life. He died in Italy but his body was brought to Vienne and buried in St. Stephen's church the origin of which was traced to him. Severus was not probably an isolated instance. There were Indian missionaries of lesser greatness who contributed to the building of the Church in Europe but whose names were lost in the womb of time.

With the checking of the Muslim expansion by Europe, the nations of the Atlantic seaboard came into prominence and the exuberant energy that animated these people began to be felt throughout the world. Their colonial ambition and missionary zeal opened up a new chapter in world history, and soon India too began to feel the impact.

The first European missionary to come to India was Friar John of Monte Corvino, who on his way to China, stayed thirteen months in Mylapore during the years 1291-92. He preached the gospel to the Hindus and baptized over one hundred persons. But the major part of his missionary life was spent in China and he was made the first Archbishop of Peking in 1307 by Pope Nicolas IV.

The founding by Pope Innocent IV in 1252 of 'The Society of Wayfarers for Christ' may be said to have started the new era of European missions. The Society was composed of Fransiscan and Dominican Friars. The rumours of the existence of Christians in several parts of India and the stories of the miracles current in Europe at the shrine of St. Thomas in Mylapore fired the imagination of the members of the newly founded Society. The vigilance of the Turk who sat at the gates of the East gave rise to many difficulties in embarking upon missionary activities in India, but a party of five missionaries succeeded in passing the gate. They were the French Dominican Friar Jordanus, the Franciscans Thomas of Tolentino, James of Padua, Peter of Siena and the Georgian lay Brother Demetrius, a scholar and linguist. They started from Avignon and after several adventures on the way reached Ormuz in 1321. From here they set sail to Malabar with the intention of continuing their journey to Mylapore either by land or by sea. But a rough sea cut short their voyage and their ship could not sail beyond Salsette where they disembarked. Leaving the four brethren in Thana, Jordanus travelled to Broach where he wished to commence his missionary work. When he reached Surat news was brought to him that the four Franciscans had fallen foul of the Muslim governor of the Province and were put to death. It appears the governor, hearing that the missionaries were not paying proper respect to the name of the Prophet of Islam in their preachings, summoned them before him and questioned them on the subject. He wanted to know their candid opinion about the Prophet and his mission and the missionaries, when pressed for an answer, told him exactly what they thought of the Prophet; and they paid the price. Jordanus returned to Thana just in time to give a Christian burial to the martyrs. After working for some time in this region where he made a few converts the Friar returned to Europe.

In the year 1331 Jordanus again visited India, this time as the Bishop of Quilon. He must have told the Pope many things about the Christians of Malabar whom he had not seen and his intention was probably to convert the Syrians to the Latin rite. The innovation, however, did not interest the Syrians. He gave them up as an incorrigible sect of Christians who believed that St. Thomas was Jesus Christ.

Knowing the Syrians as we do, this forerunner of Archbishop Menezies must have carried with him bitter memories of the Syrian opposition to the Latin rite.

CHAPTER IV

THE COMING OF THE PORTUGUESE AND THE MISSION OF ST. FRANCIS XAVIER

PEPPER, once again, comes into prominence. The Turks having closed the age-old overland trade routes to India, the much valued Indian goods, especially pepper, became rare in Europe. The Italian city states that had thrived on commerce were nearly ruined. Other nations had risen in Europe with ambitions to force a way to the wealth of the fabulous East. The accounts of travellers showed that in India itself European traders would be welcome if they could only get past the barrier erected by the Turk.

A frantic search was now made by Europeans to discover new routes to India. Medieval geographers had thought that they knew all about the land surface of the earth, but the great oceans held out promise of unlimited possibilities. Old maps and ancient accounts of mariners' adventures were fished out of libraries and bold sailors set out in all directions to explore the Seven Seas. The newly risen maritime kingdoms of Spain and Portugal were the pioneers in this new activity. Columbus worked on the theory of the global earth and sailed westward to reach the East. Other sailors, less bold, followed the routes of Pharaoh Necho's seahawks and sailed along the African coast to the south to find out if Africa was really a pensinsula or a continuation of Asia. Bartholomew Diaz reached the southernmost point of Africa and named the cape, Cape of Good Hope, as it gave promise of great things. It was, however, given to Vasco da Gama to realize the hopes held out by the discovery of the Cape. Rounding the Cape he struck boldly into the Arabian Sea and on the 20th May 1498 dropped anchor at Calicut, the then principal port on the West Coast, in the dominions of the Zamorin. The barrier the Muslims had erected between India and Europe was at last by-passed.

The news of the arrival of the Portuguese spread throughout Malabar. The Zamorin, the ally of the Arabs, viewed the new-comers with suspicion. The Arab presaged his doom. The Rajah of Cochin, smarting under many wrongs he had suffered at the hands of the Arabs, was eager to court the friendship of the Portuguese and build up the trade of Cranganoor lost to Calicut with the rise of the Muslims. The greatest rejoicings were, however, of the Syrian Christians. Impoverished by the loss of trade to the Arabs and fallen in prestige and power on that account, they entertained wild hopes of deliverance and re-establishment of their lost glory by Portuguese friendship and patronage. They promptly sent ambassadors to Vasco da Gama who himself was eager to befriend his co-religionists in the strange land he had reached.

The result of the first contact between the Syrians and the Portuguese was one of extreme cordiality. They ate and drank together, went on pilgrimages to Mylapore and entered into trade contracts especially as the inland trade of pepper was still in the hands of the Syrians. The Syrians so trusted the Portuguese that in 1502 they presented Vasco da Gama, then resident in Cochin, with the Rod of Justice of the extinct Valiar Vattam dynasty in token of their friendship.

It will be seen that there was but an interval of four years between the first landing of Vasco da Gama and the presentation of the Rod of Justice by the Syrians, and neither the Portuguese nor Syrians had time and opportunity for mutual study. While the Europeans of the Mediterranean region had some knowledge of India and her people gained through commerce, travel and hearsay, the Portuguese who came from the Atlantic seaboard knew very little about Indians and their way of life. To Vasco da Gama and his company all Indians looked alike. Their ideas of Christianity in India, when they had any ideas at all, were derived mainly from traveller's tales and the legends connected with the mythical Prestor John. Some Portuguese writers thought that the kings of Malabar, Ceylon and Pegu were Christians while others imagined that the whole population of India were Christian living under a powerful Christian emperor. So confused were the ideas prevailing among the Portuguese about Christians in India that Vasco da Gama and his party actually paid a visit to a Hindu temple and worshipped the idol imagining it to be an image of Virgin Mary. The story of this visit is worth narrating.

Gama, after obtaining the reluctant permission of the Zamorin to establish a factory in Calicut wished to see a church and worship in it. Due to the incompetence of the interpreter (it was during the first visit of Gama and a decent interpreter who knew Portuguese and Malayalam was impossible to procure) the idea was mutilated and the distinguished visitor was taken to a Hindu temple. We will do well to remember that while the Portuguese knew little about Indians, Indians knew less about the Portuguese. Except that they belonged to the Christian community generally held in high esteem in Malabar as a clean and high caste, the Hindus then did not know much about the Portuguese. If they knew they were the unclean Parangis they had later come to be known in India, the Hindus would not have allowed the Portuguese to come anywhere near their temple. Anyway, the account of the visit left by Ferna Lopez de Castanheda is amusing:

"The Kotwal took Vasco da Gama to a Pagoda of his idols, telling him it was a church of much devotion, and he thought so the more as he saw above the chief gates seven bells, and before it a copper pillar as high as a ship's mast, on the capital thereof was a big bird of the same copper which appeared to be a cock. And the church was as big as a monastery, made entirely of hewn stones and roofed with bricks which bade fair to be a fine building within. And Vasco da Gama was much pleased to see it, and he thought he was among Christians. And when we had entered with the Kotwal, we were received by some men, naked from the girdle upwards and covered downward with certain cloth up to knees, and with another cloth thrown over the shoulder. They had nothing on their head, and had certain number of threads from the top of the left shoulder which passed under the right shoulder in the way the Deacons wear the stole when they serve at Mass; and these men are called Cafres and in Malabar they serve in the

Pagodas. With a sprinkler they sprinkled water from a font on Vasco da Gama and the Kotwal and our people; next they gave them ground sandal to put on their head, as we here put ashes, and also on the brawn of their arms; ours did not put it there as they were dressed, but they put it on their head. And as they went through that church, they saw many images on the walls, and some of them had teeth so big that they came an inch out of their mouth, and others had four arms, and they were so ugly of countenance as to look like devils. This made ours doubt somewhat whether it was a church of Christians, and when they had come before the chapel, which was in the middle of the body of the church, they saw it had a summit, like a Cathedral, also of hewn stone. And on one side of this summit there was a brass door admitting one man and they went up to it by a stone stair-case, within the chapel which was a little dark. There was placed in the wall, an image which was descried from outside, because they would not let them go inside, signifying to them that only the Cafres could enter there; and there pointing to the image called it Sancta Maria, giving them to understand that that was their image. And as it appeared so to Vasco da Gama he knelt down and ours with him and they prayed. And Joao de Saa, who doubted whether that was a church of the Christians, because of the ugliness of the images that had been painted on the walls, said, while kneeling down, 'If this is the devil, I worship the true God.' And Vasco da Gama, who heard him looked towards him, smiling. And the Kotwal and his people who stood before the chapel, prostrated themselves on the ground with their hands in front, and this three times, and then they rose and prayed standing."* The temple was, in all probability, of Kali, also worshipped in Malabar and Tamil districts as Mari Amma, Mother of Epidemics.

Such ignorance of the Portuguese about Christianity in India did not last long. With their rise in power and dominance of the Indian Ocean, clergy and missionaries of various orders came to India in large numbers and they obtained a fairly sound idea of

* Quoted in *Jesuits in Malabar* by Feroli S. J.

the religions and peoples of India. They realized that India was inhabited mainly by Hindus and Muslims, and barring the St. Thomas Christians numbering at that time about 200,000 souls there were no Christian communities worth the name in India. They also found that the St. Thomas Christians, though enjoying self-government in all social and civil matters, were formally subject to local Rajahs; that they followed the Syrian rite and obtained Bishops from Western Asia; that they were good businessmen and agriculturists as well as soldiers and could put in the field, in an emergency, 20,000 fighting men, quite a respectable army judged from local standards at the time; that their Bishops, not being subjects of local Rajahs, were virtually independent and had an army of their own.

The Syrians too found out many things about the Portuguese which in their original enthusiasm they had either overlooked or failed to notice. They found that their rites differed from those of the Portuguese; that the way of life of the Portuguese was incompatible with Syrian notions of respectability and ceremonial purity. With the rise of Portuguese power a large number of them settled down in the ports of Goa, Calicut, Cochin and Cranganoor and their way of life became a scandal to all respectable Indians. The beef and pork eating Portuguese were held in contempt as unclean both by the Hindus and Muslims. In sexual morals they appeared to recognize no 'law and their attitude towards the people of the land was arrogant and contemptuous. The Portuguese soon earned for themselves a notoriety for lawless living and the term 'Parangi' by which the Portuguese were known to Indians degenerated into a synonym for an unclean barbarian. This general contempt for the Portuguese began to be shared by the Syrians too. And when the Portuguese expressed a desire to marry Syrian Christian girls, the Syrians thought that the time had come to keep the foreigners at a respectable distance.

This contempt for the Portuguese as a nation was, no doubt, uncharitable and was occasioned by an inadequate knowledge of them. Indians judged the great Portuguese nation by the standard

THE MISSION OF ST. FRANCIS XAVIER 49

of life of common soldiers, sailors and adventurers who had settled in Indian ports. As is well known, these classes, whatever their professed religion or nationality, are not particularly noted for correct living. The fact that they lived far away from their native land and the restraining influence of social codes, added much to the licence in the Portuguese settlements. Further, few Portuguese women cared to come to India and the men were, by necessity, driven to form permanent or semi-permanent connections with Indian women of no great repute. The only people with whom the Portuguese could have entered into respectable matrimonial relations were the Syrian Christians, and these lofty sons of Brahmins and kings disdained to associate themselves with the unclean 'Parangis'.

Anyway, the contempt of Indians did not seriously hinder the Portuguese rise to power. The Arabs were quickly driven off the main ports of India and the Indian Ocean and even the Pacific began to be dominated by Portuguese fleets. The maritime trade of India passed into the hands of the Portuguese and those Arabs who wished to trade with the East did so by the permission of the Portuguese.

The Portuguese were no nation of shopkeepers like the English who came later and obtained mastery over India. They still lived in the age of chivalry and were romantics, conquistadors and, above all, crusaders. Flushed with victory in the long and bitter Iberian wars with the Moors, the Portuguese had emerged as a nation overflowing with exuberant energy and as the liberators of Christendom. Europe and Africa could not hold them. They roved the high seas from one end of the world to the other in search of adventure. They lavished wealth, energy and life on their pet causes with an abandon that astonished the shrewd, calculating British businessman interested only in his dividends. They were less mature than the Italians, the lineal descendants of the Romans but more energetic, bouyant and daring, and revelled in those fantasies peculiar to adolescence. The Portuguese did not believe that there was any good in Hinduism or Islam but were firmly convinced that salvation lay only through a European

Christ. Hence most of their activities were inexplicable both to Indians and Europeans of the older civilisation.

One of the main motives of Portuguese expansion, as we have seen, was the crusading spirit. Their zeal for spreading Christianity in the East won for them the admiration and blessings of the Pope, and Alexander VI intervening in the dispute between the Spaniards and the Portuguese divided the world between them, giving the Portuguese the East as their portion in colonial, commercial, political and religious expansion. In 1514 Pope Leo X established the *Padroado* by which the Portuguese obtained certain ecclesiastical rights over the Christians and Churches in the East, which was later to cause infinite trouble to the Pope himself. This was yet to come, with the decay of the Portuguese power and the rise of other European nations. For the present we are concerned only with the phenomenal rise of Portuguese power in the East and their Christian zeal. Wherever the Portuguese flag flew, missionaries burning with zeal for the spread of Christianity appeared. The state actively supported the church and where the reasonable persuasion of the missionary failed to impress the arms of the state did.

Vasco da Gama's own chaplain, Dom Pedro de Covilham, of the Order of Redemption of Captives, was the first Portuguese missionary who was martyred in India. In 1510 the great Portuguese Admiral Albuquerque conquered Goa and rebuilt the city and made it the capital of the Portuguese Empire in the East. The earlier settlements of Cranganoor, Cochin and Calicut on the West Coast became subordinate to Goa and this city quickly rose to wealth and fame and passed into European legend as Golden Goa, the fabulous city of oriental splendour and luxury.

Goa was not only the metropolis of political and civil authority of Portuguese Empire in the East but also the headquarters of Ecclesiastical authority and missionary activities. In 1534 Goa was raised to a Bishopric and in 1557 to an Archdiocese with Cochin and Malacca as suffragans; the Inquisition was established in 1560.

The Franciscans and Dominicans were the pioneers in missionary work in Portuguese India. Within a short period they brought the majority of the population of the city of Goa under Christian influence. Their work extended to Cochin, Cranganoor and along the Coast as far as Mylapore. The greatest of their gains was, however, in the Fishery Coast where their work led to far reaching political consequences. An incident similar to the 'War of Jenkin's ear' brought about a revolutionary change in the political and religious atmosphere of the Fishery Coast and led to the naval action of Vedalai which broke the Arab power on the West Coast. The incident deserves some detailed notice.

Fishermen in India are a caste by themselves, condemned as untouchables by the higher classes, who eked out a living by an occupation more precarious than farming, itself not very profitable or reliable but the main occupation of the lower castes in India. Pearl fishing was, however, an organized industry in Tuticorin and the neighbouring coastal region. The actual pearl fishers, known as Paravars or Bharatars, were as poor as their brethren occupied in regular fishing but the Arabs who controlled pearl fishing and carried on the trade were the richest merchants in the East. The Arabs were staunch allies of the Pandyans in whose dominions were situated the pearl fisheries of South India; the revenue they derived from this industry was quite considerable and they usually took no notice of the complaints of extortion on their subjects by the Arabs. The Paravars were oppressed alike by their own kings and the Arabs but the latter were in immediate contact with them and there was constant friction between the Arabs and Paravars. Groaning under the double tyranny of the Pandyans and the Arabs, the miserable fishers had another menace to contend with. The Fishery Coast at that time was notorious for the activities of pirates and these, when hard up for plunder on the high seas, raided the defenceless villages of the fishers and carried away able-bodied men and desirable young girls to be sold as slaves. All told the plight of the pearl fishers was anything but enviable.

As the Portuguese power was rising in Malabar, some of the pearl fishers happened to have a quarrel with the Arab overseers under whom they were working and in the fray some Muslims did violence on a Paravar woman. Her infuriated husband and his friends caught the ravisher and cut off his ear lobe. This was but the spark that lit up a huge conflagration. The news of the rape of the fisherwoman spread like wild fire in the Fishery Coast and an excited mob of fishers murdered a good many Muslims.

This mutiny of the Paravars and murder of members of the powerful community of Arabs had to be avenged. The Nayacker of Madura the overlord of the Paravars nodded ascent, and the Muslims started a systematic massacre of the Paravars. They fled but were hunted. Any one who presented the head of a Paravar was rewarded five panams (the panam is a silver coin of less than eight annas in value). This high price had soon to be reduced to one panam because of the large number of heads that were daily presented for cashing. The wretched Paravars went into hiding and lived in constant dread of annihilation.

To these hunted men came an Indian Christian with a message of hope. This interesting personage was a merchant named Joao de Cruz, a native of Calicut. De Cruz was a Hindu by birth who was sent by the Zamorin to Lisbon in the year 1513 to study higher commerce as the lad gave promise of a brilliant commercial career. In Lisbon together with Commerce he studied Christianity, embraced this religion and received his Portuguese name. Loaded with honours from the King of Portugal, de Cruz returned to India to advise the Zamorin on his commercial policy but found his patron cold and aloof. His conversion had upset the Zamorin's mental balance. Nothing daunted, the enterprising de Cruz started business on his own with the help of some Portuguese gentlemen of influence. But misfortune dogged his heels in all his commercial activities. He lost many ships in the sea and in a voyage was himself shipwrecked. He escaped with bare life, having lost his wife and children in the sea. He was heavily indebted to the Portuguese Factor at Cochin and this dignitary thought the moment most opportune to demand his money. Poor de Cruz could not pay and the Factor had him thrown into prison.

The impoverished merchant had, however, some credit with

2. Thomas Clears His Doubt

(Guercino : *Vatican Museum*)

3. St. Francis Xavier

the king of Portugal to whom he now wrote of his misfortunes and King John not only asked the Commandant of Cochin to release de Cruz but to accord him facilities for further commercial activities and give him two years' time to pay off his debts. Thus freed, de Cruz, in a desperate attempt to retrieve his lost fortune started trading in imported horses near Cape Comorin and it was here that he came to know of the plight of the Paravars. No wonder de Cruz could not make good in business, for he was no businessman; in his sympathy for the wretched Paravars he left his horses in Comorin and proceeded to the heart of the Fishery Coast to work for the deliverance of the Paravars. He contacted the headmen of the fishers who were living in hiding and informed them of the powerful new enemies of the Arabs who had established themselves in Cochin; and advised them that the only way to save themselves from the fury of the Arabs was to embrace Christianity and put themselves under the formal protection of the Portuguese. The Paravars jumped at the idea. A deputation of fifteen Paravars immediately proceeded to Cochin and were baptized. Soon the Portuguese missionaries appeared in the Fishery Coast, baptized over 20,000 Paravars and in accordance with their usual practice declared they were all under the protection of the King of Portugal. "And that is how," says a contemporary writer, "Our Lord saved so many souls by means of one torn ear-lobe."

The Muslim traders of the Fishery Coast naturally viewed these activities of the Portuguese with alarm. They had probably no intention of annihilating the Paravars as they were very good fishers and the Golden Goose of the Muslims; they only wanted to drive home to the Paravars that no rebellion would be tolerated whatever the provocation. The conversion of the Paravars and the transfer of their allegiance to the Portuguese were quite unforeseen events and it became clear to all Muslims who traded with the Indian ports that they would not be left the undisputed masters of the Indian ports they had so far been. Open hostilities now broke out between the Portuguese and the Arabs, and wherever the two met they fought. These indecisive minor actions had but a nuisance value and the Muslims organized a powerful confederacy against the Portuguese in which the Zamorin, the age-old ally of the Portuguese took an active part. A great fleet was equipped against the Western intruders. The Muslim admiral viewing his formidable armada was more than satisfied. He declared a victory before the battle was won and asked the Zamorin to start preparations for celebrating it. But the Portuguese proved that they were not the unruly, God-forsaken ruffians the Indians and Arabs had taken them for. With the help of the Rajah of Cochin and their Indian Christian allies they inflicted a crushing defeat on the Arabs in the famous naval action of Vedalai. This battle once for all broke the Muslim naval power and the supremacy of the Arabian Sea passed on to the Portuguese. The victory of Vedalai was celebrated with great enthusiasm both in Portugal and in India. The Zamorin realized the hopelessness of his situation and sued for peace and the Portuguese granted it on their own terms. Henceforward the power of the Zamorin waned and that of Cochin rose.

It was easy enough to convert 20,000 Paravars overnight as it were who found in conversion the only means of saving their lives, but to bring them to the Christian way of life was a more difficult matter. Though the Arabs were overcome, the hostility of the Pandyan had to be contended with. The inhospitable climate made life for Portuguese missionaries in the Fishery Coast extremely difficult. It was at this time that St. Francis Xavier appeared in the Indian mission field and started his momentous work.

Of all the missionaries Europe has sent out to India, Xavier was undoubtedly the greatest. He was that rare phenomenon, the ecstatic and man of action combined, which appears in the world once in several centuries. With a mystic bent of mind he combined an overwhelming compassion for suffering humanity and a flair for affairs which made his personality irresistible.

Xavier was of noble birth and started life as a gay courtier in Navarre, but the gaiety of court life did not hold him long. After a brilliant academic career he joined the staff of the then famous

Paris university as a lecturer in philosophy. This was the time when Ignatius Loyola was planning his spiritual militarism and Xavier fell under his influence. He joined the newly founded Society of Jesus and abandoning the peaceful atmosphere of the university plunged into the field of missionary work in the East.

Francis Xavier landed at Goa on 6th May 1542. This city, as we have noticed, was the capital of the rising Portuguese Empire in the East and one of the richest ports in the world. The powerful Portuguese Viceroy, the terror of all sea-going nations in the East had his headquarters there. He levied tribute from all vessels plying in the Indian Ocean whether for trade or for conveying pilgrims to and from Mecca. Goa had a very large cosmopolitan population of Hindus, Muslims, Indian Christians, Portuguese and Armenians, and the naval and army personnel and their requirements attracted a large number of businessmen and contractors. Building activity was in full swing and armies of labourers and overseers toiled at the construction of churches, monasteries, palaces and dwellings for the common folk. The clergy who catered to the needs of the Christians and the missionaries engaged in expanding the church were also numerous.

Xavier, before leaving Europe, had obtained from King John of Portugal, a zealous Christian, a letter highly recommending him to the Viceroy and asking him to give full support to the missionary. The Pope had appointed him Papal Nuncio to India and the Far East and had given him authority over all churches and missions in the Portuguese Empire in the East. Thus he had the backing of the most powerful political and ecclesiastical authorities of the time; but Xavier depended for the success of his mission not on the authority of king or Pontiff, but on his own devotion to the great cause he had undertaken for Christ.

Xavier's fame had preceded him and when he disembarked from the ship most of the highly placed civil and ecclesiastical authorities of the city and a large crowd were at the wharf to welcome him. A gaily decorated palanquin was ready for his conveyance. When the distinguished visitor came down the gangway of the ship, it was noticed that he was barefooted and clad in rags. A divine joy radiated from his face and he struck the crowd as a man not of this world. He dismissed the palanquin and signified his intention to walk to the hospital first. The grandees of Goa walked behind him, and on reaching the hospital he started washing the sores of lepers.

Xavier did not like the metropolitan atmosphere of Goa. He knew there was much to be done among his own community of Europeans in Goa, but there were greater needs to be catered for. He was struck by the abject distress of the lower classes of Hindus who were treated as subhumans by high caste Hindus, Muslims and Christians alike and it was the social and spiritual needs of these miserable creatures that claimed his attention first. He was quick to realize that Portuguese arms were respected and feared most in the low lying coastal regions and if the fisherfolk inhabiting this region were converted the Portuguese were in a position to give effective protection to the neophytes who were likely to be persecuted by high caste Hindus and the Arabs who were beginning to look upon all Christians as their enemies.

Soon after his arrival in India Xavier visited the Fishery Coast and ministered to the needs of the newly converted Paravars. The progress of his mission was not without difficulties. The transfer of their allegiance brought upon the Paravars the ire of the Pandyan and his powerful army was mobilised against them. The Paravars deserted the coastal regions and took refuge in the islands, and feeding the refugees was the special care of Xavier. A good number of Paravars fled to Travancore and the Rajah gave them protection; this offended the Pandyan and an invasion of Travancore appeared imminent. A Pandyan army actually marched on Travancore but did not proceed farther than the Amboli pass. A legend says that Xavier stopped the army by performing a miracle. Xavier's standing with the king of Portugal and the Viceroy at Goa was well known to South Indian potentates and a stern warning from the saint was probably responsible for the withdrawal of the Pandyan army. In recognition of this signal service, Xavier was invited by the Rajah of Travancore to his capital and was received with great honour.

Francis Xavier obtained permission from the Rajah of Travancore to do missionary work in his kingdom. For several good reasons he confined his missionary activities to the coastal region, mainly among the fishers. For one thing Xavier believed that the down trodden, poor inhabitants of the coast stood in greater need of him than the well-to-do classes of the interior who lived in lofty seclusion; for another, he realized that it was easier for the Portuguese to interfere and afford protection to the neophytes if any trouble similar to that experienced by the Paravars arose.

Xavier, no doubt, came in contact with the Syrian Christians. In his reports he spoke well of them and their Bishop. He did not waste his time probing into the details of their ritual or trying to change the way they put on clothes, but was inspired by the larger interests of Christianity and of humanity. The passion for details in ritual and ceremonial comes out of an inordinate love of book knowledge and an idle love of speculation. Xavier was concerned with men and women and souls in agony; he had given up books when he left Paris.

After spending three crowded years in India, the eagle eye of the missionary turned eastward. His was a soul which could not find peace as long as a single country existed in the world in which Christ was not known. Xavier was now fired with a zeal to preach Christ in the Land of the Rising Sun, the farthermost corner of the known world. An incident which filled his mind with annoyance at the indifference of the civil authorities of Goa towards his mission hastened his departure from India.

Some fishermen living in Manar coming to know of the advantages the Paravars enjoyed under Portuguese patronage sent a deputation to Francis Xavier to visit them. Xavier was then busy in Travancore and could not visit them himself but sent a priest who baptized a large number of the fishermen. These men were at that time under the king of Jaffna who found in the conversion of the fishers a potential danger to himself. The Portuguese, as a matter of course, claimed all their converts for subjects, and the king of Jaffna naturally feared that the conversion of the fishermen was but the thin end of the wedge which was eventually to lead to his ruin. The conversion of the Paravars and the destruction of the Arabs were fresh in his mind. So he sent an army to Manar and ordered the fishermen to return to their old faith. The fishermen refused and about 700 of them were butchered by the soldiery.

News of the massacre of the fishers reaching Xavier, he immediately proceeded to Goa to impress upon the Viceroy the need for doing something effective in the matter. Besides, information had reached him that the brother of the king of Jaffna was favourably disposed towards Christianity. The time appeared opportune for intervention. The Viceroy was at first favourably disposed towards the proposal, but later he changed his mind for some unknown reason and Xavier's bright hopes were dashed.

In the meantime the lure of the East became irresistible and he left India in the beginning of the year 1545. He reached Moluccas and after working three years here had to come back to India without proceeding to Japan. Reaching India in January 1548, he remained in this country for fifteen months, mainly engaged in organizing Jesuit missions in India and the East. The work of an organizer and director did not hold him long. The call of Japan came again, and in February 1549 he sailed from India to the strange Land of the Rising Sun.

Xavier worked in Japan for two years but the brilliant achievements of this remarkable man here is outside the scope of this book. Suffice it to say that after founding the church and winning the veneration of all who came in contact with him in Japan, Xavier returned to India and landed in Cochin in January 1552.

What he saw in India filled his soul with anguish. The affairs of the Society had fallen in a bad way. Incompetent and unworthy men filled responsible posts and quarrels for power and position among the clergy and laity became scandalous. Xavier now showed that he was not only a missionary and organizer but a stern disciplinarian. He took vigorous measures to combat corruption and jobbery. Those who needed correction were admonished; the incorrigible were removed from office. Within a short period he mended the affairs of the Society; and then the old passion for mission work again seized him. There was yet one important country in the East which he had not visited. This was China. While he was in Japan, Xavier had occasion to notice that the Japanese looked to China as the mother of all civilisations and had the greatest respect for the culture and traditions of this great and ancient land. Now the tireless missionary decided to preach the Gospel to the people of this part of the globe.

He tried to interest the civil authorities of Goa in his mission. The proposed enterprise appeared so dangerous to the gentlemen of Goa because of the well-known hostility of the Chinese to all Europeans especially the Portuguese, that far from encouraging him they dissuaded the missionary from undertaking the hazardous mission. Individuals were, however, helpful. Iago Pereira, the Captain of the vessel that took him to Japan put his heart and soul into the missionary's design. After overcoming considerable opposition from several quarters, Xavier set sail from Goa in April 1552 with the Celestial Empire as his destination never again to return to India he loved so well. Encountering many difficulties on the way, which only added to his zeal, this bold messenger of Christ reached the island of Sancian off Canton. This was the nearest point to the mainland where foreigners were permitted to disembark. Further progress proved difficult. While Xavier was absorbed in plans to cross over to the mainland, the Master called His tired worker from the field of labour. For on the 2nd December 1552, thousands of miles away from home and friends, exposed to biting colds in the sands of Sancian, this courtier, scholar, philosopher, administrator, mystic and arch-missionary breathed his last. There was none to comfort him in his last moments except the Eternal Comforter. And his was the death of the true missionary.

Not only Christendom, but both East and West that knew him mourned Xavier's death. His body was brought to Goa and to this day it remains intact, a lasting symbol of the immortality of his work.

No mission worker in the East has earned such great tributes from Christians and non-Christians alike as St. Francis Xavier. Born of noble parents and brought up to be a courtier, gifted with all the qualities that would have carved for him a brilliant worldly life, Xavier's renunciation itself was great; but his sincerity, devotion to the Christian cause, compassion for suffering humanity, his exhuberant energy that treated the whole globe as too small for his labours and his success in spite of great hazards make him by far the greatest saint and mission worker Europe has ever sent out to the East.

It was not the reward of heaven or the fear of hell that inspired Xavier to his momentous work, but his compassion for mankind and all consuming love for Christ. He transcends all sectarian bounds and belongs to humanity and not to a particular denomination. The following hymn, attributed to Xavier, shows up the springs of emotion that welled up within him and overflowed to fill the world:

> My God, I love Thee: not because
>   I hope for heaven thereby,
> Nor yet because who love Thee not
>   Are lost eternally.
> Thou, O my Jesus, Thou didst me
>   Upon the Cross embrace;
> For me didst bear the nails, the spear
>   And manifold disgrace,
> And griefs and torments numberless,
>   And sweat of agony—
> Yea death itself: and all for me,
>   Who was thine enemy.
> Then why, O blessed Jesu Christ,
>   Should I not love Thee well?
> Not for the sake of winning heaven
>   Nor of escaping hell!
> Not from the hope of gaining aught,
>   Not seeking a reward;

> But as Thyself hast loved me
>   O ever loving Lord!
> So would I love Thee, dearest Lord,
>   And in Thy praise will sing:
> Solely because Thou art my God,
>   And my most loving King.

Xavier, though a laborious worker, was also a mystic. He used to commune with God and fall into fits of ecstasy. He woke up from these mystic experiences crying 'Enough, Lord, enough'. His face always radiated a mysterious joy, not of this world, and any one who came in contact with him was immediately fascinated by it. But it was not this mystic personality alone that brought about the success of his mission. His will to suffer was even greater than his mystic powers. This side of his personality was once illustrated with particular force in an incident by which he saved a friend. While journeying from Goa to Cochin, he found himself on board the ship in the company of a Portuguese gentleman of rank whose way of life was a byword in wickedness among the Portuguese and Indians alike. Xavier by engaging conversation made friends with the man and tried to interest him in spiritual matters. But the man proved too difficult even for Xavier. He scoffed at religion and often revolted the saint by his loose and blasphemous talk. Xavier, however, did not despair. He persisted and the man, though not particularly interested in divine subjects, proved a good listener as Xavier himself was a man of wide experience and could be a brilliant conversationalist when he wanted. Throughout the journey, the man, however, could not be converted. The ship dropping anchor at Cranganoor, Xavier invited him for a stroll in a palm grove on the beach and as the two were conversing, Xavier suddenly bared his shoulders and started scourging himself till blood came out of the flesh. The bewildered man immediately understood the significance of the saint's strange action and implored him to desist. It is related he became a penitent and died a good Christian.

Such was Xavier's strange will to suffer for his brethren.

Xavier is said to have converted seven hundred thousand men to Christianity. He established schools for instruction of the neophytes and wherever he could worked for the spiritual and material advancement of the converts. He also established on a firm foundation the Society of Jesus in India which did such splendid work in the mission field in the East.

CHAPTER V

ROBERT DE NOBILI—THE ROMAN BRAHMIN AND THE MADURA MISSION

THE work of St. Francis Xavier and the early missionaries was, as we have seen, confined mainly to the lower classes inhabiting the coast. Christianity was firmly established by these pioneers all along the regions dominated by the Portuguese, but Portuguese influence extended only to a negligible part of the country and real India, even in the South, remained aloof from Christian influence.

The later missionaries had time to review the work of their predecessors and study its effect on Indian population. The first thing they noticed was that the conversion of the lower classes was leading to a general feeling in India that Christianity was a religion good enough for Parangis and outcastes but not for respectable Indians. The fishermen from whom the bulk of the neophytes were drawn were unapproachables to the three higher castes and even the better class of Sudras treated them as untouchables. The freedom of social intercourse extended by the Portuguese to the converted fishers did nothing to raise the prestige of the Portuguese, already low as we have noticed in a previous chapter.

It was not merely the licentious life of the Portuguese settlements in the country that revolted Indians. The very construction of European society and some of its perfectly legitimate and desirable usages were objectionable from Indian standards. A casteless society was promiscuity to the Hindu. Beef eating and indifference to ablutions were abominations in the eyes of the Hindus which prevented all social intercourse between Europeans and the better classes of Hindus. The Syrian Christians had always appreciated these Hindu prejudices and had maintained a sort of caste superiority and ceremonial purity which had obtained for them the status of a high caste among the Hindus.

Another thing that struck the later missionaries was the general indifference of high caste Hindus to the religion of the Europeans as separate from their political prestige. The motive of conversion of the Paravars and other communities of fishers was either hope of deliverance from their oppressors or material advantage. The better classes of Hindus, especially Brahmins who were quite well off under Hindu kings did not care to be converted; nor did they show any interest in the religion of the Parangis. True, some discontented chieftain at times approached the Portuguese with a pretended interest in Christianity followed by requests of political help; but when this was denied or delayed, the enquirer lost his interest in Christianity.

The vigilant and energetic Jesuits of the Counter Reformation who were planning the conversion of India and the Far East did not fail to take notice of these facts. They realized that without impressing the upper strata of Hindu society Christianity could make no real headway in India. For obvious reasons, the methods adopted in the conversion of the Paravars could not be applied to the lofty, intellectually complacent Brahmin who laid down laws for kings and subjects alike and dominated the social, religious and political life of the Hindus. Before trying to convert him, it was necessary to know the religious views he held. Hence the bolder and more brilliant members of the Society of Jesus started studying the language, religion, literature and social theories of the Hindus, and the result was an eye-opener to many a missionary. Hitherto Europeans had treated the Hindus as a band of abandoned infidels bereft of all true knowledge and grace of God. But a closer study of the Hindus convinced the more enlightened of the European missionaries that far from being savages the Hindus were a civilized people, inheritors of a great tradition and culture comparable to that of the Greeks and Romans from whom Christianity had learnt and adopted much.

This knowledge led Father Robert de Nobili of the Society of Jesus to introduce a bold and original method in his missionary work. He rightly judged the power of the Brahmins as the leaders of the religious and social life of the community and as the counsellors of kings. If Brahmins as a class could be persuaded to accept Christianity he knew that the conversion of others would follow as a matter of course. His extensive study of Hinduism and its social theories made him draw a sharp line between religious and social codes, and he maintained that there was no need for bringing Christianity to India as a violent revolutionary change but that Christ could live in India without hat, pants and boots; that eating, drinking, clothing, washing and fashions in hair dressing had nothing to do with the fundamentals of Christianity, and Indian Christians could be allowed to follow their traditional notions in these matters. He dismissed caste as a social convenience, the cord and the Kudumi (the tuft of long hair worn by South Indians) as marks of social distinction and held that Hindus, on conversion, need not give these up.

Agreeable to these notions, Father Robert de Nobili along with his disciple Father Vico, appeared in Madura clad in the saffron robe of the Sadhu with sandal paste on his forehead and the cord on his body from which hung a cross. He took up his abode in the Brahmin quarters of the city. The Hindus with their traditional respect for holy men came to pay homage to the strange Sanyasin. Madura was, at that time, a great centre of Hindu culture and its stately temple harboured many a learned Brahmin whose one delight was the study of things spiritual. Some of these learned men were interested in the new arrival and went to his Ashram to discuss and to question. At first the enquirers were refused admission by the disciple on the plea that the holy man could not be disturbed in his meditation. This but added to the curiosity of the Brahmins of Madura. Pressure for audience became insistent, and gradually the more prominent of the enquirers were admitted to the holy man's presence. De Nobili's profound knowledge of Tamil and Sanskrit and the religion of the Hindus stood him in good stead in dealing with these enquirers. He did not, however, degenerate into a disputant but always maintained the dignity of the teacher. De Nobili gave out that he was a Brahmin from Rome. Knowing the notoriety the Portuguese had obtained all over India for unclean living, he dissociated himself from this community and swore he was no Parangi.

Strictly speaking, de Nobili was quite justified in his claims. By a wide interpretation, the word 'Brahmin' means a priest and as such he was not wrong in maintaining he was a Brahmin. By the term Parangi or Ferangi, Indians as a rule meant the Portuguese and Father Robert was an Italian. The Italians, as the inheritors of the traditions of the Roman civilisation had, throughout the middle ages, held the newly risen Iberians as half-baked upstarts and Father Robert probably shared his countrymen's views about the Portuguese.

There was nothing in the way of life of the Roman Brahmin to cause resentment to the most exacting Indian Brahmin. He performed the ablutions as neatly as the most punctilious Brahmin. He lived on frugal fare, abjuring wine, fish and meat. He never looked at a woman. He abandoned the use of leather shoes and trod on clean wooden sandals as gracefully as a Hindu teacher. He gave audience, sitting cross legged as the meditating Yogi, clad in saffron clothes and hallowed by the aroma of the sandal paste. He discoursed on profound subjects in perfect Tamil and showed deep insight into the religion and philosophy of the Hindus.

It should not be imagined that Father Robert adopted this way of life out of sheer hypocrisy. He loved it. He was something of an ascetic and believed that a meagre vegetarian diet and strictness in personal habits enjoined by Brahmins were in conformity with the higher life. The Brahmin mode of dress was best suited to the climate of South India and the ablutions were refreshing in the tropical heat. In his own words, he became an Indian to save Indians even as God became man to save mankind, and there was nothing demeaning or irreligious about that. While he gave up his nationality for India, de Nobili certainly did not give up his religion.

The Brahmins of Madura did not know what to make of their Roman compeer. Hinduism, as is well known, is strict in the observance of social rules but exceedingly liberal in the matter of belief and as long as the Roman conformed to the formal behaviour enjoined on Brahmins, no one could raise any objection to the doctrines he preached. To those who questioned his claim to Brahminhood Father Robert showed documentary evidence to prove that he belonged to a clan of the parent stock that had migrated westward from ancient Aryavarta. Here too he was right, for research has shown that the Romans and the Hindus belong to the same Aryan race! This documentary evidence and his own exemplary life brought conviction to the doubting, and Father Robert was generally accepted in Madura as a Roman Brahmin. He even wrote a fifth Veda propounding Christian doctrines.

The Roman Brahmin collected numerous disciples and commanded universal respect. A modified form of baptism was introduced for the initiates which differed from the orthodox form in some minor details. Father Robert's disciples were all drawn from the higher castes, and he became a power in Madura. Kings and nobles wished to befriend him. His fame for ascetic virtue was such that when once the king of Madura invited him to the palace de Nobili politely declined the invitation on the plea that moving out of doors his eyes might light upon some woman which would impair his vow of celibacy. Such ostentatious display of strictness had the desired effect. In India a teacher is respected not for the greatness of his doctrines but for the holiness of his life.

With success and power came opposition to de Nobili. The Brahmins of Madura began to view the activities of the Roman Brahmin and his followers with uneasiness. They had their own suspicions about de Nobili's claim to Brahminhood. But the faith the people had in him, the royal patronage he enjoyed and the saintly life he led which left nothing to be desired by the most exacting standards made the acrimonious attacks of his enemies ineffective.

But opposition came from other quarters which proved more serious. Before de Nobili's arrival in Madura, the Franciscans were working among the lower classes and on their leaving the field their work was continued by a Jesuit missionary named Fernandez. Father Fernandez was a staunch adherent of the old school and a bitter critic of the 'accommodation theory' of de Nobili. He together with certain missionaries of his way of thinking viewed the activities of the Roman Brahmin with alarm and sent representations to higher authorities stating that while de Nobili was trying to convert Brahmins to Christianity he was in reality converting Christianity to Brahminism. The cord, the Kudumi and sandal paste were made much of in these representations. Father Fernandez even went out of his way to teach his low caste followers that there was in fact no distinction between his own flock and de Nobili's Brahmin converts as all Hindus lost caste the moment they accepted Baptism. He further declared that both de Nobili and himself were pure Parangis. The worthy Father did not make a public declaration of his convictions because of the authorities in Goa and Cochin who were favourably disposed towards de Nobili, but one of his agents did. One fine morning a Paravar convert of Father Fernandez appeared in Madura and boldly denounced Father Robert as a Parangi impostor and claimed equality with his Brahmin followers on the strength of his conversion and loudly declared that they had no right to the cord and the Kudumi.

This public accusation was turned to good account by the Brahmin enemies of Father Robert and they stirred up the people against him. De Nobili's own disciples who had firmly believed that he was a Rishi from the West and his message the fulfilment of the Veda, were seriously perturbed and wanted an explanation from their Guru. The unfailing resourcefulness of the man saved him. De Nobili asserted with great vehemence that the accusation of the Paravar was malicious and inspired by an unholy desire to claim equality with his superiors. He gave written avowal to the following effect:

"I am no Parangi; I am not born on their soil, nor am I allied to their race. In this God is my witness, and if I lie, I am willing not only to be deemed a traitor to God and to be given over to the pains of hell hereafter, but also to suffer every conceivable chastisement in this world. I am born in Rome. My family are of the rank of noble Rajahs in this country. The holy spiritual law which I proclaim has been preached in this very country by other men, Sanyasis and saints alike. Whoever says this law is peculiar to Paravars and Parangis lies: for since God is Lord of all castes, His law must likewise be observed by all."

De Nobili was strictly right. His written avowal has been much criticized by his enemies as a piece of imposture, but enlightened Christian opinion can find nothing blameable in it. Father Robert was born in Rome, a fact he admits. The Italians are as different from the Portuguese as the Burmese are from the Singhalese. That he was of noble birth, none can deny. The law of Christ was for all alike; nor was true knowledge confined to Jews; the seers and saints of India were not denied true knowledge and they too had prescience of the redemption of man through God incarnate.

Father Robert's ideas on caste were strangely modern. He maintained that caste was a social convenience and had nothing to do with the fundamentals of Hindu religion, a view held by all enlightened Hindus at present. "By becoming a Christian," says de Nobili, "one does not renounce his caste, nobility or usage. The idea that Christianity interferes with them has been impressed upon the people by the devil, and is the great obstacle to Christianity. It is this that has stricken the work of Father Fernandez with sterility." What de Nobili wanted to teach was not socialism or practical democracy but Christianity.

The personality of Father Robert and his thorough grasp of Hinduism won the day and the storm blew over. But the persevering Father Fernandez and his company would not accept defeat, and fresh complaints were continuously made to the ecclesiastical authorities in Goa, Cranganoor and Cochin, and Father Robert was called upon to appear before the authorities to answer the charges in person. His brilliant defence of his methods always silenced his enemies. He could explain with ease and conviction the most outlandish and seemingly pagan of his activities. Those who railed against caste were asked to explain the propriety of maintaining social distinctions in Europe. Did a nobleman of rank dine with a plebian? When seats could be reserved in churches for the lordly, where was the harm in having separate congregations in India for the high and the low? Europe certainly did not practise social equality at the time, then why should India do so? In India social distinctions were more clearly defined than in Europe, but why should Europeans insist that Indians who accepted Christianity should discard their ancient usages and adopt European customs? Father Robert was not a social reformer but a Christian missionary.

Then there was the cord and the Kudumi. The cord, it is true, has some religious significance but its social significance at the time was greater. It was the mark of the three higher castes and in the people's mind was associated with nobility of birth. Hence while de Nobili retained the cord, he did not accept it in its entirety. Instead of the triple cord used by Hindus he introduced a quintiple cord symbolizing the Trinity and the two natures in Christ's person. The cord as such, he maintained, had no great place in the fundamentals of Hinduism and could be adopted by Christians. One cannot but admire de Nobili's profound grasp of Hinduism and contempt for his ill-informed critics. For Hinduism does maintain that the cord is non-essential to the higher life and many a Hindu teacher has discarded the cord to signify his emancipation from caste. As regards the Kudumi, only the stupid could maintain that Jesus Christ wanted men to dress their hair in a particular way.

The social inequalities and degradation imposed by the rigours of the caste system could not have possibly escaped the notice of the observant de Nobili. But he was a spiritual teacher and the abolition of caste was the concern of the social reformer. His mission was to enthrone Christ within the existing framework of Indian society and he left it to Indians themselves to bring about necessary social reforms. Moreover, it was then too early to abolish the caste system, for it must be remembered that de Nobili started his work in Madura in the first decade of the 17th century.

De Nobili's sincerity, zeal and extensive knowledge of India and her people always scored for him well deserved victories over his adversaries. He tore the arguments of his ignorant accusers to pieces; he convinced the enlightened and confounded men of little knowledge. But his enterprising enemies carried the war outside India. Rome began to get continuous reports of a disquieting nature about the activities of the Madura Mission. But when enquiries brought matters to the fundamentals, Father Robert's accusers could do no more than fumble about the cord and the Kudumi and exhibit a vague uneasiness about the way de Nobili and his followers looked. Anyway report after report reached Rome and de Nobili became a problem to Christendom in general and to the Pope in particular. The controversy raged in Goa, Cochin and Cranganoor and even in Europe de Nobili's strange activities led to heated disputes. The Pope was finally pressed for a verdict. After an exhaustive enquiry into the subject, conducted by able doctors of law and doctrine, de Nobili's methods were declared quite valid and in the year 1623 Pope Gregory XV in a notable bull ruled as follows:

"Brahmins are kept from confession of Christ by difficulties about the cord and the Kudumi. Desiring to procure the conversion of these nations, after suitable discussion we accord to the Brahmins and other Gentiles the cord and the Kudumi, sandal paste and purification of the body. These should not be received in idol temples, but only from priests after they have blessed them."

Thus de Nobili won his final victory. But he had to pay a heavy price. The charges he had to answer in person constantly necessitated his absence from Madura, and the controversy became so widespread and public that it was all too plain to the Brahmins of Madura that though de Nobili was not a Parangi, he had some intimate relations with them and that they held authority over him. This made his position in Madura difficult.

De Nobili now abandoned the role of the recluse and took to the life of the other well-known Hindu teacher, the wandering Sadhu. With a band of devoted followers de Nobili wandered all over South India, from village to village, from city to city, teaching, comforting and baptizing. His converts were drawn from all sections of the community and the higher castes enjoyed all their traditional social privileges. The wandering pilgrim commanded the respect of all who came in contact with him. Churches sprang up all over South India. The followers of de Nobili had no political advantages to gain by conversion. A genuine yearning for a God of Mercy and Righteousness who desired devotion and a contrite heart was the only motive for conversion. The congregations of the Madura Mission increased day by day, and the fame of the Mission spread not only throughout India but all over Christendom.

For over forty years did de Nobili work in India. He went to Ceylon to spend the evening of his life in meditation and prayer, but his spirit could find no peace away from the plains of the South he loved so dearly. He returned to India and when the end appeared nigh, retired to the shrine of St. Thomas at Mylapore where he lived in a mud hut. Old, feeble and blind he continued the austere life of the Sadhu till the very end, which came on the 16th of February in the year 1656 at the age of eighty.

Not less than 100,000 Christians are attributed to him. His contribution to Tamil literature was also considerable. Even in his old age he kept four secretaries busy writing down the outpouring of his soul.

De Nobili loved India and Indians and their way of life. In his deep insight into human nature, in his sympathy with Indian culture and traditions, in his recognition of the prophetic presage of Indian sages of the coming of the Saviour, he stands alone among the Europeans of his time who were inclined to treat the Hindus as a God-forsaken set of idolaters.

Critics are not even now rare who consider de Nobili as an impostor and his work as a gigantic fraud. In support of their arguments they point out the rapid decline of the Madura Christians and their virtual disappearance which they attribute to want of spiritual vitality. But the Christian communities of Madura suffered many things of many men. The brutal soldiery of Tippu were their worst enemies. If the nascent community could not survive the anarchy that overwhelmed South India soon after it was founded and the violent persecutions of Tippu and petty chieftains, the blame does not fall on the founder or his methods. Before passing rash judgement on de Nobili we will do well to remember that the communities Apostle Thomas himself founded on the plains of the South India perished soon after his departure and the lamp at his shrine had to be tended by Muslim admirers of the saint. Nor is it correct to judge the work of de Nobili by his formal adherents alone; for his life and doctrines penetrated farther than the church he organized and nowhere in India except Malabar is Christian influence so marked even at present as in the Tamil countries.

The great work of de Nobili was continued by John de Britto, another Jesuit, a greater intellectual and zealot than de Nobili himself. His proficiency in Tamil was such that he was acclaimed the greatest of contemporary Tamil writers. His labours in the Madura Mission were as arduous as those of de Nobili himself. "In the greater church of all Christ's followers, his eminence as a disciple, intrepid, selfless, and enduring in all great qualities that add to the vigour of the Christian life is assured. He is not only among the first since the Apostolic days, he is really with Robert de Nobili, the greatest among missionaries in India of the Church of Rome, and one of the greatest in the wider Church of Christ."*

This praise of a protestant missionary is well deserved. Britto worked in the Madura Mission for over sixteen years. His zeal and sacrifice and his sufferings won for him many adherents. But unfortunately he had to contend with anarchical political conditions in the regions he worked. The old Tamil kingdom had collapsed and there was a desperate scramble for power by petty tyrants. The enemies of de Nobili and de Britto found their long awaited opportunity in the turmoil, and desperate political upstarts were available to do the direst deed. The Madura Christians were violently persecuted and de Britto shared their sufferings and had to undergo imprisonment and torture. He was released and

* William Robinson of the L.M.S. mission.

soon after went to Portugal, but the call of India was irresistible and he returned to Ramnad, where the conversion of a local chieftain led to trouble with the Rajah. De Britto was arrested, tortured and put to death.

After the martyrdom of de Britto in 1693, the affairs of the Madura mission fell in a bad way, but in the year 1707 another celebrated Jesuit missionary reached India bent upon continuing de Nobili's work. He was Father Joseph Beschi. He was an Italian and emphatically renewed the claims of de Nobili for Roman Brahminhood, a position which John de Britto because of his Portuguese origin could not claim. Beschi, however, adopted a line of approach to the Hindu heart which differed considerably from that of de Nobili. This was also inspired by a sound understanding of Hindus and Hinduism. Though the ascetics and wandering Sanyasins commanded great respect among Hindus, there were also religious heads among them who lived like princes and awed the public by their aloofness and worldly power. They were learned and venerable men who commanded the homage of influential communities and were competent to pronounce judgement on all disputed points of religious law and practice. They officiated during the coronation ceremonies of princes and chieftains and were their preceptors and advisers. While living a strict religious life, they usually confined themselves to the four corners of their palaces and appeared in public only on grand occasions.

De Nobili and de Britto had impressed South India by their ascetic and wandering life, but Beschi decided to assume the role of the High Priest of the Madura Mission. In his personal life he was an ascetic, but for overawing the people he adopted a showy life. He travelled in ivory palanquins, surrounded by numerous disciples. The silk umbrella, the insignia of royalty, was carried before the vehicle in which he travelled. He reclined on superb couches, and attendants fanned him with fly whisks of yak or peacock tail.

Father Beschi's scholarship in Tamil was even greater than that of de Britto. His books are read with delight by all sections of

Tamilians, Christians and non-Christians alike. His literary distinction won for him the friendship of Chanda Sahib, the Nawab of Vellore, who presented him with four villages in the Trichinopoly district which yielded an annual revenue of Rs. 12,000.

The Madura Mission reached the zenith of its glory under Father Beschi. The congregation spread throughout the Tamil country and the number of Christians was about 200,000. But with the death of Beschi in 1742 decline set in. The over-enthusiasm of the Jesuits brought them into conflict with the other orders of the Catholic Church and with secular authority. Their activities were viewed with suspicion and distrust. In the general atmosphere of antagonism the critics of the Jesuits of the Madura Mission succeeded in getting the support of influential ecclesiastical authorities who denounced the activities of the Mission as a fraud. In 1759 when the Order of Jesuits was suppressed in Portugal, the Madura Jesuits were, without notice, deported from the shores of India.

This was the virtual collapse of the Madura Church. Its founders were busy in enlarging the sphere of their activities and increasing the number of their following when misfortune overtook them. Given time they would have organised the Madura Church on a sound basis, built up a hierarchy of responsible Indians, and this would have given rise to a powerful community of Christians comparable to the Syrians of Malabar. But before the structure was complete, the rains came, the wind blew and the builders were called away.

After the withdrawal of the Jesuits, the Portuguese power itself was scarcely felt in India. New Nations had risen in the West who had driven away the Portuguese from the Indian seas. In India itself there was confusion and anarchy. Political turmoil, neglect and active persecution all but annihilated the Madura Church. When, during the early years of the nineteenth century the Abbe Dubois visited India, he found but a scattered community without any leaders, organisation or status. About 60,000, the Abbe tells us, had been forcibly converted to Islam by the soldiers of Tippu.

CHAPTER VI

THE SYRIANS AND THE PORTUGUESE

THE cordiality that existed between the Portuguese and the Syrian Christians of Malabar during the first few years of their contact did not last long. If anything, the two nations as they came to know more about each other began to develop mutual contempt. The Syrians, as we have seen, looked upon the Portuguese as an unclean people not good enough for social intercourse.

The Portuguese, on the other hand, could see nothing in the Syrians to justify their aloofness and superiority complex. Compared to the powerful Portuguese, lords of the Eastern Seas and rolling in wealth amassed by the trade with the East, the Syrians were a poor community. They were subjects of Hindu Rajahs and had no independent status. The way of life of the Syrians appeared to the Portuguese more pagan than Christian, and the generality of the Portuguese could not escape a feeling that the Syrians were no better than Hindus for whom they had the utmost contempt. Hence they could attribute the aloofness of the Syrians only to perversity.

Discerning men among the Portuguese, both among the clergy and laity, had visions of a fusion of the two communities to the advantage of both. The Syrians had excellent military traditions and could put in the field in an emergency a respectable army of 20,000 fighting men, and with the superior discipline and equipment of the Portuguese a combined army could be quite formidable both on land and sea. A Syrian community loyal to the Portuguese could also obviate the need for drawing recruits from Portugal, a tedious process at the time because of the difficulties of communication; in an emergency the Portuguese were usually at a loss to know how to raise a reliable army in India. Intermarriages and free social contacts between the Portuguese and Syrians would have created quite a powerful Christian kingdom in India.

But the Syrian Christians had different views. They were inveterate conservatives, and to them pride of race and ancient traditions were dearer than political and economic advancement, and they persistently rejected all Portuguese proposals to befriend and fraternize. Where women were concerned, they followed Brahmin notions of purity and the giving of a Syrian Christian girl of good family in marriage to a Parangi of whatever position was unimaginable to them.

The clergy had an additional interest in bringing the Syrians under Goa. The Portuguese power was rapidly rising in the East and the ecclesiastical authorities in Goa thought they were the natural guardians of all Christians who lived in regions where Portuguese political influence was felt. It irked them to note that while most of the Christian communities of the Indian Coast owed allegiance to Goa, the Syrians who were the most important received their Bishops from elsewhere. Further, the Syrian rite which they could not understand was thought to contain many errors inspired by Nestorian influence. All told, the Portuguese considered it desirable to bring the Syrians under the authority of Goa.

That the Syrian Church stood badly in need of reforms, no impartial person can deny. With the rise of Muslim power the Malabar Church, as we have seen, lived in practical isolation and the arrival of Bishops from overseas was far from regular. The area ruled by the Syrian Bishop was too unwieldy to be effectively controlled from one centre, and at times when the arrival of a Bishop was delayed nothing prevented bold Cattanars (as the clergy among the Syrians were called) from propounding their own doctrines independent of the Archdeacons. The fact that the Syrians were distributed under three independent Rajahs also made cohesion difficult. Besides, some of the Cattanars had large families and poor relatives and a few at least were not above imposing exactions on their flock and demanding exorbitant fees for the administration of spiritual comforts. The Bishops themselves were foreigners who did not know the language of the people and the virtual rulers of the community were the

Archdeacons whose office was hereditary in the Pakalomattam family converted by St. Thomas and invested with authority over the Christians of Malabar. The evils of hereditary rule in the ecclesiastical field are too obvious to be enumerated here. Besides, long association with the Hindus had led the Syrians to borrow many of the beliefs and practices of their neighbours which were not in conformity with orthodox Christian principles.

All this shows that the Syrian Church did stand in need of reforms at the time. St. Francis Xavier knew this. But he knew that India had greater needs and hence he devoted his time and energy for catering to these. He was, however, well disposed towards the community and had great regard for their Bishop, Mar Jacob Abuna. The Portuguese were inclined to treat him with scant respect and Xavier wrote to the king of Portugal strongly recommending him to his favour and asking him to issue instructions to his Governors, Procurators and Captains to treat the venerable old Bishop in a manner befitting his honoured position. Further, "Your Highness should write to him recommending him very much to recommend you to God, for Your Highness needs more to be favoured by the Bishop in his prayers than the Bishop needs the temporal favour of Your Highness. He has been working much amongst the St. Thomas Christians, and now in his old age he is very obedient to the customs of the Holy Mother the Church of Rome."

This leaves us in no doubt as to his allegiance, and he was certainly no Nestorian.

Mar Jacob Abuna was a friend of the European missionaries, and he too felt the need for reforms in his Church. With his co-ordination the Franciscans established, in 1545, a college in Cranganoor with the intention of instructing young Syrians in the Latin rite so that these young men could bring about the necessary reforms in the Syrian Church. A few Syrian youths were educated here but when the young zealots came out of the college to preach their innovations, the general body of the Syrians would not only not accept the innovations but threatened to excommunicate the innovators. This was an eye-opener to the Portuguese.

They were now convinced of the futility of reasonable persuasion in dealing with the Syrians and decided to have recourse to more direct methods. Ecclesiastical power had by now passed on to the Jesuits and these, in their dealings with the Syrians betrayed a complete lack of understanding of their tenacious attachment to traditions and tried to force their will on the community.

With the death of Mar Jacob Abuna in 1549, the Portuguese started direct interference with the Syrian Church. To fill the vacant see, Patriarch Abdiso of Geziresh, who was formally subject to Rome, sent Bishop Mar Joseph to Malabar. The Portuguese who had assumed guardianship of all Christians in South India by virtue of the *Padroado* thought the right of appointing Bishops for the Syrian Christians belonged to them. The Syrians maintained that the *Padroado* was inapplicable to the Syrian Church which had been ruled by Bishops from Western Asia from time immemorial but applied only to the neophytes the Portuguese converted. Well, the *Padroado* was an agreement between the Pope and the king of Portugal who were the final authorities in the dispute; but the Pope was in Rome and the king of Portugal in Lisbon and the difficulties of communication provided the authorities of Goa the necessary excuses for doing what they liked.

So when the vessel taking Mar Joseph to Malabar touched Goa in November 1556, the Portuguese interested him in the excellent possibilities of Goa as a health resort, disembarked him there and the vessel sailed without the Bishop. They then wrote to Lisbon and Rome pointing out to the authorities there the impropriety of permitting Eastern Patriarchs to send Bishops to Malabar when they were so near Malabar to look after the Syrian flock. Pending a reply, Mar Joseph was detained at Bassein where he lived as a virtual prisoner. The Portuguese had ample opportunities to study Mar Joseph and his companion, and it is interesting to note that those who moved closely with them had nothing but praise for them. This is evident from a letter written by Father Antonio da Porto to the king of Portugal. Extracts from this letter are reproduced below:

"I discussed with them many times passages of both the Old and New Testaments, and found that their points of view conformed with that of our doctrines, and as regards the literal meanings, I found they had as much faith as those who were born and lived in the place where the events took place. . . . In the Articles of Faith and the Sacraments of our Holy Mother the Church, I often discussed with them what is fundamental and necessary, and in no way or word found them differing from us. As regards their life and good habits, they were such that they were a good example not only to myself, but to the new Christians of this country and the Moors were astonished at their good life and their good doctrine and practice. The Portuguese being more enlightened were so edified by their good life and practice that few spoke with them once without returning to speak again; and many cherished for them great devotion and visited them many times, although they lived in this jungle. They are men who do not eat meat because they belong to the Order of St. Basil, as observed by the Carthusians; they do not eat fish either in Lent or in Advent or on the days of fasting, nor do they drink wine on these days. They are very quiet and retiring, so that they never get out unless absolutely necessary, spending all their time in prayer and contemplation and in studying the Sacred Scripture and the saintly doctors on Scripture which they have."

They were found to be such staunch Catholics that the worthy Father taught them how to say Mass in Latin. Although they learnt Latin with alacrity and had no objection to saying Mass in this language, when the Portuguese suggested the introduction of the Latin rite in Malabar and the desirability of bringing the Syrian Church under Goa, the Bishop stoutly refused. This naturally offended the Portuguese and Mar Joseph's detention continued.

In the meantime news reached Goa that a Syrian Bishop of obscure origin had appeared in Malabar and was teaching heretical doctrines. This upset the plans of the Portuguese. They now thought Mar Joseph a lesser evil and allowed him to proceed to Malabar.

Mar Joseph was as much convinced of the need for reforms in the Malabar Church as the Portuguese themselves, and earnestly set to work in this direction. He won the admiration of the Syrians and persuaded the Chaldean Bishop then working in Malabar to go back to where he came from. Mar Joseph now introduced certain reforms in his Church. Among other things he "removed many errors from the Mass, declared some censures void, introduced the sacred vestments, counselled confession, and corrected many other false opinions." The Portuguese, however, thought the reforming zeal of the Bishop inadequate and Father Carneyro, a Jesuit missionary, went about preaching from Parish to Parish and telling the Syrians that they were no better than heretics. Mar Joseph and the Syrians resented this and their antagonism led to the withdrawal of Father Carneyro from Malabar. While he was in Cochin, on his way to Goa, an arrow shot by an unknown hand wounded the Father, and the Portuguese thought that Mar Joseph had something to do with it. They soon discovered serious errors in his teachings and denounced him to Lisbon and to Rome. The Bishop was first asked to go to Goa and thence to Europe. Mar Joseph, confident of his own orthodoxy and allegiance to Rome, was ready to answer any charges and prove his innocence. He promptly proceeded to Goa and from there sailed for Lisbon.

Mar Joseph was a man of great charm and the picturesque Syrian won the admiration of the court of Lisbon. He became a favourite of Cardinal Henry and Queen Catherine. His doctrines were examined, and Cardinal Henry found that his only heresy was his unbelief in the necessity for bringing the Syrian Church under Goa. It was a waste of time to send him to Rome to answer charges of heresies which he had never held. So Mar Joseph was sent back to India and peremptory orders were issued to the Archbishop and Viceroy of Goa to send him to his see in Malabar without delay or hindrance.

He reached Malabar in 1565, but no sooner had he taken charge of his flock than reports of fresh heresies reached Goa from the Jesuits of Cochin and Cranganoor. The authorities at Goa found the charges serious and again denounced Mar Joseph, this time direct to Rome. The Pope ordered an enquiry and Mar Joseph had again to go to Goa to prove his innocence. In the First Council of Goa held in 1567, Mar Joseph was found guilty of all the charges framed by his accusers. With irrefutable evidence of his heresies the Bishop was again sent to Lisbon by the triumphant authorities of Goa who did not fail to point out what a fool the arch-heretic of Malabar had made of Cardinal Henry.

Undismayed Mar Joseph again went to Lisbon. Here he produced irrefutable evidence of his innocence. He gave out in detail the reforms he had already introduced in the Malabar Church; for the rest he proved that most of the accusations of the Jesuits rose out of their innocence of Syrian Christian social structure and were purely social matters which had nothing to do with the fundamentals of Christianity. Mar Joseph had no difficulty in convincing Lisbon that the accusations were inspired not by a love of reform but solely by a desire for bringing the Syrians under Goa. Lisbon not only acquitted the Bishop honourably but strongly recommended him to the Pope's favour and sent him to Rome.

It did not take Rome much time to find out that Lisbon was right. The personality of the genial Syrian was irresistible. The Pope and the Cardinals were so impressed by him and his brilliant defence that they seriously thought of making him a Cardinal. But the hand of fate interfered and this most remarkable and interesting figure in Syro-Portuguese history passed away in 1569.

While Mar Joseph was being shuttled about between Goa and Europe, the Syrians had not been keeping quiet. During the first deportation of Mar Joseph to Lisbon, they applied to Patriarch Abdiso for another Bishop in place of Mar Joseph. The Patriarch sent them Mar Abraham. This prelate differed from the saintly and learned Mar Joseph in many respects. He was less genial and learned, but had greater worldly wisdom and energy; he met the Portuguese on their own ground, returned blow for blow, met cunning by cunning, hypocrisy by hypocrisy and abduction by elusion. Benefiting by the experience of his predecessor, Mar Abraham studiously avoided the Portuguese and eluding their vigilance managed to reach the Serra, the hinterland where the agricultural population among the Syrians lived. The Serra was sufficiently far removed from the ports to be safe from the long arm of the Portuguese. He started governing the Syrians from the Serra when Mar Joseph, after proving his innocence in Lisbon returned to Malabar loaded with honours. Mar Abraham now did not know what to do with himself. He sounded Mar Joseph on the desirability of dividing the Malabar Church into two dioceses, but Mar Joseph thought this unreasonable. While he was thus left without a flock and wandering in Malabar, the Portuguese who were smarting under the grievance of his appearance in Malabar without their permission, kidnapped him, accused him of several heinous heresies and sent him to Europe. Before the ship carrying him reached the Cape of Good Hope, Mar Abraham reached patriarch Abdiso, having escaped on the way. The Bishop interested the patriarch in his scheme of the division of the Malabar Church, especially as the area could not be effecttively administered by one Bishop and as it was essential to put the Malabar Church on a higher status to offset the designs and claims of the Portuguese. As Mar Joseph had established direct relations with Lisbon and as the troublesome Portuguese at Goa were not likely to respect his decision, the Patriarch sent Mar Abraham to Rome to get orders from the Supreme Pontiff. Rome was by now quite distracted with this endless trouble between the Portuguese and the Syrians and sent Mar Abraham back to Abdiso to decide between the two Bishops and gave instructions to the Archbishop of Goa to abide by the decision of the Patriarch.

The Patriarch decided in favour of Mar Abraham, created the new See of Angamali for him and sent him to Malabar. Fearing no harm from the Portuguese because of the Pope's Bull and the Patriarch's letter, Mar Abraham reached Goa in 1568 on his way to Malabar. The Portuguese however could not resist the temptation of detaining Mar Abraham who had eluded them so many times. Besides Mar Abraham had reached Goa at an opportune moment. Mar Joseph had just left India on his second deportation and if the Malabar Church were sufficiently starved for Bishops, the Syrians were likely to swallow any Bishop, even Portuguese. Hence the Portuguese at Goa rejected the letter of the Patriarch as unauthorized and maintained that he had no right to appoint a Bishop or create a see; as for the Pope's Bull they respectfully told Mar Abraham that His Holiness had been misinformed and if the matter would be represented to him in its true light he would gladly revise his hasty decision, and in anticipation of this revision they imprisoned Mar Abraham in a Dominican convent.

Mar Abraham did not imagine that the Portuguese would be so disrespectful of authority. Anyway, the prelate did not wait for further orders from Rome. A master in elusiveness, he escaped from the convent and made straight for Cochin. Reaching this port, he calmly presented the Pope's Bull to the Portuguese authorities here, who, quite innocent of the designs of Goa, allowed him to proceed to the Serra and accorded him all facilities to make his journey expeditious and comfortable. By the time orders were received in Cochin from Goa for the arrest of the absconding prelate, Mar Abraham was firmly entrenched in the heart of the Serra as the Archbishop of the Syrian Christians of Malabar. Angamali was a mountainous region inaccessible to the Portuguese and from here he ruled the Syrians without much interference from them.

For once the Portuguese were baffled. They did not, however, give up hope. In the year 1575 Mar Abraham received a polite invitation from the Archbishop of Goa to attend the Second Council of Goa. The tone of the letter, however, suggested that Angamali was subordinate to Goa and Mar Abraham was duty bound to attend. The Syrian Archbishop was too shrewd to miss its implications; hence while he refused to attend the Council, he wrote to Rome his reasons for the refusal. He also prevailed upon the Rajah of Cochin in whose kingdom Angamali was situated to write to the Pope that Mar Abraham who enjoyed his patronage was constantly harassed by the Portuguese and had been twice captured by them without reason and had to make good his escape. At the insistance of the Archbishop the Rajah had made it plain to the Pontiff that Mar Abraham was an obedient son of Rome and his refusal to attend the Council of Goa was inspired solely by a fear of the Portuguese who had become notorious for double dealings.

The design of the Portuguese on the See of Angamali had by now become plain to everybody, and Mar Abraham vigorously fought for the independence of his ancient Church. He addressed Pope Gregory XIII on the matter to whom he sent a Profession of Faith. He then informed his own Patriarch of the evil intentions of the Portuguese and warned him that if he did not take active steps to combat them, the Malabar Church would be grabbed by Goa. He got influential members of the Syrian community to send a petition to the Patriarch impressing upon him the need for appointing at least five Bishops under the Archbishop of Angamali because of the extensive area covered by the Archdiocese and the difficulty of administering it from one centre; the petitioners also made it plain to the Patriarch that the Portuguese were thoroughly hated by the Syrians and if a Latin Bishop were appointed to the See of Angamali even with the permission of the Patriarch, the turbulent element among the Syrians would not hesitate to remove him by force if necessary. These vigorous measures had the desired effect, and the Portuguese realized that Mar Abraham was a man who would not willingly accept their yoke. Hence they waited and prayed for something to turn up.

Although he fought valiantly all the attempts of the Portuguese to reduce his church to their subjection, Mar Abraham, like Mar Joseph believed that reforms were needed in the Syrian Church. He appreciated the learning of the Jesuit Fathers of Vaipicotta Seminary and accepted, as his adviser, Father Roz, a learned Jesuit. In 1583 he convened a Provincial Synod at Angamali, consisting of his own clergy and two Jesuits from Vaipicotta. The need for several reforms were impressed upon, and the Jesuits and the Syrian clergy unanimously agreed as to the ways and means of giving effect to them.

The relations between Mar Abraham and the Jesuits improved to such an extent that the Archbishop decided to attend the Third Council of Goa held in 1585. Mar Abraham, however, was gifted with a keen memory and he attended the Council only on receiving an assurance of honourable treatment from well placed Portuguese officials and a personal undertaking by Father Valignani that he would conduct him safe to Goa and back. The affairs of the Serra were freely discussed in the Council at Goa and Mar Abraham promised to give effect to all the reforms recommended by the Council.

On the Archbishop reaching the Serra, complaints that he was not giving effect to any of the reforms reached Goa; further that he had lapsed into Nestorian heresy. These charges were carried to Rome, and Pope Clement VIII expressed sorrow on the lapses of Mar Abraham and asked the Archbishop of Goa to enquire into the charges. This was the order Goa had all along been waiting for. But before the instructions reached Goa, Mar Abraham fell seriously ill and Goa could neither summon him nor send any one to torture a dying man with enquiries. Mar Abraham did not survive the illness but died in the year 1597.

The death of Mar Abraham gave the Portuguese, at long last, the opportunity for successfully carrying out their designs on Angamali. And with the hour came the man. He was Alexio de Menezies.

Alexio de Menezies was an ecclesiastic of extraordinary ability and resources. He enjoyed the special confidence of Lisbon and Rome and was appointed Archbishop of Goa in 1595. He was well connected and the Viceroy of Goa had the greatest regard and respect for him. Menezies considered the reduction of the Syrians to Goa as his life mission. The ascending power and prestige of the Portuguese and the respect their arms inspired in the East lent considerable support to the plans of Menezies. He had, however, no original plans; his success was mainly due to the extraordinary vigour and want of scruples with which he pushed forward the plans of his predecessors.

Menezies' first attempt was to impress Rome and get the

THE SYRIANS AND THE PORTUGUESE 87

necessary authority from the Pope for the execution of his schemes. The interminable reports of heresy of the Syrian Bishops the Portuguese constantly sent Rome began to bear fruit; Rome was inclined to believe that there was something in it. The Portuguese were in a favourable position to present their case forcefully while the Syrians could only send an occasional petition which in all probability never reached Rome. Besides it appeared at the time that in a short while Portuguese expansion would embrace the whole Eastern world, and Rome was inclined to the view that it would be desirable to bring the Syrian Church under the Portuguese. Hence, as we have already seen, Pope Clement VIII had ordered the Archbishop of Goa to enquire into the charges against Mar Abraham, and by the time the order reached Goa the Syrian Bishop had fallen seriously ill. Menezies could not summon Mar Abraham to Goa nor did he wish to conduct an enquiry at Angamali when the Syrian Bishop was on his deathbed. So he decided to abide his time; meanwhile he took certain preliminary measures for the successful execution of his plan.

Menezies decided that no Bishop owing allegiance to Rome or elsewhere should reach Malabar without his permission and ordered a general blockade of the Indian Seas. The Captains of all Portuguese vessels had strict instructions to ascertain the identity of all Syrians and Armenians and return any Bishop of these nationals to where he came from. In case of doubt, the suspect was to be detained and referred to Goa. Similarly all the civil and ecclesiastical authorities of the ports were ordered to be vigilant and not to let any Bishop or doubtful persons from Western Asia pass the ports without instructions from Goa. These orders were strictly enforced on land and sea and no Bishop escaped the vigilance of the Portuguese. One Bishop, however, tried to run the blockade; he was captured at Ormuz and sent back to Babylon. Another tried to travel through Mogul India to Malabar but he never reached his destination.

During this blockade of the Indian Seas, Mar Abraham died and pending the arrival of a new Bishop, Archdeacon George of the

Pakalomattam family acted as the interim head of the Syrian Church in conformity with traditions. This arrangement, for obvious reasons, did not suit the convenience of Archbishop Menezies who appointed Father Francis Roz, the Jesuit adviser of the late Mar Abraham, as the Vicar Apostolic of the vacant See of Angamali.

The design of Menezies was now quite clear to Archdeacon George. He was an able man and did what he could to retain the independence of his ancient church. But not being an ordained Bishop he lacked the authority and self confidence of Mar Joseph and Mar Abraham; his own sovereign, the Rajah of Cochin, was a staunch ally of the Portuguese to whom he was much indebted, and was but vaguely interested in the religious quarrels of the Syrians; and most important of all, George had to fight a more powerful and masterly tactician than the Bishops had, for all accounts show that Menezies was one of the most energetic and determined men Portugal had ever sent out to India.

With the appointment of Francis Roz as the Vicar Apostolic, Archdeacon George stirred up the Syrians. There was resentment throughout Malabar and the Syrians did not permit their Vicar Apostolic to enter their churches. Menezies now retraced his steps. He realized that he had acted hastily and cancelled his orders in connection with the appointment of Father Roz as the Vicar Apostolic. He confirmed Archdeacon George as the Vicar but appointed Father Roz and the Rector of Vaipicotta Seminary as his advisers. George gracefully accepted his own confirmation, but thought himself competent to rule the Syrians without the advice of Father Roz and the Rector.

News of the capture of the Babylonian Bishop and the blockade of the high seas by the Portuguese now reached the Serra. The enraged Archdeacon ordered a general assembly of the Syrians and a large number of Cattanars and laity gathered at Angamali; the Archdeacon made every Cattanar and layman swear that he would accept no Bishop appointed by Goa and pending the arrival of a Bishop from Western Asia would obey him as the head of the Syrian Church. He exhorted the people and the clergy to resist all European innovations in the Syrian Church as a retaliatory measure against the Portuguese blockade. The whole of the Serra was thoroughly roused and when disaffection was at its worst and the feelings against the Portuguese most bitter, Archbishop Menezies decided to visit the Serra; a measure that speaks abundantly for the courage of the man and his sincerity. In fact, it was this bold and original move to study the affairs of the Serra in person and to befriend the Syrians that paved the way for the success of his eventful mission; for once in their midst, the Syrians found that Menezies was one of the born leaders of men and they accepted his leadership almost as a matter of course.

On the 1st February 1599, Archbishop Menezies landed in Cochin and sent an invitation to Archdeacon George to go and meet him. He solemnly declared in the invitation that the Archdeacon's personal liberty would be most scrupulously safeguarded, and his erroneous action in rousing the Syrians against his Archbishop had been pardoned.

Archdeacon George did not know what exactly to make of this invitation. The Archbishop's fame had preceded him and it was widely known in Malabar that he was a man powerful enough to give orders to the Portuguese Governor of Cochin, the most respected and feared political authority on the Malabar Coast. His standing with the authorities at Goa and Lisbon was also reputed high. Hence it would have been indiscreet for the Archdeacon to decline Menezies' invitation. George decided to go to Cochin and meet the Archbishop. But he could not make out what the Archbishop exactly wanted. The fame of the Portuguese for kidnapping Syrians had not yet died down, and the Archdeacon started from the Serra for Cochin at the head of an army of 3,000 picked Syrians whom he called his bodyguard.

It was now the turn of Menezies to be mystified. He was not, to be sure, frightened of the Syrians kidnapping him. The Rajah of Cochin in whose territory Angamali was situated could be depended upon to see to that, even if the Portuguese were unable to protect him at the moment. But the Syrians could be quite violent when excited, and it was unnecessary, any way, for the

Archdeacon to bring so many of them armed to the teeth; so he sent word to the Archdeacon reiterating his first assurances of personal safety of the Archdeacon and pointing out there was no need to bring 3,000 armed men as a bodyguard. On this the Archdeacon left the major part of his army behind and proceeded to Cochin.

In the meeting, the persuasive Archbishop did not find much difficulty in having his own way with the Archdeacon. The public profession of faith of Mar Joseph and Mar Abraham and his own prestige stood the Archbishop in good stead. When asked to sign the clause in which the allegiance of the Syrian Church was to be transferred to Goa, the Archdeacon, however, hesitated. Again the personality of Menezies prevailed. He pointed out to the Archdeacon that it was unreasonable for him to owe allegiance to Babylon when he, Menezies, had confirmed him in his office and Babylon was not in a position to afford help in case the local Rajahs proved hostile; the all-powerful Portuguese fleet was always ready at Cochin to fly to his aid in case of an emergency. Archdeacon George knew he was fighting a losing battle and he signed the instrument.

According to the agreement a Synod of all the Cattanars and leading laity was to be held under the auspices of the Archbishop in order to purge the Syrian Church of its errors and bring it under Goa. When the people came to know about the agreement, they were considerably perturbed and there was resentment all over the Serra. But Menezies soon won over the people to his side. Until now, as we have seen, the Archbishops of Goa had been negotiating with the Syrian Bishops through intermediaries and the dilatory process of correspondence. Menezies abandoned this slow and roundabout method and decided to address the people direct. He undertook a tour of the Serra, and wherever the mighty Archbishop appeared the people were greatly impressed by his personality and sincere concern for the Syrian Church. In this ecclesiastical tour Menezies took care to put forth the greatness of Portugal in dazzling splendour and the Syrians who had seen neither royalty nor episcopal pomp in such magnificence were swept off their feet. He celebrated Easter at the important Syrian centre of Kaduthurithi with such showy publicity that the people wondered how such a lofty personage could condescend to be in their midst. His liberality was as magnificent as his greatness. He lavished money and presents on the people with the abandon of an emperor who had won a battle and plundered a rich kingdom. Archdeacon George thought this was bribery, but the worthy Archbishop said his liberality was inspired by Christian charity.

Anyway, the Archbishop became sufficiently popular with the Syrians to administer the sacrament of Confirmation in Syrian Churches and ordain priests for them without the permission of the Archdeacon. In fact the Syrians vied with one another for the privilege of receiving confirmation and ordination from so great an ecclesiastic. All told, before the Archdeacon knew what was happening Menezies had secured for himself more than a majority for the forthcoming Synod.

Menezies now knew his Syrians well. He found that the people generally had nothing in common with their Bishops. The local language of the people, Malayalam, was as different from Syriac as was Latin. The Portuguese missionaries knew more about Syrians and their way of life than Persian or Babylonian Bishops. Menezies thought that Babylon was a weakening link, a mere memory with no vitality. Goa, on the other hand, was a living force with infinite prestige, in close proximity to the land of the Syrians, and he felt sure that the Syrians would accept its authority if properly presented. Anyway, Menezies left nothing to chance. He ordered the priests of Vaipicotta, Cochin and Cranganoor to launch an intensive campaign among the people to familiarize them with the proposed innovations. This campaign and his own extensive tours had the desired effect.

The Archdeacon was now thoroughly alarmed. When he had signed the agreement mentioned elsewhere, he had but a hazy idea of the exact nature of the reform. He had, in all probability, thought that his traditional authority over the Syrians would be respected. But in the Archbishop's tours, his ordaining priests and administering sacraments without anybody's leave, the general attitude of Menezies suggested that there existed no such person in the Serra as an Archdeacon. The Archdeacon remonstrated with the Archbishop, but by now the latter was in a very sound position to ignore the Archdeacon. He took no notice of the plaints of George. In sheer despair the Archdeacon excommunicated his Archbishop.

Menezies now produced his trump card. He sent an urgent note to the Rajah of Cochin asking him to impress upon the Archdeacon the need for treating him with due respect. The Rajah was a staunch ally of the Portuguese and had benefited much by the alliance. He was greatly flattered by the presence of Menezies in his dominions. The manner in which the prelate ostentatiously ordered the Governor of Cochin about left the Rajah in no doubt as to the power and prestige of Menezies. Hence the Rajah felt greatly hurt on hearing that one of his own subjects had the audacity to excommunicate the distinguished visitor. He was but vaguely interested in the quarrels of the Christians. Menezies, it is said, had supplemented his request to the Rajah with a handsome present in cash. How far this is correct is not known. What is known is that Archdeacon George received peremptory orders from the Rajah to behave himself.

This completely crushed the Archdeacon. The rest of the story was all a one-sided affair. The Archdeacon cancelled his order of excommunication and wooed his powerful rival. Menezies pressed his advantage hard and George was immediately asked to accept the following ten conditions as a preliminary step to the convening of the Synod:

1. Abjuration of all doctrines the Archbishop considered heretical.

2. A declaration to the effect that the Law of St. Thomas is the same as the Law of St. Peter.

2. Acceptance of the Profession of Faith which the Archbishop had sent him from Goa on the death of Mar Abraham.

4. Submission of all Syrian books in the Archdiocese for correction or burning as the Archbishop thought fit.
5. Rejection of the authority of the Patriarch of Babylon and severing all connection from him.
6. Recognition of the Pope as the Supreme Head of the Church of Christ.
7. Rejection of all Bishops not approved by Goa.
8. Acknowledgement of the Archbishop of Goa as his ecclesiastical superior.
9. Circulation of letters commanding all Cattanars in the diocese to attend the forthcoming Synod, and the acceptance of the degrees of the Synod as binding on the Archdeacon and all those under his authority.
10. The attendance of the Archdeacon, in person and without a bodyguard, in the Archbishop's visitation of the parishes.

The Archdeacon put off signing the document as long as he could on some pretext or other. But the excuses for delay were, however, satisfactorily settled for him by Menezies and George had to sign it.

Preparations for the Synod were now made in right earnest. The date fixed was 20th June 1599, the third Sunday after Pentecost, and the place Diamper (Udayamperoor, in Malayalam) a Christian centre a few miles south west of the port of Cochin. The Archbishop and the Archdeacon sent out separate circulars commanding all Cattanars to attend it. Those who could not attend had to produce valid reasons for absence without which, they were warned, they were liable to be excommunicated. Each parish had to send four representative leaders from the laity. The object of the Synod was given in detail in the circular Menezies had sent out which has been carefully preserved. Among other things, the circular mentions:

"We give you all, and every one of you in particular, to understand that the most Holy Father, Pope Clement VIII our Lord Bishop of Rome, and Vicar of our Lord Jesus Christ upon earth, at this time presiding in the Church of God; having sent two briefs directed to us, one on the 27th January, in the year 1595, and the other on the 21st of the same month, in the year 1597; in which by virtue of his pastoral office and that universal power bequeathed to the supreme, holy, and Apostolic chair of St. Peter over all the churches in the world by Jesus Christ, the Son of God, our Lord and Redeemer, he commanded us upon the death of the Archbishop Mar Abraham, to take possession of this Church and Bishopric, so as not to suffer any Bishop or prelate coming from Babylon, to enter therein, as has hitherto been the custom, all that come thence being schismatics, heretics and Nestorians, out of the obedience of the Holy Roman Church, and subject to the Patriarch of Babylon, the head of the said heresy; and to appoint a governor or Apostolic Vicar to rule the said diocese both in spirituals and temporals, until such time as the Holy Roman Church shall provide it with a proper pastor; which being read by us we were desirous to execute the Apostolic mandate with due reverence and obedience; besides, that the same was incumbent on us of right as the metropolitan and primate of this and all other churches of the Indies and the oriental parts.

"But perceiving that our mandate in that behalf had no effect, what we had ordered not having been obeyed in the said diocese, so that what our most holy father, the Bishop of Rome, had designed, was like to be frustrated; after having laboured therein for the space of two years, schism and disobedience to the Apostolic See, having been so rooted in that diocese for a great many years, that the inhabitants thereof instead of yielding obedience to the Apostolical and our mandates; on the contrary, upon the intimation thereof did daily harden themselves more and more, committing greater offences against the obedience of the Holy Roman Church; after having commended the matter to God and ordered the same to be done through our whole diocese, and after mature advice by what methods the Apostolical mandates might be best executed; and being also moved by the piety of the people and the mercy God had shown them in having preserved so many thousand souls in the faith of our Lord Jesus

Christ, from the time that the holy Apostle St. Thomas had preached to them until this date, notwithstanding their having lived among so many heathens, and been scattered in diverse places, their churches and all belonging to them having been always subject to idolatorous kings and princes, incompassed with idols and pagodas, and that without holding any other Christians before the coming of the Portuguese in these parts; we being likewise desirous that the labours of the holy Apostle St. Thomas, which still remained among them, should not be lost for want of sound doctrines; and as the Apostolic mandates might not be frustrated, and determined, and having provided for the government of our own church during our absence, did prepare to go in person to take possession of the said Bishopric, to see if by our presence we might be able to reduce them to the obedience of the Holy Roman Church, and purge out the heresies and false doctrines sown among them, and introduced by the schismatical prelates and Nestorian heretics, that had governed them under the obedience of the Patriarch of Babylon; as also to call in and purge the books containing these heresies; and according to our pastoral duties so far as God should enable us to preach to them in person the Catholic faith.

"Accordingly, going in the said Bishopric, we set about visiting the Churches thereof; but at that time, Satan, the great enemy of the good of souls, having stirred up great commotions, and much opposition to this our just intent, great numbers departing from us, and forming a schism against the Holy Roman Church; after having passed through many troubles and dangers, out of all which, God of the great mercy, not remembering our sins and evil deeds was pleased to deliver us, and to grant us an entire peace, for the merits of the glorious Apostle St. Thomas, the Patron of this Christianity, but chiefly of his own great clemency and mercy, which make, that does not delight in the death of a sinner, but rather that he should return and live; and by coming all to the light of truth may join us in the confession of the Catholic faith, approving our doctrine and intention and submitting themselves to the obedience of the Holy Roman Church; which being by us observed, after having returned thanks to God, we thought fit, in order to the compassing and securing of all those good effects, to assemble a diocesan synod in some commodious place near the middle of the said diocese, there to treat of all such matters as faith and divine worship, the good of the church, the extirpation of vice, the reformation of the Christians of the said diocese, and the profit and peace of their souls; to which end, having pitched upon the town and church of Diamper, we do hereby let all the inhabitants and Christians of the said Bishopric, as well ecclesiastic as laicks, of what state or condition soever, to understand, that we do call and assemble a diocesan synod in the said town of Diamper, on the 20th June of this present year, 1599, being the third Sunday after Whitsuntide."

The Archdeacon's circular had probably a different tale to tell, but it has not been preserved. Anyway, the Synod met as scheduled and it was a thoroughly representative body. From among the St. Thomas Christians, 153 Cattanars and deacons, and 671 procurators of the people attended it. Besides the Archbishop and a large number of European priests, important Portuguese civil authorities including the Governor of Cochin were present. Matters were freely discussed through the services of able interpretors, and the decrees were read out, and amendments suggested and carefully and elaborately discussed. The Syrians had been tutored in advance, and they had no difficulty in accepting most of the decrees. But on the second day when the formula for the Confession of Faith was read out, there was general disapproval as the formula seemed to leave in doubt whether the Syrians were Christians at all before the advent of the worthy prelate. The tactful Archbishop rose to the occasion, solemnly confirmed his conviction of the adherence of the Malabar Church to Christ from the time of St. Thomas onwards, and maintained that the Confession of Faith was mere reaffirmation of old beliefs with necessary improvements. This quietened the Syrians, and after this there was little opposition.

The proceedings went on for eight days, and Menezies made all the representatives of the Syrian Church accept on solemn oath the reforms he wished to bring about. It is not possible to give in detail here all the decrees of the Synod, and their amendments. Suffice it to say that the Syrian Church was made dependent on Goa and the old connection with Babylon was severed. Of the reforms mention may be made of some of the more important.

The Cattanars had been indifferent to their duties and they were enjoined to say Mass every day. Simony, which was rampant among some sections of the clergy, was strictly forbidden. Priests were forbidden to marry, and those who were already married were discouraged to have anything to do with their wives. New sacraments were introduced, and confession was made compulsory before receiving Holy Communion. All Syriac books were surrendered for correction or destruction, and some of them were burnt.* The Syrian rite and language were, however, retained. The Syrians were enjoined to show better missionary zeal. Veneration of the saints of the Roman Calendar was introduced and churches were to be adorned with images and paintings. The casting of horoscopes and cures according to Parsiman,† a Persian work, was forbidden. Early baptism was made compulsory. The use of bells and candles was introduced in the churches. One of the decrees forbad people from sleeping in the churches;‡ another condemned untouchability and other caste regulations but permitted them as a concession to the social prejudices of the Syrians and in recognition of the need for maintaining prestige in a caste ridden country.

The Synod of Diamper has been a matter of bitter controversy in Malabar and elsewhere. The tone of the Syrians in general and of the Syrian Catholics in particular indicates that the Synod was

---

* Some historians find in this a parallel to Omar's destruction of the Alexandrian library. This is, no doubt, an exaggeration. But it is quite certain that many books of historical value were lost together with those that were objectionable and superstitious.

† The Parsiman, supposed to be a work on medicine and strange cures, taught, among other things, the seduction of women by love charms, preparation of poison and destruction of enemies by magic and casting out devils from possessed individuals.

‡ The Syrian churches were at times used as inns by pilgrims.

imposed upon them by the unscrupulous and crafty Menezies from purely political motives without the sanction of the Pope. This is not, however, the whole truth. That Menezies had political motives is quite true; that he often stooped to unfair means in gaining his end is also true. But it must be borne in mind that the Syrians themselves had sound reasons for an alliance with the Portuguese, and the interest Menezies showed in their welfare convinced the intelligent, at any rate for the time being, that friendship with the Portuguese and their patronage would definitely advance their interests. The Portuguese expansion at the time was so vigorous that it promised to embrace in its wide sweep the whole of India if not Asia. The Syrians, as we have seen, had suffered much at the hands of the Muslims and some of the petty chieftains were inclined to treat their ancient privileges with scant respect. And Menezies they knew was a man who was sincerely interested in them and was in a position to promote their welfare. The genuine enthusiasm he inspired throughout Malabar shows that few, except Archdeacon George and his close associates, took him for a merciless tyrant overrunning a defenceless people, and all were inclined to view him as a leader and a patron. The fact that one day while the Synod was in progress seventy-five Syrian representatives demanded an assurance from the prelate that if they took the oath of allegiance to Goa, the king of Portugal should take them under his protection and exempt them from certain taxes they had to pay, supports this statement. It may be mentioned that Menezies readily agreed to this and on a sign from the mighty prelate, Don Antonio, the Governor of Cochin, knelt before the Archbishop and accepted the responsibility for protecting the Syrians on behalf of his royal master. Lest this should alarm the Rajah of Cochin, Menezies that very day wrote to the Rajah to say that the protection the Portuguese extended to the Syrians was confined to spiritual matters and they had not the slightest intention of interfering with the legitimate authority His Highness exercised over his Syrian subjects in temporal matters.

Soon after the termination of the Synod, the Archbishop

decided to give effect to the reforms personally. The danger of leaving this important task to the Archdeacon and the Cattanars was quite obvious, and with the thoroughness that characterised all his actions Menezies proceeded to enforce the reforms. In order to effect this the Archbishop undertook an extensive tour of visitation of his newly acquired diocese. Wherever the Archbishop went with his pompous retinue, unprecedented popular enthusiasm welcomed him. Newly composed songs in his praise greeted him in every parish and the path he trod on was thickly strewn with flowers. His Grace gracefully responded to the enthusiasm of his flock and in one parish, according to a legend, cakes distributed by the prelate to the children contained each a hidden gold coin. Even the Hindus were greatly impressed and the whole of Malabar vibrated with a new energy and the prestige of the Christians rose very high indeed. The innovations the Archbishop introduced were immediately and enthusiastically accepted. For once the old prejudice against the Parangi was forgotten.

This enthusiasm was not, however, universally shared. In some parishes the subtle humour of the Syrian Christian asserted itself. In old Palur, for instance, a stage show organized for the entertainment of the prelate had some interesting features of topical interest. Palur was situated in the northernmost extremity of the diocese and the parish was under the Zamorin who had always viewed the activities of the Portuguese with suspicion; hence the parishioners were in a better position than the Cochinites to give expression to their feelings.

The main characters of the farce were St. Peter, St. Thomas and St. Syriac, the patron saint of the parish. The subject matter was the activity of Archbishop Alexio de Menezies. In a conversation between St. Peter and St. Thomas the latter accused St. Peter of sending to Malabar Menezies 'a very enterprising man, who by sheer violence, has maintained the cause of the Portuguese'. St. Thomas maintained that their ancient usages, introduced by him, personally, were good enough for the Syrians. St. Peter agreed that the usages introduced by St. Thomas were good, but the innovations were better. A lengthy dispute now followed, and St. Syriac was called in to judge between the two. St. Syriac instead of deciding between the Apostles, passed judgement between the Patriarch of Babylon and the Archbishop of Goa. He maintained that the Patriarch of Babylon was the true pastor of the Syrians and the Portuguese Archbishop 'who declares to the contrary is a heretic, against whom it is necessary that the Indian Christians should be on their guard. They ought not to surrender their faith to him; and the oaths he exhorted at Diamper are manifestly null and void."

Menezies did not find the performance very interesting. He suppressed it and declared that the originators of the drama and its principal characters were possessed of the devil.

Such incidents were, however, rare, and the Malabar Church as a whole was delighted with the change and their new Archbishop.

Soon after the tour of visitation, Archbishop Menezies left Malabar, having realized the greatest ambition of his life. There was great rejoicing in Goa and Portugal on the successful termination of the Archbishop's enterprise. In 1601, Menezies secured for his faithful assistant and adviser, Francis Roz, the See of Angamali, which was now made a Diocese Suffragan of Goa.

But the story does not end here. The successful end of Menezies' mission was but the beginning of the real trouble. Francis Roz found his flock too turbulent for him. The new Bishop was more learned than able. He lacked the drive and initiative of Menezies and the problem that met him at every step baffled him. He too, like Menezies, undertook a tour of his vast diocese; but though well received the Bishop's tour proved but a shadow of the pageant of his great predecessor. Roz was a good man but he failed to impress.

Besides, by now the Syrians had sufficient time to recover from the feverish enthusiasm Menezies had worked them into. The magnificient illusion the arch-showman from Goa had created vanished with his departure, and the Syrians had now time to contemplate in retrospect the happenings of Diamper. Before the

Synod, the Syrians, though nominally under Bishops sent from Babylon, were virtually independent and much of the internal administration of the diocese was left to the Cattanars and the Archdeacon. The Latin Bishop, on the other hand, in his zeal for the purity of law and practice actively interfered with the rights and privileges of the Cattanars and in the daily life and usages of the people. Another serious cause for discontent was the reduction of the See of Angamali to a Bishopric from Archdiocese and its subjection to Goa. Politically the Syrians had gained little or nothing by their allegiance to Goa. They just remained where they were. Calm deliberation now convinced them that Diamper was an All Fools' Day.

Further Archdeacon George was far from broken; he had only bowed before the inevitable. With the departure of Menezies to Goa he again raised his head. He fomented trouble and courted the Rajah of Cochin for favours and help in his schemes against the Portuguese. The Rajah himself, like the Syrians, had by now recovered from the spell the magician from Goa had cast over him and he too realized that his interests lay not in a union of Syrian and Portuguese Christians but in a division of the two. The Syrians alone could be a serious threat to his position, and able Bishops had successfully challenged the authority of weak Rajahs; and he had always appreciated the political need for keeping the Syrians engaged in their religious quarrels. A combination of Syrians and Portuguese could be a standing danger to his position and he repented of the support he had lent to Menezies' scheme. Now that Menezies was gone and Roz did not command the prestige that Archbishop did, the Rajah of Cochin ignored him and actively sided with the Archdeacon.

Roz, however, realized the importance of raising the See of Angamali to an Archdiocese. He also felt the need for transferring the See to Cranganoor. The Archdeacon and his party were particularly strong in Angamali and Roz felt he would be much more comfortable at Cranganoor, a port under Portuguese influence. At the request of Roz, the See of Angamali was raised to an Archdiocese and transferred to Cranganoor.

This, far from solving his difficulties led to greater troubles for the poor Archbishop. Cranganoor was under the jurisdiction of the Bishop of Cochin and he objected to the transfer of the see as an encroachment by Roz into his dominions. This led to a bitter controversy between Roz and the Bishop of Cochin which Goa found difficult to settle. In the meantime the trouble between the Jesuits and other orders was gaining momentum and with this added incentive for quarrel, Portuguese priests and their partisans often came to blows in the ports of Cochin and Cranganoor, to say nothing of farther south where a state of open war between the various orders existed. Roz was drawn into these disputes, and this left Archdeacon George plenty of time and opportunities to seize power and consolidate his position. He was no more the inexperienced young man who met Archbishop Menezies but an older and wiser man, a mature tactician and strategist. While Archbishop Roz was busy in his quarrels with his own nationals, Archdeacon George became the most powerful man in the Serra. The Cochin Rajah and the European enemies of Roz actively supported him, and his voice became powerful enough to be heard even in Rome.

On the 16th February 1624, the much harassed first Latin Archbishop of the Syrians died at the age of 67. The following sad legend on the porch of Sts. Gervase and Protase aptly summarizes the latter part of the Archbishop's life: "On account of the continuous wars, he could stay neither in Angamalee nor in Cranganoor."

Don Esteben de Britto who succeeded Roz was a man of peace. He was overwhelmed by the authority the old Archdeacon exercised over his diocese and was distracted by quarrels with the Dominicans. He followed the line of least resistance and when he found that Archdeacon George would give him no peace till he had received written confirmation of the powers he had seized, the obliging Archbishop signed a document of virtual abdication in his favour. The signing of the deed coming to the knowledge of the authorities in Cochin and Goa, they almost gasped. Britto himself felt that he had acted somewhat foolishly.

Hence when in 1636 Count Linhares, the Viceroy of Goa, happened to visit Cochin, the matter was represented to him and the Count brought pressure on the Rajah of Cochin who asked the Archdeacon to surrender the document. George readily complied with His Highness' request and the Viceroy took away the precious document with him.

Later, however, it was noticed that the document was still in the Archdeacon's possession, and the surrendered one was a copy with a forged signature. Till his death which occurred on the 25th July 1640 Archdeacon George was the virtual ruler of the Syrians under de Britto. The Syrians still revere him as one of their greatest countrymen who successfully fought the Portuguese domination and did much to retrieve the position lost to Menezies at Diamper. De Britto appointed Thomas de Campos, a nephew of George as his successor, and a year later Britto himself died.

After this, the Portuguese influence generally and of the Jesuits in particular began to decline and the Syrian Church again worked for severance from Goa and applied to Babylon for a Bishop. A Patriarch by name Ahtallah now appeared in Mylapore at the shrine of St. Thomas and wrote to the Syrians that he would be shortly proceeding to take charge of the see left vacant by Mar Abraham. The news was received with the greatest rejoicing in Malabar and as he started from Mylapore in 1653 for Cochin by sea, large congregations from all over Malabar moved to Cochin to receive him. About 100,000 Syrians including some 40,000 armed men congregated in Cochin to receive the Patriarch. The Portuguese were thoroughly alarmed and the ship that carried the Patriarch cast anchor in stream and did not come anywhere near the harbour. The impatient Syrians demanded the immediate surrender of the Patriarch and the Portuguese replied by manning their guns into position on the walls of the fort. An appeal to the ruler of Cochin proved futile; he could do nothing against the Portuguese or the Syrians. In the resultant excitement, a wild rumour spread throughout the crowd that the venerable Patriarch was murdered and thrown overboard by the Portuguese. The furious Syrians wanted to storm the Portuguese fortress, but wiser counsels prevailed. Some of the responsible leaders managed to lead the mob away to Mattanchery, close by, without unnecessary bloodshed. At the church at Mattanchery the Syrians decided that no Syrian worth his name should owe allegiance to Goa and the Portuguese. Every one was asked to swear by the cross of the Mattanchery church, made famous by this day's events, that he would not accept the authority of Goa. To make the oath effective, it was necessary for every individual to touch the cross while swearing, and what with the eagerness of the crowd and the unmanageability of their number, this presented a difficult problem. But a happy idea struck an ingenious brain and long ropes were tied to the cross in all directions, and Syrians held to the ropes and swore to an undying hatred of the Portuguese and a determination to end once for all the authority of Goa. This event is known in Syrian Christian history as the Revolt of the Coonen (crooked) Cross.

The difficulties of administration had now to be solved. The authority of the ruling Bishop was rejected but there was no Western Asian Bishop at hand to take charge. In this predicament twelve Cattanars representing the Apostles ordained a Bishop of their own, and the choice naturally fell on Archdeacon Thomas. He ruled the Syrians taking the title of Mar Thoma I. From now on the Syrian Church enters its modern phase, and the further history of this interesting Church will be continued in a later Chapter.

CHAPTER VII

CHRISTIANITY IN MOGUL INDIA

THE Jesuits of the Counter Reformation had, in their ambitious plan, the conversion of the whole world, and those who worked in the Indian field did not confine their activities to the South. Their eagle eyes scanned the great subcontinent ruled by the Moguls and thought it a rich field promising excellent harvest, but did not know how and where to begin their mission. And then an opportunity presented itself, an invitation from the great Akbar himself to go to Agra and instruct him in the Christian religion.

The Mogul dynasty was founded in India by Babur, of the house of Chengiz Khan and Timur, by his defeat of Ebrahim Lodi, the then king of Delhi, in the historic battle of Panipat in 1526. Babur and his son Humayun could not do much to consolidate their conquests as a good many turbulent chieftains and petty rulers had yet to be subdued. It was given to Humayun's son Akbar to consolidate his predecessors' conquests and establish the Mogul Empire on a firm basis. He ascended the throne in the year 1556 at the early age of thirteen. The Emperor, though young in years, was old in experience, and from the very start showed those qualities of leadership which has won for him universal esteem.

The early Moguls, though nominally converted to Islam, had retained most of the religious traditions of the Mongols and were happily free from fanaticism. They accepted the superior culture of Arabia and Persia, no doubt, but had no great regard for the dogmas of Islam and kept an open mind in matters concerning the Great Unknown. And Akbar was gifted with a keen intellect and an insatiable thirst for knowledge.

The vast majority of his subjects were Hindus and Akbar realized the need for conciliating them for the stability of his vast dominions. He entered into matrimonial relations with the Rajputs and employed several chieftains of this noble race in high places in the army and in civil administration. This benevolent attitude towards Hindus, very rare among Muslim monarchs of the Middle Ages, was not actuated by mere political considerations but also by Akbar's genuine love for their traditions and culture. He often imitated the Hindu way of dress and manners.

By nature Akbar was an eclectic and a liberal, and inclined to the secular view of the state. It irked him to note that Muslim divines dictated to him state policies based on the Islamic law while most of his subjects were non-Muslims, and throughout his life he assumed an attitude of studied antagonism towards the doctors of Islam. The dogmas of Islam did not satisfy his spirit of enquiry into the mysterious. He was fearless in his search for truth, and invited learned men of all religious persuasions to his court and listened to regular philosophic discussions between rival parties. Brahmins, Jains, Zoroastrians and Muslims freely propounded their views, and as it happens in such arguments many prophets and holy men came in for a good deal of criticism. Akbar enjoyed these controversies and wished to have some learned Christian priests also among the disputants.

Akbar, no doubt, had some knowledge of Christianity gained from the Armenians who were in his kingdom but he was attracted to the Jesuits by a report from Bengal that they had refused the benefits of religion to certain Portuguese who had deprived the Mogul Government of certain legitimate dues and persisted in keeping their illgotten gains. Such high sense of religious duty was rare at the time, and Akbar sent an invitation to one of the Jesuits, Father Julian Pereira, to visit him. Father Pereira arrived in Agra in 1578 and was immediately dragged into religious wranglings with the Muslims. But Pereira was more dogmatic than learned and proved no match for the chief Mullah of the court, nicknamed the Sultan of Mecca. So he requested Akbar to apply to the Jesuit College at Goa for some learned priests if he wished to have an intellectual exposition of Christianity. Akbar was interested and he despatched an ambassador to Goa accompanied by an Armenian Christian named Dominic Pires with the following Farman:

"Order of Jalal Ud Din the Great, King by God appointed. Fathers of the Order of St. Paul, know that I am most kindly disposed towards you, and I send Abdulla, my ambassador, and Dominic Pires to ask you in my name to send me two learned priests who should bring with them the chief books of the Law and the Gospel, for I wish to study and learn the Law and what is best and most perfect in it. The moment my ambassadors return, let them not hesitate to come with them and let them bring the books of the Law. Know also that as far as I can, I shall receive most kindly and honourably the priests who will come. Their arrival will give me the greatest pleasure, and when I shall know about the Law and its perfection what I wish to know, they will be at liberty to return as soon as they like, and I shall not let them go without loading them with honours and gifts. Therefore let them not have the slightest fear to come. I take them under my protection. Fare you well."

Although the Jesuits were only too glad to get a footing in the capital of the Mogul Empire, the letter considerably intrigued both the civil and ecclesiastical authorities of Goa. The Portuguese had come to look upon all Muslims as their enemies, mainly because of their traditional hostility to the Arabs, and the sincerity of Akbar's motive was doubted. The real intention of the emperor was suspected to be far removed from thirst for Christian knowledge. One possible explanation that offered itself was that Akbar wished to get some European priests to his capital and detain them as hostages for the redress of some fancied grievance he might have had against the Portuguese; another that he had an exaggerated idea of the glamour of Portuguese women and wished to get Portuguese wives for his harem through the good offices of the Fathers. The Jesuits were, however, determined to avail themselves of the God-given opportunity, and accordingly the first 'Mogor Mission' was formed under Rudolf Aquaviva, an Italian Jesuit. Antony Monserrate, a Spaniard, and Francis Henriquez, a Persian convert from Islam, together with the leader constituted the first Mogor Mission. They started from Goa on 17th November, 1579, accompanied by Akbar's emissaries, travelled by way of Surat, Mandu, Ujjain, Narwar, Gwalior, and after the usual delays incidental to travel at the time, reached Fatehpuri Sikri on 27th February 1580.

The welcome the Fathers received in Akbar's court set at rest all their suspicions about the intentions of the Emperor. It became clear to them that Akbar was inspired solely by a desire to know more about Christianity from the Jesuits. Hopes ran high, and the Fathers, from the very kindly and almost fraternal treatment they received from the Emperor, imagined that his conversion would be the easiest thing in the world. It gave them no little satisfaction to imagine that while their compeers in the South struggled among the poor and the lowly, they were in a position to address themselves to the highest in the Indies and bring about the conversion of the Mogul Empire through the agency of the Emperor and his court.

Familiarity with Akbar and his genius soon disillusioned the Fathers on this point. Akbar studiously cultivated the friendship of the Jesuits, and was always most kind and considerate to them, but days and months passed by in elaborate discussions and long sermons without anything of importance happening. The Emperor had learnt from the Fathers all that an enquirer could possibly learn, and still the eagerly awaited baptism did not take place. Slowly the depressing truth dawned upon the Fathers that the Emperor in inviting the Fathers had no intention other than providing greater variety to his religious discussions which he indulged in as a sort of intellectual diversion.

So the Fathers continued to enjoy material favours without gaining substantially in spiritual matters. The Emperor gave them enough money and excellent houses to live in, and supplied them food from the royal table. He often visited them in their house, and walked hand in hand with the Fathers. He even sought their opinion on state affairs, and asked them to tell him openly and without demur if there were any lapses in his personal conduct or in his capacity as the head of the state. The Fathers took advantage of this and pointed out to him the undesirability of polygamy and his indifference to the message of Christ. He took their advice with becoming humility but did nothing to give the Fathers satisfaction on these points.

In their religious disputes with the Mullahs, the Jesuits often attacked Islam and the Prophet with much vehemence. This brought them a good many enemies in the city. Akbar himself, though he professed general agreement with the Fathers in their opinion of Islam, pointed out to them the need for propounding truth in a more modest manner as there were turbulent elements in his kingdom whom he himself found difficult to keep under control. When the feelings between the Jesuits and the Mullahs assumed alarming proportions, Akbar suggested the fire ordeal*, which cooled the ardour of the disputants.

As time passed on, the Jesuits began to lose all hope of converting the Emperor. They began to suspect that he was insincere in his praise of Christianity, and if anything, his idea was to found a religion of his own and emulate the Prophets. They wrote about him as follows:

"The Emperor is not a Muhammadan, but is doubtful as to all forms of faith and hold firmly that there is no divinely accredited form of faith, because he finds in all something to offend his reason and intelligence; for he thinks that everything can be grasped by reason. Nevertheless he at times admits that no faith

---

* The fire ordeal was the trump card of Akbar and his son Jehangir. Different versions of the ordeal were reported by travellers, though no one appears to have been subjected to it. According to one account, the Mullahs were to throw the Koran and the Jesuits the Bible into a fire pit, and the book that would not be consumed by fire was to be considered the true one. In another version, the disputants themselves were to jump into the fire pit with their respective scriptures, and the party that held the true book was expected to come out unhurt with the book. On good authority we know that the Jesuits refused to tempt the Lord in this manner, but stories were current in India at the time of Bernier's visit (in Aurangazeb's reign) that a Florentine Jesuit in Jehangir's time (probably Father Corsi) agreed to undergo the ordeal while the Mullahs refused, and the priest was, on that account, known as Atesh or Fire-eater.

commends itself so much to him as that of the Gospel, and that when a man goes so far as to believe this to be the true faith and better than others, he is near to adopting it. At the Court some say that he is a heathen and adores the sun. Others that he is a Christian. Others that he intends to found a new sect. Among the people there are various opinions regarding the Emperor: some holding him to be a Christian, others a heathen, others a Muhammadan. The more intelligent, however, consider him to be neither Christian, nor heathen nor Muhammadan, and hold this to be the truth. Or they think him to be a Muhammadan who outwardly conforms to all religions in order to obtain popularity."

The Fathers, any way, gave up all hopes of a speedy conversion of the Great Mogul, and the personnel of the first 'Mogor Mission' returned to Goa in 1583.

A second Mission was despatched, again at Akbar's invitation sent through a Greek subdeacon named Leo Grimon who happened to be in Akbar's court at the time for what purpose it is not known. Leo gave the Jesuits at Goa a rosy picture of the Mogul court, of Akbar's pronounced antagonism to Islam and his eagerness for immediate conversion to Christianity. Hopes running very high, two fathers, Duarte Leitao and Christoval de Vega, with a lay brother Estevao Rebeiro started immediately from Goa. On the Mission reaching Lahore where Akbar was then residing they found that Grimon had misinformed them on the state of affairs at the court. The Emperor received the missionaries with his usual kindness, but a powerful faction at the court was strongly opposed to Christianity and the Mission, thoroughly disillusioned, left Lahore in disgust soon after its arrival in this city.

The failure of the second Mogor Mission was attributed to the impatience of its members, and every one including Akbar was greatly hurt by the precipitate departure of the mission, and a further attempt was considered desirable. Accordingly the third mission was formed under the able leadership of Father Jerome Xavier, a grand nephew of St. Francis Xavier, with Father Emmanuel Pinheiro and a lay brother Benedict de Goes as his assistants. This mission reached Lahore on the 5th May 1595, and did good work for years, the personnel having been replaced from time to time from Goa.

Father Xavier and his assistants enjoyed royal patronage as in the case of the first mission, and on more than one occasion it was thought that Akbar would embrace Christianity. His antagonism to Islam became more marked as he grew older and he even prohibited the building of new mosques. The Jesuits were appointed tutors to Prince Salim. Permission and funds were given to them to build a church at Lahore, and both the Emperor and the Prince often visited the new church when the building was completed. Salim himself was very favourably disposed towards Christianity and gave the Fathers a large sum towards the cost of building the church.

Prince Salim as he grew up began to develop rebellious tendencies and even instigated the murder of Akbar's favourite minister Abul Fazal. Later he went into open rebellion. The missionaries, however, managed to maintain good relations with the father and the son.

In 1606 Akbar died. Though it is generally believed that he died a Muslim, stories are current which purport to say that he was baptized a Christian on his death-bed.

Prince Salim who succeeded Akbar as Jehangir, continued his patronage of the Jesuits, but he was an erratic genius, a much lesser man than his able, astute, wise and energetic father. In his time Europeans of note other than the Portuguese penetrated into India and Jehangir himself was much amused to note that there was anything but unanimity among Christians themselves about Christianity. The Jesuits had now to contend with considerable opposition from the English. The first Englishman who courted Imperial favours against the Jesuits was Capt. William Hawkins. Reaching Surat in an English ship in 1608, he proceeded to Agra armed with a letter from James I, and reached this city in the month of April in 1609. He has recorded many complaints against the Jesuits. He went in fear of his life because of plots for his assassination, inspired he said by Jesuits; the poor man went so far as to marry an Armenian lady 'in order to avoid being poisoned' by the Jesuits. He entered into religious controversies with the Jesuits and presented the Protestant version of Christianity to Jehangir. With all his efforts, however, the influence of the Jesuits prevailed, and giving up all hopes of winning over Jehangir to his side Hawkins left Mogul India in disgust.

In 1612 an English squadron appeared in Indian waters, and defeating the Portuguese fleet that attacked it gave an inkling of coming events to Indians. English prestige rose high and when Paul Canning went to Agra as the envoy of King James he was well received by Jehangir. Canning too, like Hawkins, suffered much at the hands of the Jesuits and wrote bitter things about them.

Jehangir had a child's curiosity in European music and pictures, and at times the foreigners went to ridiculous extremes to please His Majesty in these matters in order to win his favour. Canning, for instance, had one of his followers, who was a cornet player, perform before Jehangir, and the Emperor was delighted by the performance; upon this, the Jesuits asked Canning to instruct his cornet player to teach two of their men how to play on the instrument, and added that this was an Imperial Farman. Canning point-blank refused. The Jesuits then produced a Neapolitan juggler much to the amusement of Jehangir.

With the arrival of the famous embassy under Sir Thomas Roe in 1615, the quarrels between the Jesuits and the English took a more decorous form.

On the whole, the Jesuits were better favoured than the British, and Father Corsi had the ear of the Emperor. Jehangir, in his ostentatious regard for the Jesuits and their religion went, on one occasion, so far as to order two of his nephews to embrace Christianity. The baptism of the princes gave rise to wild hopes and even Hawkins who was at the time at the court took part in the celebrations. The news was received in Spain with great rejoicings and king Phillip III sent a personal letter to Jehangir congratulating him and adopting the royal neophytes as his godchildren. Soon after, however, there was a rupture between the

Portuguese and Jehangir and the latter promptly ordered his nephews back to Islam.

Jehangir moved freely with Christians of all denominations and was once even heard to swear by the face of his father that he would embrace Christianity. This swearing took place, it appears, after an over-indulgence in wine. Manucci shrewdly observes that the Emperor's preference for the company of Christians was inspired not by a love for Christianity but by a love of pork and wine. This was probably true, but Islam had its compensations too. For once he asked the Jesuits rather bluntly what he would do with his numerous wives if he turned Christian. Jehangir's attitude towards religion was typical of the hedonist who because of his responsible position could not afford to deny God. He took from all religions what was convenient for him.

A favourite story inspired by Jehangir's love of the miraculous was the Legend of the Sagacious Ape. A juggler from Bengal, so goes the story, brought a monkey to Jehangir's court claiming that the animal had insight into religious truths. Jehangir had the names of twelve prophets written, each on an identical looking piece of paper, and after careful shuffling, the pieces were offered to the monkey and the animal is said to have taken out the paper on which Jesus' name was written. Jehangir, suspecting that the owner of the monkey who knew Persian had made some secret sign to the animal, wrote the names in the official code but the result was again the same. A courtier gave a more rigorous test; he secretly removed the piece of paper on which Jesus' name was written and offered the remaining eleven pieces to the monkey; the sagacious ape carefully examined all the pieces but could not find the name of Jesus on any of them; it worked itself into a fury, tore all the eleven pieces, attacked the courtier and wrenched from his hand the precious document and kissed it devoutly.

The truth of the story was vouchsafed by reliable eye witnesses and Sir Thomas Roe and his chaplain Terry attributed it to "one of the many tricks of the Jesuits". The Jesuits themselves disclaimed all hand in the affair, but the story got wide publicity in the Roman Catholic world and even poems were composed in Spain in honour of the Sagacious Ape.

Except for a brief period of two years (1613-1615) when Jehangir was much annoyed by the activities of some Portuguese who, in their quarrel with the English, happened to capture a vessel in which the Queen Mother had some interest, the Jesuits enjoyed continued patronage in the Mogul Court. Towards his old age, Jehangir's leaning towards Christianity became definitely marked, and stories got currency in India that he had privately embraced Christianity but could not confess it publicly because of his fear of the Mogul aristocracy. In his old age Jehangir, however, became politically unimportant, the Empress Nurjehan having taken over control of the state for all practical purposes. Nurjehan was not particularly fond of Christians. On 28th October 1627 Jehangir died and with him the hopes of the Jesuits of converting the Mogul Emperors to Christianity.

Akbar and Jehangir inspired rich Christian legends but poor congregations. The Jesuits were solely occupied with attempts to convert the Emperors and paid little attention to the conversion of the people.

Shah Jehan who succeeded Jehangir, though not a bigot, was a staunch believer in the greatness and glory of Islam and he was, more than any one else, responsible for putting forth Islam in all its splendour in India. The Taj Mahal, the Juma Musjid at Delhi and several other noble edifices and some great works of art like the Peacock Throne were inspired by and constructed under his supervision. He was indifferent to Christians but just tolerated the Jesuits as the pastors of the little community of Europeans and other Christians at Agra and elsewhere. What is known as the Hugli incident made him, for some time at least, a deadly enemy of Christians, and for a brief period he actively persecuted them. This incident and its repercussions deserve some detailed notice.

There was, at the time, a considerable number of Portuguese in Chittagong and the Arakkan Coast, mostly renegades whose main occupation was piracy. They actively supported the king of

Arrakkan in his depredatory incursions into Mogul territory and were a constant source of trouble to the low lying coastal districts of Bengal. To make matters worse, a Portuguese adventurer named Tavares founded the port of Hugli, towards the close of the 16th century, and this caused a large influx of Portuguese and Eurasian population into the Port. Hugli was independent both of the Mogul Governor of Dacca and the Portuguese Viceroy of Goa and the city was a law unto itself. By their mastery of the sea nearby, the Hugli Portuguese managed to divert all the trade of Bengal from the Mogul port of Satgaon to Hugli and this city soon rose to eminence as one of the richest ports on the bay of Bengal.

The citizens of Hugli were not particularly noted for the correctness of their lives. The main wealth of the city was from a flourishing slave trade maintained by kidnapping Mogul subjects from the coastal regions of Bengal. It was the boast of the Hugli Portuguese that they made more Christians in a year—by forcible conversions, of course—than all the missionaries in the East in ten. The seriousness of their activities was brought home to Agra when two beautiful slave girls belonging to Empress Mumtaz were kidnapped by them. Shah Jehan himself had an old axe to grind. In his abortive insurrection against his father, Shah Jehan had applied to Hugli for help which the city refused. Nor did she care to send an embassy to congratulate Shah Jehan on his accession to the throne.

Shah Jehan now issued peremptory orders to the Governor of Dacca to exterminate Hugli. The Governor was only waiting for the order. He made secret but extensive preparations for the assault. The Portuguese were informed of the move by their agents and the missionaries at Agra, but the rulers of Hugli had an exaggerated idea of their own strength and belittled the mighty power of the Mogul. On 26th June 1632, an army of 70,000 men and a fleet of 500 vessels attacked the city from land and sea. The little band of 300 Portuguese soldiers and a hastily recruited army of civilians and slaves put up a stiff resistance but they were hopelessly outnumbered and the city fell to the Moguls.

The carnage was terrible. A few of the inhabitants escaped to the jungles of Saugar island and the rest were either put to the sword or captured and sent to Agra.

About 4,000 male and female captives, all Christians, reached Agra alive, and the treatment meted out to them was anything but in keeping with the liberal traditions of the earlier Moguls. Able bodied men and desirable women were sold as slaves. A few escaped death by accepting Islam. Some were forcibly converted and a good number were thrown to elephants to be trampled upon for the diversion of the Emperor and his ladies. A general outburst of violence against Christians marked the arrival of the captives at Agra. The church was plundered, the bells were removed, and the doors walled up. The Jesuits fell into disgrace and dared not move out of doors for fear of the mob. Even the Armenian nobleman Mirza Zulqarnain, who had held a high post in the Mogul administrative service, was imprisoned and had to buy his liberty on payment of a huge sum. The missionaries were forbidden to convert any one, and all public worship by Christians was stopped by Imperial orders. Some free Christians were even forcibly converted on some pretext or other.

Fortunately, however, this outburst of violence did not last long. Shah Jehan, his prestige restored and thirst for revenge satisfied, relaxed the rigour of his orders against Christians due mainly to persuasion by some of the nobles of the older school. But all royal patronage of the Jesuits was withdrawn for good, and the court and people alike began to look upon Christians as undesirable aliens, and missionary activities as objectionable. Thus fallen into evil days, the mission just lingered on in Agra without being able to make any headway.

The hostility of the Muslims was bad enough for the Jesuits, but they had some trouble with their co-religionists too. A few Franciscans had appeared in 'Mogor' from somewhere, and the Jesuits thought their work as an encroachment upon their rights. There was some tussle between the two orders, but the meek Franciscans gave up the fight and withdrew. But the Jesuits

4. Akbar Meeting the First Jesuit Mission
(Courtesy : *Historical Research Institute, St. Xavier's College, Bombay*)

5. De Nobili and a Disciple
(Courtesy : *Historical Research Institute, St. Xavier's College, Bombay*)

6. A Mogul Painting of the Assault on Hugli
(*Shah-Jehan-Nama*)

had more serious trouble from one Dom Matheus de Castro Melo, a colourful personality, who deserves some detailed notice.

Dom Matheus was the son of a Goan Brahmin couple who had embraced Christianity. Matheus was a brilliant young man and received education under the Franciscans in Goa. A Portuguese nobleman interested himself in Matheus and on his recommendation the young man was sent to Portugal for higher studies and thence to Rome. Here he was ordained a priest and later, in 1637, appointed Bishop of Chrysopolis.

The Indian Bishop proved more of a nationalist than an ecclesiastic and his career was marked by hostility towards Europeans in general and the Jesuits in particular. He had probably suffered much at the hands of colour prejudiced priests and laymen. It irked him to note that the Jesuits excluded all Indians from their order and he put it down to their jealousy of Indians. It was the considered opinion of His Lordship that Indian converts, especially Brahmins, were any day more intelligent than the generality of the Jesuits.

Dom Matheus came to India in 1639 for what precise purpose it is not known, but soon after his arrival he quarrelled with the Archbishop and Viceroy of Goa. He left Goa in disgust, went to Arabia, managed to visit the tomb of Muhammad, and then proceeded to Rome. Here in 1645, he was appointed Vicar Apostolic of Ethiopia, but in 1648 he was in Arabia again where he quarrelled with the Jesuits and excommunicated one of them. In 1650 he was, however, in India as the Vicar Apostolic of 'the kingdom of the Great Mogul, Adelkhan (Bijapur) and Golconda'. After making a futile attempt to drive away the Portuguese from Goa, he proceeded northwards and reached Agra on the 1st February 1651. Here Father Botelho, who was then in charge of the Mogor Mission, received him with due respect but the Vicar Apostolic was not satisfied with the affairs of the Mogor Mission. Admonition proving of no avail, Dom Matheus openly sided with the enemies of the Jesuits whether English, Dutch or Indian and went about telling every one that the Jesuits were Portuguese spies. His propaganda proved quite successful and Shah Jehan ordered the arrest of Father Busi of the Mogor Mission and the poor priest was released only through the intervention of Mirza Zulqarnain. The Jesuits, however, did not keep quiet. They accused the Bishop, as usual, of sedition and heresy and he had to leave India for Rome to answer these charges. In the year 1679 he died at the mature age of 72.

It is unfortunate that the little we know of this remarkable Indian Bishop is from the picture painted by his enemies. He was not, in all probability, as black as he was painted. All the Jesuits at the time were not saints and the universal hostility their activities inspired must have given the independent Bishop much cause for complaint. One of the accusations against the Bishop was that he used to remark that though he had travelled all over Europe he had not come across one edifice which could approach in beauty and chasteness of design the then newly built Taj Mahal.

Anyway, when the Bishop left India the Jesuits "rendered thanks to God and quoted the verse: 'imperavit ventis et facta est tranquillitas magna'—'He rebuked the winds and there was a great calm'."*

Though Shah Jehan was unfavourable to Christians, the Jesuits began to expect great things of Prince Dara, his eldest son. Dara was a charming person with a taste for literature and art, and held liberal views on religion. He was particularly fond of Hindus and Christians and moved freely with the Jesuits. He had inherited the genial temperament and diversity of interests of his great grandfather Akbar, but little of his political genius. In the war of succession that rocked the Empire during Shah Jehan's old age, Dara was ignominiously defeated by the cunning Aurangazeb. Aurangazeb seized the throne, imprisoned Shah Jehan and disposed of his brothers one by one.

Aurangazeb ascended the throne in 1658 and reigned at Delhi while Shah Jehan lived in captivity at Agra. Aurangazeb is well known for his bigotry which led to the ruin of the Mogul Empire.

* *The Jesuits and the Great Mogul*, Edward Maclagan.

Though he did not indulge in active persecution of non-Muslims, throughout his long reign he adopted a steady pro-Muslim policy which was humiliating to his non-Muslim subjects. The Jeziah was imposed for the first time in Mogul India. The missionaries were exempted from the tax as Christian Faquirs possessing no property, and that too by the intervention of the Portuguese lady Dona Juliana who wielded considerable influence in the court as the keeper of the seraglio. No conversion from Islam was permitted but Hindus and Christians were lured to Islam by economic help and other incentives. Nor were forcible conversions rare. The accidental repeating of the Kalma was seized as a valid excuse for forcible conversion and even where there was no actual repeating of the Kalma it was enough if some fanatic swore that he heard it repeated.

Under these conditions the missionaries found it practically impossible to convert any one to Christianity, and the small Christian communities attached to the mission suffered want and privation. They gave up all hope of any large scale conversions where the Imperial influence prevailed, and diverted their attention to other fields. There were some missionary activities at Kaffiristan, Nepal, Nagpur, etc. during this period but none proved successful. The mission to Kaffiristan was sent on the report of some Armenians who had heard rumours of a mysterious Christian community existing in the mountain fastness of the Hindu Kush, but the missionaries failed to locate the community.

In Bengal, however, there appeared some promise of success as the Augustinians had already made some headway in certain places in this province. Their work was considerably accelerated by the zeal of a Don Antonio de Rozario, a young zealot from a Zamindar family of Bengal. Rozario was an inspired man. He was a "small, dark, wizened figure with slender means and little education, but full of the most remarkable zeal for the propagation of his faith, and endowed with an extraordinary persuasiveness of discourse. On hearing him, it was said, one had either to become a Christian or drown himself." By his own efforts he converted about 20,000 Hindus to Christianity, mainly low class men living near his patrimony west of Dacca. He wanted priests to minister to the needs of the new community and the Jesuits jumped at the idea. But when they started work among the neophytes they met with considerable opposition from the Augustinians who thought the field was theirs and the Jesuit activity was an encroachment. Goa settled the dispute in favour of the Jesuits but these now experienced considerable opposition from the Muslim authorities, and Rozario himself came into trouble. The Missionaries also found the climate unbearable. Nor did the Augustinians keep quiet. Goa was far off and Rome still farther, and they actively interfered; and between the Augustinians and the Jesuits, the 20,000-Christians of Rozario relapsed into Hinduism.

The Jesuits had some standing at Jaipur at this time mainly because Jaisingh Sawai, the celebrated astronomer Rajah, wished to have learned European astronomers in Jaipur. Jai Singh ruled from 1699 till 1743, and the famous observatories at Jaipur, Delhi, Muttra, Ujjain and Benares were constructed by him. He came to know that some of the Jesuits were proficient in astronomy and applied to Father Emmanuel de Figueredo, the Superior of the Mogor Mission at the time, for men learned in the science. Figueredo replied that he should apply to Portugal itself for really learned men and the zealous Rajah sent the Father himself as the head of a mission to Portugal for astronomers. In 1729 Father Figueredo returned with de Silva, a well-known astronomer and he settled down in Japiur. De Silva's descendants are still found in the state.

Jai Singh's thirst for astronomical knowledge was insatiable and he wrote to all the Jesuit centres in India and to Rome for European astronomers. Quite a number of Jesuits proficient in the science collected at Jaipur and they were given every facility for doing missionary work in the state. In spite of this encouragement, congregations were few probably because the learned fathers were better astronomers than missionaries. Jai Singh died in 1743. Under his descendants both astronomy and the Jesuits suffered neglect, and the Mission had to close down.

Aurangazeb died in the year 1707 and with his death began the decline of the Mogul Empire. The fanatical policy he followed bore fruit, and a vigorous Hindu revival under the leadership of the Maharathas shook the foundations of the Empire. The Empire had already been drained of its resources by Aurangazeb's constant wars with Shivaji and his successors and with the death of the old tyrant rebellion started everywhere, and chief after chief, viceroy after viceroy declared independence. The successors of Aurangazeb were weak men who could not stem this surging tide of rebellion. They did, however, keep up a shadow of the old glory till 1739 when the Persian invader Nadir Shah swept over India like a cyclone, sacked Delhi and carried away the accumulated treasures of the Empire to Persia. India was now left without a master and rival groups warred on one another for supremacy till all were swept aside by the forceful impact of British colonial expansion.

The Mogor Mission had nothing spectacular to show compared to the work of the Franciscans and Jesuits in the South. For one thing, Portuguese influence was not felt in Mogul India; for another, Muslims were hard to convert. The main obstacles to the conversion of the Muslims were monogamy, and the dogmas of Trinity and Incarnation.

Under Akbar and Jehangir, as we have seen, the missionaries had full freedom to preach and convert. The methods adopted by the Jesuits in reaching the people was not street preaching; they usually attracted Hindus and Muslims to their church by the display of religious pictures, and by showy ceremonials. On these occasions, the missionaries went among the crowd explaining to men and women the meaning of the pictures and ceremonials and pointing out the superiority of Christianity to Hinduism and Islam. The crowd listened with interest but conversions were few. In fact conversion by the missionaries was mainly confined to the servants of Europeans and Armenians, and even in these cases complaints often reached the Emperor that the missionaries had bribed the convert.

Though they were hard to convert, Indian Muslims, compared

to their brethren farther West, were generally tolerant towards religious innovators of all kinds. Except for brief periods of outbursts mainly inspired by political motives, persecutions were extremely rare in the Mogul Empire and Muslims, probably because of their association with the Hindus, took religious discussions in good spirit. The eccentric English wanderer Coryate wrote that he vehemently disputed religion with a Muslim in Multan and would have been 'roasted on a spitt' in Persia or Turkey for what he said against the Prophet. On another occasion the same zealot acted as Muezzin in a mosque, and ascending the minaret called the Faithful to prayer by the astounding Azan, "There is no God but God, and Hazrat Isa (Prophet Jesus) is the Son of God."

Though there were no Christian congregations of importance in Mogul India, there were quite a number of individuals who wielded considerable influence in the court and elsewhere. The Mogul army had a sprinkling of Europeans, especially in the artillery section, but none of them rose to any eminence. The Armenians were, however, different. There were, in all important Mogul cities, quite a large number of them engaged in trade; a greater number found employment in the Imperial and Provincial services. Persian was the official language of the Moguls who looked to Persia as the centre of Asian culture. Armenians who were proficient in Persian and familiar with the culture of Persia easily found employment under the Moguls. They lived on excellent terms with Europeans, and the Jesuits derived considerable help from them.

Of all the Armenians in Mogul India, the greatest was Mirza Zulqarnain. He was not, strictly speaking, an Armenian but the son of Mirza Sikander a merchant from Aleppo who took service under Akbar. Sikander was an able official and was well thought of by Akbar and Jehangir. He was a generous patron of the Jesuits; in his will he set apart "Rs.2,000 for the Church and Christians of Lahore, Rs.4,000 to the Church and Christians of Agra and Rs.3,000 for a grave for himself with a chapel."

Sikander's son Zulqarnain was adopted in boyhood by Akbar himself, and when he came of age was appointed Governor of Sambhar. He held this post under Jehangir too, but when prince Khurram (Shah Jehan) rebelled against his father, Zulqarnain remained loyal to Jehangir and this brought him greater honour and rank.

On Shah Jehan's accession to the throne, the Christian nobleman fell out of favour. He was demoted and transferred to Gorakhpur but was recalled in the persecution of 1633 and imprisoned. With some difficulty, he bought his freedom on payment of a large sum. Gradually, however, Shah Jehan's hostility wore down and in 1649 Zulqarnain was restored to his old province of Sambhar as its Governor. Two years later he resigned, and spent his days in retirement.

Zulqarnain was a staunch Christian and a constant ally of the Jesuits. From time to time, especially under Shah Jehan, pressure was brought upon him to embrace Islam, but the Mirza stoutly refused to be bullied or cajoled. He, like his father, was a generous patron of all Christians and gave unstintingly to relieve want and destitution. He was known among Europeans as the 'Father of the Christians of Mogor'. The Jesuit mission received from him more than Rs. 40,000 for various charities. The wanderer Coryate received Rs.20 from this 'noble and generous Christian of the Armenian race'. Dom Matheus, the Bishop of Chrysopolis, received Rs. 100.

Zulqarnain was a versatile genius, and was an excellent poet and musician. His knowledge of Hindustani was profound. He died in or about the year 1656. None of his descendants rose to the eminence of Zulqarnain, and nothing is known at present of this noble Mogul family.

Another Armenian celebrity of the time was Kwaja Martinus. He was not an official but a prosperous businessman. He is said to have visited Rome in pilgrimage. He had given the Jesuits Rs. 10,000 towards the cost of building the church at Agra. We know little about his private life, but his remains rest in the Santos Chapel at Agra.

Then there is the legend of Akbar's Christian wife. Akbar is said to have had a Christian wife named Miriam but there is no historical background to the story. One version of the legend is that she was Portuguese, another that she was Armenian. Closely connected with the legend of Akbar's Christian wife is the story of the Indian Bourbons. A member of this noted family is believed to have migrated to India and settled down in this country marrying a sister of Akbar's Christian wife. Many families in Agra, Narwar, Gwalior and Bhopal during the rule of the East India Company used to trace their descent from the Bourbons, and travellers' tales are plentiful which attribute the origin of these families to this or that Bourbon. The modern Indian Bourbons have little to boast of except a glorious ancestry of doubtful origin.

An interesting personage who wielded considerable influence in Delhi towards the decline of the Mogul Empire was the lady Dona Juliana Diaz de Costa. Her father was a Portuguese captive from Hugli who bought his freedom by payment of a ransom. Juliana was born in Agra probably in the year 1657, though accounts are not wanting which suggest her nativity in Cochin or Bengal. She married while young and had children, but little is known about her husband. She joined the service of Aurangazeb's wife, and was entrusted with the education of the young princes. By her intelligence and ability she won the regard of the queen and wielded considerable influence in Aurangazeb's seraglio. On this Emperor's death in 1707, his successor Bahadur Shah who had been under her tutelage showered honours upon her. She was given an allowance of Rs.1000 per month and was allotted the palace of Dara Shukoh for her residence. In addition, four villages near Okla were endowed on her, and the revenue from these was quite considerable.

Juliana was an ardent supporter of all Christians without distinction of nationality or denomination, and the English and the Dutch shared her munificence with the Jesuits. She endowed the Jesuit mission at Delhi with one lakh of rupees, and gave financial aid for the despatch of a mission to Tibet. Though wealthy,

Juliana lived a simple, frugal life. She died in July or August 1734 at a mature age, and her body was brought from Delhi and buried in the church at Agra.

The great Christian figures of Mogul India left no descendants of consequence. Their progeny perished with those of their masters.

CHAPTER VIII

BEGUM ZEBUNISSA JOANNA SAMRU—THE CHRISTIAN PRINCESS OF SARDHANA

DURING the troublous days that followed the disruption of the Mogul Empire, security of person and property was practically unknown in India. The power of warring chieftains was short lived, and their span of life shorter still. The country was in a constant state of war, and many an astute statesman and powerful ruler met with an untimely death. Hence the romantic story of the life of Begum Samru, a girl left destitute at a very young age, who carved out a kingdom for herself and ruled it as independently as circumstances would permit at the time and died full of years and honour is itself of interest; but the fact that she was a Christian and a staunch supporter of all Christian activities and ended her days leading a saintly life makes her story doubly interesting.

The eighteenth century was essentially the age of European adventurers in India. With the death of Aurangazeb the Mogul power declined rapidly and the momentous struggle for the crown of India started between the Maharathas, the Sikhs and the British. Every chieftain or adventurer who owed allegiance to the Mogul became virtually independent and sold his services to the highest bidder when he himself was not in a position to expand his power independently. European adventurers who, by the very nature of their nationality and interests, had no loyalty to any of the rising Indian powers took full advantage of the situation, and those who were energetic and unscrupulous enough managed to carve out semi-independent kingdoms for themselves. During this century European leadership was considered superior to Indian, and all Indian rulers wished to have European Generals in their army. The Sikhs, the Maharathas and the Sultans of Mysore had large numbers of Europeans in their army. They, however, entertained few Englishmen in their service because of their jealousy of the rising power of the British and the suspicion of loyalty of British officers.

The rapidly rising power of the British was probably responsible for the Indian predilection for European Army Officers. During the reign of Shah Jehan and Aurangazeb, the Mogul Army had quite a good number of Europeans in it but they were not generally considered superior to Indians, though in the artillery section Europeans were specially proficient. But in the eighteenth century Europeans came to be looked upon as definitely superior to Indians, and a good many Europeans came to India as soldiers of fortune attracted by the excellent opportunities the country afforded for really enterprising men. Of these adventurers, Walter Reinhardt proved a remarkable man. He was of German extraction, came to India at a young age and served under the French. When the British took Chandernagore in 1757, Reinhardt became a refugee but he soon obtained a position under Gurgin Khan, the Armenian General of Mir Kassim.

It was while serving under Mir Kassim that Reinhardt was discredited with the cold-blooded shooting of fifty-one Englishmen. The British factor at Patna, Mr. Ellis, for some fancied grievance he had against the Nawab, attacked the city without warning or provocation but was defeated and captured with his men. Mir Kassim who had suffered many things of many Englishmen, in a fit of temper, ordered the English captives to be shot and the work was entrusted to Reinhardt who executed it promptly and efficiently. It is related by the British that no Indian officer would undertake this work and Reinhardt volunteered. The English was naturally horrified at his cold-blooded action and they have left us accounts of Reinhardt which depict him as a detestable blackguard, blacker than Lucifer. They tried their utmost to capture the villain, but Reinhardt who knew the British well, managed to keep himself sufficiently far from their spreading influence to die a natural death as the ruler of a principality he founded in Hindustan.

The accounts of his enemies show Reinhardt as a morose, cruel, unscrupulous devil, and the name Samru by which he was known in India is believed to be a corruption of 'sombre' the nickname the British gave him. Another explanation of the name 'Samru' is that once he enlisted in the British army under the name of Summers which was corrupted into Samru. Whatever the origin of his name, Samru thoroughly hated the British. He might have shared this sentiment with the French when he was in their service, or he had probably suffered some personal humiliation at their hands. Moreover the eighteenth century British in India were not a very lovable community, and Samru had probably thought that India was not likely to miss very badly the fifty-one Englishmen shot by his orders.

In the battle of Buxar (1764) Mir Kassim and the Nawab of Oudh were defeated by the British and Samru fled westward. He was a fine soldier and leader of men, and managed to build up a respectable regiment of mercenaries officered by European adventurers like himself, and roamed about Hindustan in search of a patron. His fame as an able general and stern disciplinarian had by now spread throughout India, and Jawahar Singh, the Jat Chief of Bharatpur engaged him in 1765. In the same year the Jat Chief made an unsuccessful attempt to capture Delhi, and during the seige, Reinhardt came across the girl who was to play an important part in his life and in contemporary history.

The girl's Muslim name was Farzana, but her origin is obscure. She is mentioned as a Kashmiri in some accounts, but her father Lutaf Ali Khan, was of noble birth. His son by another wife ill treated Farzana and her mother, and the two were driven out of the house, and left to eke out a living as best as they could in those troublous times. One account shows that the two were in a dancing troupe when Reinhardt met them. Farzana was then in her teens, and her beauty and intelligence at once attracted the rough German, a connoisseur of women, who had a well stocked harem in proper Muslim style. He granted her the status of wife and she came to be known as Begum Samru.

The Begum was as astute and clever as she was beautiful. The misfortunes of her childhood had made Farzana precociously self reliant and responsible. She took an active interest in the affairs of her husband and made herself familiar with the management of his army and his estates, and cultivated good relations with the officers most of whom were Europeans.

Jawahir Singh of Bharatpur, Samru's patron, died in 1772, and his successor did not possess the grit required to hold the turbulent Jats together. The Mogul Nobles of Delhi took advantage of his weakness and the prevailing dissentions, attacked him and inflicted a severe defeat on the Jats in the battle of Barsana. The Moguls were, however, so impressed by the section of the Jat Army commanded by Samru that Najaf Khan, the Premier Noble, on behalf of the Emperor offered his patronage to Samru. Samru realized that the Jat cause was as good as lost, and after protracted negotiations finally accepted the Mogul offer. Reinhardt was presented to Shah Alam on 21st May 1774 and received the jaghire of Sardhana from the Emperor. The revenue from this principality was to defray the expenses connected with the maintenance of a standing army which was to be at the disposal of the Emperor at the time of need. The jaghire of Sardhana was situated in the fertile Doab between Aligarh and Muzzaffarnagar and yielded a revenue of six lakhs of rupees.

Samru himself was getting tired of his roving life, and after his marriage with Farzana seriously thought of settling down as a chieftain with a kingdom of his own. He made the town of Sardhana the headquarters of his jaghire, and started exploring the possibilities of developing the area. But Reinhardt did not live long to enjoy his newly acquired possession. Four years after receiving the jaghire from the Emperor he died on 6th May 1778, of a neglected cold.

On Reinhardt's death trouble about succession arose. Farzana had no children, but Reinhardt had a son by another wife; this young man was, however, a fool utterly incompetent to take charge of Samru's army and his jaghire. Hence both the European and Indian officers of the army requested the Begum to take charge of her late husband's possessions and his army, and the Emperor gave his formal sanction. Thus Farzana became the Princess of Sardhana, with an army of her own and a fairly big sized principality as her kingdom. Samru's disciplined and well trained corps was 4,000 strong with 82 European officers, 200 horse and a good train of artillery; not a very big army, quite true, but quite a respectable one compared to the indisciplined, loosely held Indian armies of the time.

On Reinhardt's death, the command of the Begum's army was held by a German named Pauli. He was implicated in an intrigue, the exact nature of which is not known, and was decapitated. A M. Marchand had entertained some hopes of marrying the Begum, but Pauli's fate cooled his ardour and he gave up the idea.

Under the influence of Reinhardt and her European officers, the outlook of the Begum had by now become definitely Christian and her stepson Zafar Yab and herself were baptized at Agra on 7th May 1781 by Fr. Gregorio. The Begum was given the Christian name Joanna and her stepson Louis Balthazaar Reinhardt. From now on, till her death she remained a staunch Christian and a benevolent patron of all Christians irrespective of nationality and denomination.

After the death of Pauli the Begum began to search for an able European officer to command her army and soon she found the proper man. He was George Thomas, the celebrated Irish adventurer. Thomas, after serving in South India under various flags, took the road to Delhi and hearing of the Christian princess of Sardhana went to her and offered his services. The princess was an excellent judge of men and the daring Irishman immediately received a commission. His ability and qualities of leadership won for him special favours and he received rapid promotions and became the commander of the Begum's forces. He reorganized and disciplined the army and the Princess of Sardhana became a power to be counted with in Delhi and the surrounding areas.

The affairs in Delhi at the time were in a peculiar state. The Mogul power counted for little or nothing, but the prestige of the Emperor was as high as ever. Such was the grip the Mogul name had obtained on India under Akbar, Jehangir, Shah Jehan and

Aurangazeb that a superstitious awe still clung to the word Mogul, and no one dared to gaze on the dead empire without permission. The warring chiefs of the time were always anxious to arm themselves with an Imperial Farman for the enjoyment of rights they had usurped. Even the Rohila ruffians who wished to murder the Emperor thought it desirable to have a formal death warrant signed by the Emperor for his own execution before they could kill him.

And with the hour came the man. Shah Alam II, the then heir to the Mogul title, was essentially a man of peace. He signed Farmans with supreme impartiality. When the power of Mahdaji Scindia was in the ascendant, he appointed him Amir-ul-Umra or Premier Noble and as such the virtual ruler of Delhi. When Scindia was defeated by the Rajputs and the Rohila Chieftain Ghulam Qadir threatened Delhi, the Emperor promptly deposed Scindia and elevated Ghulam Qadir to the position of Amir-ul-Umra. Scindia retrieved his fortune and drove Ghulam Qadir out of Delhi when the Emperor reinstated Scindia in his old office. So much for the power and prestige of the Mogul Emperor.

We may, however, give here an account of the part Begum Samru played in driving out Ghulam Qadir from Delhi as it shows at once the spirit of the lady and her loyalty to the Mogul cause though bestowed upon an imbecile. Ghulam Qadir was the Rohila Chieftain of Saharanpur, notorious for his treachery and cruelty. On hearing of the defeat of Scindia at the hands of the Rajputs, and his retreat to Gwalior, Ghulam Qadir with the avowed intention of plundering Delhi appeared on the bank of the Jumna opposite Delhi Fort with a strong force. He managed to win over Manzur Ali, the influential Nazir of the Emperor, and with his help crossed over to the citadel. Shah Nizamuddin, the deputy of Scindia, finding the situation hopeless fled the city, and Ghulam Qadir together with his accomplice started exploring the palace for treasures. Now a most unexpected thing happened.

Begum Samru, hearing of the unenviable predicament of

the Emperor acted with surprising promptness and speed. She proceeded to Delhi by forced marches and encamped on the bank of the Jumna. This unexpected move of the Begum considerably disconcerted Ghulam Qadir. Her army had the reputation of being the very best in and near about Delhi, and the Rohila Chieftain knew that he had to conciliate her. He sent word to the Begum to name her terms. The Begum agreed to withdraw but wished to discuss the terms personally and hence requested Ghulam Qadir to come over to her camp secretly. As treacherous people are slow to suspect the intentions of others, Ghulam Qadir in post haste crossed the Jumna to the Begum's camp with no more men about him than two of his trusted associates. The terms were discussed with ostentatious cordiality and the Begum agreed to join his forces as soon as he crossed the Jumna back to Delhi. This promise the Begum, however, had not the necessity to keep; for when Ghulam Qadir rose to depart from the Begum's camp, he found the ferry blocked by her redoubtable soldiers, and had to flee to his own camp stationed on the other bank of the Jumna.

The Begum now crossed over to Delhi and was received by the Emperor with all the joy appropriate to the occasion. Ghulam Qadir and Manzur Ali were pardoned at the request of the Begum, and she herself was granted the title of Zebunissa (ornament of her sex) and given a robe of honour. The extent of her principality was also enhanced by the addition of several Parganas.

Ghulam Qadir did not, however, keep quiet. With the departure of the Begum to Sardhana, he again appeared in Delhi, looted the palace, violated the Zenana, and blinded the Emperor. Scindia was now roused to activity; he attacked and defeated Ghulam Qadir, who took to flight; the miscreant was chased and captured and put to an ignominious death.

During those days when treachery was the commonest thing among rulers, the Begum constantly supported the cause of the weakling Emperor and his partisan Scindia and had fought several actions against the Sikhs, the Rohilas and the Jats. Situated as her territory was in close proximity to the expanding Sikh power, it was the Begum's special care to guard her own kingdom and that of the Scindia, then representing the Emperor, against the incursions of the Sikhs. The Begum often commanded her troops in person; the battlefield had no terrors for this eighteenth-century Semiramis. "Col. Skinner had often, during his service with the Maharathas, seen her, then a beautiful young woman, leading on her troops to the attack in person, and displaying in the midst of the most frightful carnage, the greatest intrepidity and presence of mind." She was in the thick of every action and her boldness and utter disregard for personal safety inspired her soldiers and goaded them to action in the most desperate situations. And the Begum's troops were reputed to be the best in Hindustan.

In regions far removed from Delhi, where Joanna's fame reached by hearsay only, she was believed to be living a charmed life. She was fabled to have been in possession of a spell which saved her from dangers and disconcerted her enemies. There was a story current in India that Joanna had a magic veil by waving which she was capable of destroying her enemies. The fact that she survived numerous situations of peril from her very childhood onwards and lived for 85 summers during a period in the history of the country wherein the span of human life was extremely short, the people may be pardoned for their credulity.

We must, however, mention here a short period of misfortune that dogged the Begum's heels. Joanna, though she possessed an exceptionally virile mind, was, after all a woman, and for once she yielded herself to sentiments which nearly brought about her ruin, and no account of her life would be complete without some reference to this phase of her life.

Thomas, the commander of her forces, as we have seen, was a man of proved ability and loyalty, and under his guidance the Begum's army was feared and respected by all. In the year 1790 a Frenchman named Levassoult entered her service. Levassoult was a handsome young adventurer, dashing and brave, and his bearing and mien attracted the Begum, then in the prime of her womanhood and possessing the vigour and looks of youth. He rose rapidly in his mistress' favour, and had a good following among the French officers of her army. Intrigues now started to oust the Irishman Thomas, and Levassoult being a favourite of the Begum the French did not find it very difficult to persuade the Begum to believe that Thomas was more concerned about promoting his own interests than the Begum's. The absence of Thomas from Sardhana on a campaign against the Sikhs gave Levassoult and his partisans a chance to fan suspicion and the Begum was even prevailed upon to ill-treat Thomas' wife. On his return from the campaign against the Sikhs, Thomas found Sardhana too hot for him, and he left the Begum's service in disgust.

Levassoult, now left without a rival, lost no time in consolidating his position. The Begum was quite taken by the personal charm of the youthful Frenchman and when he proposed marriage, closed in immediately. But she wished to keep the matter a secret as it might have led to public scandal, Levassoult being her inferior in rank. Levassoult agreed, and the two were married by Fr. Gregorio who had baptized the Begum. The marriage ceremony was secretly performed and there were but two Frenchmen during the proceedings as witnesses. But such an affair could not be kept a secret for long. Levassoult himself was much elated by the marriage, and though he was passionately in love with the Begum, wished to play the Prince of Sardhana. A man of many parts, Levassoult's besetting sin was vanity. Even before his marriage he had imagined himself superior to his brother officers but after the marriage the tactless Frenchman openly assumed an attitude of arrogance and superiority. When the Begum entertained her officers, as was her wont on all important occasions, he began to take liberties with her much to her embarrassment and the surprise of her officers. The marriage was not known to many, tongues started wagging and the Begum and her character fell in the estimation of all.

Those who admired Thomas and were smarting under the wrongs he had suffered now assumed an attitude of hostility.

The reaction was sudden and terrific, and shows the fickle nature of loyalties at the time and the supreme need for tact, vigilance and caution in rulers. The catastrophe was precipitated by the Begum's ill-conceived plan to attack Thomas who had risen to power under his new patron, Appa Khande Rao, an ambitious Maharatha chief who entertained designs on Delhi. Thomas had caused the Begum considerable annoyance by spitefully attacking and laying waste part of her province while he was on a march past her territories. The Begum left Sardhana with her army and encamped about fifty miles south-east of Jhujjar with the avowed intention of attacking Thomas. But before her plans could materialize mutiny broke out in the army and the Begum had to beat a hasty retreat to Sardhana only to find that Legios, a friend of Thomas and an inveterate enemy of Levassoult, had already taken possession of the city. The Begum realized the hopelessness of her situation and took to flight with the intention of taking refuge in British territory. The mutineers invited Zafar Yab Khan, Joanna's stepson who was living in retirement at Delhi to take charge of Sardhana and assume the title of his late father. The young man at first hesitated; but pressed by the officers of the army he decided to march at their head to Sardhana. A detachment was also despatched to arrest the fleeing Begum and her husband.

The pursuing column intercepted the Begum's party at Khirwa, in her own territory not many miles from Sardhana. Levassoult who was accompanying the Begum's palanquin on horse, seeing the detachment and the danger they were placed in, decided to put an end to himself rather than suffer the humiliation of capture and maltreatment. The Begum who was passionately fond of Levassoult for whom she had lost so much, firmly asserted that she would follow him unto death. Incidents reminiscent of the last scene in *Antony and Cleopatra* now occurred. As the insurgents closed in, a scream was heard from the palanquin and Levassoult peeping in found Joanna in a pool of blood. Levassoult took his revolver, and shot himself dead, and his lifeless form fell from the saddle. His corpse was subjected to "every act of insult and indignity. For three days it lay exposed to the insults of the rabble and was at length thrown into a ditch."

Though the Begum had stabbed herself, the wound was not fatal. The dagger was turned off by a rib and she recovered from the swoon she had fallen into. The mutineers carried her captive to Sardhana. "She was taken to the old fort, and kept tied under a gun-carriage for seven days exposed to the scorching heat and a victim to the insults and jeers of the mob. She was denied food or drink, and would have perished of starvation but for the Ayahs who continued to be faithful to her and supplied her wants by stealth."* Zafar Yab Khan, goaded by his officers, now decided to consolidate his position. The Delhi Emperor now counted for little or nothing, and hence he thought it desirable to get his title confirmed by the British, whose growing power was effectively felt in Delhi. In support of his claim Zafar produced a letter signed by the Begum stating that she had abdicated in his favour and requesting the British to confirm him in his title. Whether or not the letter was forged or obtained from the Begum under threat, it is not clear, but the Begum who had taken care to cultivate good relations with them had a high standing with the British and they withheld confirmation of Zafar till the facts of the case were fully known.

The Begum had at least one friend in the army. He was M. Saleur, who, though he could not stay the mutiny, still thought well of her and remained loyal to her cause. Through his tactful intervention, the Begum was released from public confinement and was given a house to live in though her residence was closely guarded. From here the Begum now started working for her freedom, but she did not know whom to apply for help. At last, after much deliberation, she decided to appeal to a person whom one would have least expected her to supplicate, showing thereby her thorough understanding of men, their weakness and their strength. For Joanna appealed to no other person than George Thomas, her most bitter enemy who was even suspected to have engineered the mutiny and reduced her to her present plight.

* *Begum Samru*, Banerji.

Thomas was a peculiar man possessing most of the characteristics that distinguish the Irish as a nation apart. He could be extraordinarily bitter and violent when roused, but equally generous and large-hearted when touched by love or pity. He had, after all been a close associate of the Begum for long, and her chief adviser and loyal general; rumours were even current that he was passionately in love with the Begum and his bitterness and recent enmity were inspired by jealousy of Levassoult. The Begum knew her Thomas well and wrote to him for help.

Joanna did not mince matters. She described to him in detail her miserable plight and her fear of being poisoned by Zafar Yab Khan and his henchmen any day and told him plainly that she had no friend left in the world except her former general and ally. She sincerely apologized to him for the wrong she had done him. Would Thomas forgive her and deliver her from her enemies?

The letter touched the heart of the chivalrous Irishman. He took prompt action. Scindia was bought over by the promise of a handsome bribe, and Thomas marched to Sardhana at the head of his army. As threat of punishment of the mutineers might have endangered the life of the Begum, he encamped outside the principality of Sardhana and issued a proclamation that the Scindia as the Deputy of the Emperor took serious objection to the mutiny and usurpation of power by Zafar Yab Khan, and all officers and men of the army were ordered on pain of death, to disown Zafar Yab and reinstate the Begum. A part of the army now decided in favour of the Begum and proclaimed her the queen of Sardhana. But by the time Thomas arrived in Sardhana a counter revolution had already placed Zafar Yab back on the throne. Thomas declared that he would, on the orders of the Scindia, enforce his decision on the point of the sword and his strong stand had the desired effect. The army abided by his decision and the Begum was formally reinstated in her old charge.

Thus, after remaining in captivity and disgrace for about a year, Joanna regained her status as the Princess of Sardhana.

The lesson she learnt was bitter. Never again did she allow her sentiments to get the better of her judgement in the management of her kingdom and her army.

The Begum rewarded M. Jean Saleur by appointing him chief of her army. Zafar Yab Khan fled to Delhi where he died a prisoner. Nor did the Begum forget the prompt action of Thomas. When the fortune of that great adventurer turned and he was left without a friend in India, it was the Begum who took charge of his family. Thomas died in India while making arrangements to leave the country, and the Begum adopted his son John Thomas and provided for the family. She did everything to obliterate her connection with Levassoult and in order to placate the army took care to keep all her past association with him a secret. She even renamed her adopted heir Dyce Samru so that the soldiers and officers could feel that they were serving the legal heir of the redoubtable Reinhardt Samru whose memory they had cherished even during their revolt against the Begum.

The Begum did not enjoy her possessions for long without disturbance. The Emperor's power counted for nothing, but she soon felt the impact of British expansion. Towards the close of the eighteenth century it became clear to every ruler in India that the passing of Indian suzerainty to the British was a matter of time, and the shrewd Joanna, in spite of her late husband's inveterate hatred of them, took care to remain on the right side of the British. Her religion also attracted her to the British, and in 1791 she had, in order to cultivate their friendship, released on payment of a large ransom Col. Stuart, the British Commandant of the then frontier station of Anupshahr, who had fallen into the hands of the Sikh chief Bhanga Singh. The Begum continued the good work by cordial correspondence and it looked as though the old hostility of the British towards Reinhardt had lessened towards his widow. But the arrival of Lord Wellesly as the Governor-General in 1798 brought about a change in their dealings with the Begum. Wellesly was determined to push on the Company's dominion to the farthest limit of India, and it irked him to note that the fertile and strategic principality of

Sardhana remained independent so close to Delhi, and he wished to annex it.

Simultaneously with the rise of the British power in Hindustan proper, the affairs of the Maharathas fell into a bad way. Chief began to fight chief, and the power of the Scindia with whom the Begum had an alliance waned and dissentions started in his dominions. The British in their all absorbing desire to push their advantage treated treaties and alliances with contempt and began to annex every kingdom that came in their way without the least regard to justice or treaty obligations. It was clear to the Begum that a rupture between the Scindia and the British was imminent, and she had to decide in favour of one or the other. The situation called forth all her powers of diplomacy and tact.

The Begum was a masterful tactician and managed to remain friendly with both the British and the Maharathas. But Wellesly was a hard man to please. He had his eye on Sardhana, and appeals to justice and chivalry made by his own diplomats and army chiefs were lost upon him. He was determined to have Sardhana but was prepared to allot an equal or larger area of land to the Begum elsewhere. The battle of Assaye in which the British defeated Scindia left them the virtual rulers of Hindustan and placed them in a favourable position to force their will on Sardhana.

The Begum realized the futility of resisting the British, and after protracted negotiations agreed to give up Sardhana and accept a principality on the west side of the Jumna which they were in a position to offer her because of the defeat of the Maharathas and the British claim to territories once held by them. But when Wellesly wrote to her on 23rd Dec. 1803 that she must immediately relinquish Sardhana and the proposed territory on the west side of the Jumna would be made over to her at His Lordship's leisure, the letter brought forth a spirited reply from the Begum. The Begum's reply was addressed to Lt.-Col. Ochterlony who was arranging negotiations. The Begum wrote:

"You have written to me to evacuate and deliver over the

districts of Sardhana etc. which has been my residence for a length of years, and on which I have expended lakhs of rupees in buildings and habitations to the *amils* of the English gentlemen immediately on their arrival. My brother, it is proper that you should consider that when I go away from here, I require a place to stay in where I may reside with my family and dependants. There are near a thousand destitute persons and lame and blind people in this district for whom a place of abode is necessary. From the commencement until the present time no gentleman invested with authority has disgraced me in this manner. At the period when the English gentlemen acquired possession of Hindustan I rejoiced that from a consideration of my being of the same religion with theirs I should by some means or other be exalted in rank but the contrary has happened for they have required of me several districts possessed of me for thirty years. What may not happen to the rest? If it be the intention of the gentlemen by some means or other to dispossess me, what occasion is there for preserving appearances? Do, my brother, come and having laid hold of my hand turn me out of my abode. The world is not narrow and I am not lame. I will sit down in some retired corner and pass my time in solitude."*

The Begum naturally suspected the intentions of the British, then notorious for perfidy, and the only explanation she could think of for their haste in demanding the surrender of Sardhana was that they wanted to grab her kingdom and then enter into dilatory correspondence which would eventually end in nothing. She was not prepared to accept this if she could possibly avoid it. Though she did not openly break off with the British there was enough to show in her attitude that any day she would flee into their enemy's camp. The Maharathas took full advantage of the situation, and even made a letter available to the British intelligence agents which was supposed to have been written by the Begum signifying her alliance with Jaswant Rao Holkar then plotting against the British. The letter was a forgery and it took some time before the British discovered the fraud but in

* Quoted in *Begum Samru* by Banerji.

the meantime the Begum's sincerity was suspect. The British, however, did not consider it desirable to alienate the Begum completely at the time as they had more than enough at their hands, what with the constant trouble the Maharathas and the Sikhs were giving them. A letter dated 10th Dec. 1804 written by the Agent to the Governor-General aptly describes the situation:

"As the situation of the Begum both from the geographical position of her country, and from the nature of her military strength, is or appears to me to be, such as to render her either a most useful ally or a very troublesome enemy, without the possibility of her ever becoming formidable as a neighbouring Power, I should imagine that the conciliating her might in the present state of affairs be a simple and effectual means of restoring and preserving the tranquillity of the upper part of the Doab. Her force is said to consist of nine battalions of infantry and 40 guns. These if subsidized by the Government and opposed to the Sikhs, might as far as I can judge, completely prevent their committing depredations in the British territories and, by insuring the realisation of the collections, greatly enhance the value of the highly capable district now in question."

The Begum's discontent against the British became widely known, and Holkar and Ranjit Singh sent their agents to persuade her to join them and fight the British. The Begum and her officers, because of their nationality and religion, still wished to maintain cordial relations with the British; the shrewd Joanna must have also realized the futility of resisting the rising power of the British and the danger of openly alienating them. In this difficult situation she played her part well. Rumour spread all over the country that the Begum was in favour of accepting the offer of Ranjit Singh who promised her an annual subsidy of one lakh of rupees and a jaghire in return for military help, and the Begum did nothing to contradict these rumours. On the contrary some changes in the command were either made or ordered to be made, and this move was construed as an indication that the Begum wished to enter into hostility with the British and did not like the idea of a European commanding the army when war appeared imminent with a European power; an Indian or Armenian commander was likely to be more faithful to her cause.

It was now the turn of the British to worry. Ranjit Singh's strength was well known to the British and a powerful Sikh ally like the Begum so close to Delhi was not likely to minimise their troubles in respect of the Sikhs. The Holkar with the Rajah of Bharatpur was seriously threatening the British forces in the Doab. The Sikhs beat Col. Burn, took Saharanpur and captured Mr. G. D. Guthrie, the British Collector. Surely this was no time to force Wellesly's designs on Sardhana. In fact it became the painful duty of Lord Lake who was in charge of operations in this part of India to court the Begum and obtain the release of Mr. Guthrie which the Begum readily did as the professed ally of the British.

The Begum's activities puzzled everybody. While conducting and encouraging negotiations with the Sikhs and Maharathas, she never joined either. While assuming an attitude of hostility towards the British, she went out of her way to get Mr. Guthrie released. She engendered and propagated all sorts of rumours about imminent outbreak of hostility between the British and herself, but in her actual dealings with them her conduct was exemplary and most cordial. Ochterlony who knew the Begum well was as impatient of Wellesly's obstinacy as the Begum herself and did nothing to allay the Governor-General's fears of the Begum's disaffection. All told, the Begum's diplomacy proved eminently successful, and Wellesly did not consider the time opportune to dislodge the Begum from Sardhana.

In July 1805 Lord Cornwallis came to India for the second time and replaced Wellesly. The new Governor-General was a man of mature wisdom and pursued a conciliatory policy towards Indian rulers. Lord Lake had no difficulty in persuading Cornwallis to abandon the idea of annexing Sardhana and to reinstate the Begum in her principality for life. She too agreed to accept the suzerainty of the British and accordingly Mr. Guthrie who

THE CHRISTIAN PRINCESS OF SARDHANA

owed her much was sent to Sardhana with a letter of authority confirming her title as the Princess of Sardhana. The Governor-General wrote to her as follows:

"I have great pleasure in apprising you that reposing entire confidence in your disposition to maintain the obligations of attachment and fidelity to the British Government, I have resolved to leave you in the unmolested possession of your jaghire, with all the rights and privileges you have hitherto enjoyed. As the condition of this indulgence I have a right to expect that you will not only abstain from affording encouragement to those turbulent persons who are disposed to excite confusion and promote disorders, but that you will cordially assist in preventing their attempts to disturb the tranquillity of the Company's territories."

The Begum was now 54 years of age and looked forward to a settled and peaceful life. After the treaty with the British she withdrew from the active field and was content to live as a faithful ally of the British. She had absolute authority over her own dominion, but her relationship with other powers was defined by the treaty and she was content to leave these matters to the British. She reduced the size of her army and what was left could be made available to the British when they needed it. She did not now care to take a personal interest in the conflicts which the powers were then engaged in, but set herself to work for the development of her jaghire and the welfare of her subjects. The province of Sardhana was a fertile agricultural region and she improved the irrigation system and actively helped the peasantry. Under her constant care the lot of the peasants improved greatly and her peasants and their fields were reputed the best in Hindustan, Travellers report that Sardhana stood as a green smiling land in sharp contrast to the general devastation the country was reduced to during the protracted conflicts of the time. The annual revenue yielded about a million rupees.

The Begum often gave splendid parties in her palace, and many a distinguished European traveller was attracted to her court by her fame. Mrs. Deane, an English lady who visited Sardhana in 1810, has left us the following interesting account of the Begum's military establishment:

"We were escorted over the estate by her colonel-commandant, a respectable old gentleman of the name of Peton, a Frenchman by birth but resident at her court for many years. She has a regular cantonment here for her troops, and a strong fort containing some good houses which are inhabited by her officers and their families. Her soldiers are tall stout men, with light complexions, hooked noses and strongly marked features, being principally Rajputs who are the best soldiers, but much addicted to chewing opium, generally proud and often insolent. Their uniform is a dress of black blue broadcloth, reaching to the feet, with scarlet turbans and waistbands. Her park of artillery seemed also in excellent order; most of the large guns stood in a line in front of the palace gates."

Major Archer wrote of her as the Indian Elizabeth: "She has through a long life maintained her station and security among a host of contending powers and may bear the honour of similarity of character with our Elizabeth."

Mrs. Deane has left us a pleasing pen portrait of the Begum: "Her features are still handsome, although she is now advanced in years. She is a small woman, delicately formed, with beautiful hazel eyes; a nose somewhat inclined to the acquiline, a complexion very little darker than an Italian, with the finest turned hand and arm I ever beheld. Zophanay, the painter, when he saw her, pronounced it a perfect model. She is universally attentive and polite. A graceful dignity accompanies her most trivial actions; she can be even fascinating when she has any point to carry."

In her younger days, the Begum used to observe Purdah and when appearing in public or giving audience wore a veil; but after her treaty with the British and better social contact with them her way of life changed and she adopted many of the usages of the Europeans. She often gave parties which were attended by British officers, and on these occasions dressed in English style and sat with them at table. She was a brilliant conversationalist with a keen sense of humour. When the Governor-General or Commander-in-Chief visited Sardhana, she put forth all the splendour of her court and entertained him on a lavish scale. On these occasions she dressed in a peculiar style, half European and half Indian, wearing a turban and decked with a 'prodigious quantity of jewels'. Her Christmas and New Year parties were reputed the best in India. The British settlement at Meerut, because of its close proximity to Sardhana, was specially favoured of the Begum and often enjoyed her hospitality. She kept a fine band of European musicians under the famous M. Antoine who, on her death, was employed by Ranjit Singh who had a predilection for western music. The Begum was also a lover of Indian dancing and for the entertainment of visitors maintained a troupe of trained dancers.

The Begum was particularly considerate to European ladies and "seldom permitted them to quit her presence without bestowing upon them some token of her generosity, according to the native custom, either a Cashmere shawl or a piece of silk or a jewel, to the value of 20 or 30 guineas." Some proud Englishmen, however, felt humiliated by this generosity of the Begum. "When we recollect who the Begum originally was, the diabolical character of her husband . . . it is strange thus to find an enlightened British community, the victors of the soil, doing homage and seeking favours at her footstool, or even condescending to partake of her hospitality." So wrote one Bacon.

An amusing incident which illustrates the presence of mind of the Begum and her ability to save the most embarrassing situation by her ready wit is narrated by Pearse in his *Memoir of Lake*. In 1803 when negotiations for the transfer of Sardhana were taking place, Lord Lake wrote to the Begum to come to his camp near Bharatpur as he had some important matters to discuss with her. Some other Indian Chiefs were also invited, but the Begum was the first to arrive. "Upon this occasion an incident occurred of a curious and characteristic description. She arrived at headquarters, it appears, just after dinner and being carried in her palanquin at once to the reception tent, his lordship came out to meet and receive her. As the adhesion of every petty chieftain was, in those days, of consequence, Lord Lake was not a little pleased at the early demonstration of the Begum's loyalty and being a little elevated by the wine which had just been drunk, he forgot the novel circumstances of its being a native female he was about to receive, instead of some well-bearded chief, so he gallantly advanced, and to the utter dismay of her attendants, took her in his arms and kissed her. The mistake might have been awkward, but the lady's presence of mind put all right. Receiving courteously the proffered attention, she turned calmly round to her astonished attendants—'It is,' said she, 'the salute of a padre (priest) to his daughter.' The Begum professes Christianity, and thus the explanation was perfectly in character though more experienced spectators might have smiled at the appearance of the jolly red-coated clergyman, exhibited in the person of his lordship."

The splendid parties she gave and her social activities were mainly intended for her army officers and the British guests; the Begum herself lived a simple, plain life. As she advanced in years, she became deeply religious and lived an almost saintly life. She adorned Sardhana and other towns of her province with many a church and chapel. In 1820 she had a beautiful church built at Sardhana on the model of St. Peter's at a cost of four lakhs of rupees; the congregation at Sardhana consisted of about 2,000 Christians. Though a staunch Catholic, the Begum's interest extended to all denominations and her charity to everyone who was needy. In 1830 she had a chapel built for her Anglican subjects.

In 1831 the Begum practically retired from public life, having made her will and invested her adopted son Dyce Samru with authority. She was then 80 years of age. She gave freely of her vast wealth, and her generosity became a byword in North India. In 1834 she sent to Pope Gregory XVI an alms of a lakh and a half of rupees 'as a small token of her sincere love for the holy religion she professed.' On her recommendation the Pope raised Sardhana to a Bishopric and her own domestic chaplain Father Julius

THE CHRISTIAN PRINCESS OF SARDHANA 147

Scotti was ordained the first Bishop of Sardhana. Dyce Samru was knighted by the Pope. Nor was the Pope the only head of a church to receive her alms. She sent to the Archbishop of Canterbury fifty thousand rupees for the promotion of 'the most deserving protestant institution in England.' For the benefit of Indian protestants she gave a princely sum of a lakh and a half of rupees, one lakh of which to be set apart for the instruction and ordination of young aspirants for ministerial duties and the remainder for the liberating, on Good Friday, deserving cases of impoverished debtors imprisoned at Calcutta. About five lakhs were in addition given away for repairing and maintainance of churches in Sardhana and elsewhere. The Tibetan mission regularly received donations from her. "She subscribed liberally towards Hindu and Muslim institutions also."

Although the Begum retired from active life, she still kept good health, and it looked as though she would live for ever. She became a legend and a marvel. The saint Shakir Shah of Meerut is said to have averted her death in 1831. The Begum fell dangerously ill this year and the saint went to Sardhana to see her. He was old and feeble and on the way to Sardhana the good man died. His last words were: 'Aya Tore, Chale Ham', meaning, 'the call came for you, but I answered it'. The Begum recovered from her illness, and coming to hear of the saint's death on his way to Sardhana she had a beautiful tomb built for him.

The final call came at last, and her remarkable life of 85 summers ended in the year 1836. "She had an attack of fever and after a few days' illness during which she retained her consciousness to the last, prepared by the sacrament and prayers of the church, she quietly expired in her palace at Sardhana on Wednesday the 27th January, about half-past six in the morning. The momentous news spread all over northern India and people from far and wide hied to Sardhana and this town within a few hours of the Begum's death became a surging sea of humanity. The crowds that assembled outside the palace walls, and on the roads were immense, and one scene of lamentation and sorrow was apparent; the grief was deep and silent; the clustered groups talked of nothing but the heavy loss they had sustained, and the intensity of their sorrow was pictured in their countenances nor did they separate for the night. According to the custom of the country the whole of the dependants observed a strict fast; there was no preparing of meals, no retiring to rest; all were watchful and every house was a scene of mourning."

The body lay in state till 8 o'clock next morning when the funeral took place. "All arrangements being completed, the body was carried out, borne by the native Christians of the artillery battalion under a canopy, supported by the principal officers of her late Highness's troops, and the pall by Messrs. Dyce Sombre, Solaroli, Drever and Troup, preceded by the whole of Her Highness's bodyguard followed by the Bishop chanting portions of the service, aided by the choristers of the Cathedral. After them the Magistrate Mr. Hamilton and then the chief officers of the household, the whole brought up by a battalion of her late Highness's infantry, and a troop of horse. The procession preceded by four elephants from which alms and cakes were distributed among the crowd, passed through a street formed of the troops at Sardhana, to the door of the Cathedral, the entrance to which was kept by a guard of honour from the 30th N.I. under the command of Capt. Campbell. The procession passed into the body of the church in the centre of which the coffin was deposited on trestles. High mass was then performed in excellent style, and with great feeling by the Bishop.

"Thus terminated the career of one who, for upwards of half a century, had held a conspicuous place in the political proceedings of India. In the Begum Samru the British authorities had an ardent and sincere ally, ever ready, in the spirit of true chivalry, to aid and assist, to the utmost of her means, their fortunes and interests."

On the Begum's death Sardhana, according to the treaty between the British and the Begum, lapsed to the British and Dyce Samru was pensioned off. To the last Dyce cherished the memory of his great adopted mother. He had a tombstone erected to her memory and the work was executed by the famous Italian sculptor

Tandolini at a cost of 40,000 rupees. On the panels was inscribed the following fitting legend:

"Sacred to the memory of Her Highness Joanna Zebunissa, the Begum Sombre, styled the Distinguished of Nobles and Beloved Daughter of the State, who quitted a transitory court for an eternal world, revered and lamented by thousands of her devoted subjects at her palace at Sardhana, on the 27th of January 1836, aged ninety years*. Her remains are deposited underneath in this Cathedral built by herself. To her powerful mind, her remarkable talent, and the wisdom, justice and moderation with which she governed for a period exceeding half a century he, to whom she was more than a mother, is not the person to award praise, but in grateful respect to her beloved memory is this monument erected by him who humbly trusts she will receive a crown of glory that fadeth not away. David Ochterlony Dyce Sombre."

To this prayer of Dyce we can only add 'Amen'.

* According to lunar reckoning.

CHAPTER IX

EARLY PROTESTANT MISSIONS

THE power of the Spaniards and the Portuguese, and the material prosperity that resulted from their maritime activities, inspired the jealousy of lesser nations. Both these great nations of the middle ages were staunchly Catholic and the Pope mediating between them allotted the East to the Portuguese, and the newly discovered continent of America and countries farther West to the Spaniards. Other European powers, as long as they respected the authority of the Pope, had to abide by his decision. But with the revolt against Rome, started under Luther, several newly risen powers rejected the authority of the Pope, and of these the Dutch and the English were the most important. These Protestant nations had a double incentive in overthrowing the power of the Spaniards and the Portuguese; they wanted to show their contempt for the Pope and at the same time wrest naval supremacy from the Iberians.

Both the English and the Dutch successfully challenged the monopoly of trade enjoyed by the Portuguese in the East. The Dutch captured the Portuguese strongholds of Quilon and Cranganoor and finally, in January 1663, Cochin. The ambition of the Dutch as far as India was concerned was confined to trade, but the English began to develop political ambitions. The internal dissensions that followed the decline and fall of the Mogul Empire made matters easy for them, and from their small settlements in the coastal regions the English made inroads into the Peninsula and finally became the undisputed masters of the vast subcontinent.

Unlike the Catholic Portuguese, the Protestant nations thought, at any rate in the initial stages of their development, that they had no responsibility to preach the Gospel in the East. They hated the Catholic Portuguese and wherever they found them fought them; beyond this they thought they had no religious duty. Moreover the Protestant traders were the servants of private commercial enterprise whose sole aim was profit, and the preaching of the Gospel was the responsibility of ministers and not of traders. Nor were ministers very keen in those days to preach the Gospel. The newly formed Protestant churches were too pre-occupied with reformation at home and quarrels with Catholics to devote much attention to non-Christians.

Some of the Reformist leaders even thought that they had no mission towards non-Christians. The theologians Theodore Beza and John Gerhard, for instance, maintained that Jesus' command to preach the Gospel to the nations of the world was addressed to his immediate disciples, and their successors were not competent to continue the work. Besides, Luther himself had thought that within a hundred years of his time the world would come to an end. "Another hundred years," said he, "and all will be over. The Gospel is despised. God's word will disappear for want of any to preach it. Mankind will turn into Epicureans and care for nothing. They will not believe that God exists. Then the voice will be heard, Behold the Bridegroom cometh." As such good Protestants thought their immediate duty was the purification of their own selves for the Second Coming and not the preaching of the Gospel to the people of India and China. Many a Christian minister also thought that the work of conversion was God's and not man's. When William Carey, for instance, prior to his departure to India, suggested, in a meeting of ministers, that he would like to discuss 'the duty of Christians to attempt the spread of the Gospel among the heathen nations,' Mr. Ryland, the Chairman ordered: "Young man, sit down. When God pleases to convert the heathen, He will do it without your aid or mine." Carey, of course, refused to sit down, but that's another story.

Anyway, the East India Company did not want missionaries to come to India. There was a clause in their charter which prohibited sending out to India 'missionaries and gentlemen.' The atmosphere in which the servants of the Company lived in India was not congenial for these types of people. Besides, it was difficult to trade in India according to the precepts of the Sermon on the Mount, and business and religion did not go very well together.

We have seen that the Portuguese had earned for Europeans a bad name in India by their licentious lives. But we must remember that the Portuguese had an Archbishop and a responsible Viceroy in Goa, and Bishops, Governors and clergy elsewhere to regulate and correct the lives of their countrymen. The English settlers were not troubled by any of these. They lived as they liked. Rejection of Catholicism did not immediately make all Englishmen good Protestants. Most of the servants of the East India Company were society's hard bargains. The aim of the Governors of the Company was profit, and agreeable to official notions on such matters, they refused to interfere with the private life of their servants. The way of life of the Governors and other responsible employees of the Company was not very correct either. In their dealings with Indians, they never kept their word if they stood to profit by perfidy. The dealings of Warren Hastings, Clive and others are too notorious to deserve mention here. If this was the morality of responsible officials, that of the subordinates can very well be imagined. In their personal lives, the early English settlers in India were a reproach to their countrymen and their settlements became hotbeds of corruption, immorality, gambling, violence and drunkenness. These were not, certainly, the people who could convert Hindus and Muslims. In fact the Indians judged Christianity by the way of life of the Christians, and Terry makes the following comment about the opinion Indians held about Christianity at the time:

"It is a most sad and horrible thing to consider what scandal there is brought upon the Christian religion by the looseness and remissness, by the exorbitances of many which come amongst them, who profess themselves Christians, of whom I have often heard the natives who live near the ports where our ships arrive say thus, in broken English, which they have gotten—'Christian religion, devil religion; Christians much drunk; Christians much do wrong; much beat much abuse others'."

This being the atmosphere in which the early English lived in

India, it is not surprising that it is neither the powerful English nor the Dutch who first sent out Protestant missions to India but little Denmark. This country had an insignificant trading settlement in Tranquebar, and King Frederick IV sponsored the despatch of the first Protestant mission to India.

Ziegenbalg and Heinrich Plutschau, the first Protestant missionaries, reached India on 9th July 1706. They met with much opposition from the civil authorities of Tranquebar who were inclined to doubt the missionaries' claim of royal patronage. They were suspect and their work, apparently the isolated effort of two misguided zealots, was thought a mad enterprise. But the missionaries were determined men and neither indifference nor hostility deterred them. Their first effort was to get over the language difficulty. The two missionaries studied Tamil, attending the village school and sitting cross-legged with the urchins and tracing the alphabet in sand in the traditional manner of Indian schools. As soon as they learnt enough Tamil to make themselves understood, they started preaching.

The success of the missionaries was not spectacular, but they persisted. They were considerably handicapped by lack of funds; but worse than this was the way of life of European Christians in India which made missionary work difficult. Ziegenbalg thus describes his experience in this matter: "All our demonstration about the excellency of the Christian constitution make but a very slight impression, while they find Christians so much debauched in their manners, and so given to gluttony, drunkenness, lewdness, cursing, swearing, cheating and cozening, notwithstanding all their precious pretence to the best religion. But more particularly are they offended with that proud and insulting temper which is so obvious in the conduct of our Christians here."

Under these conditions many could not be induced to embrace Christianity. But the missionaries never gave up hope and were successful in converting a few; these were mostly poor or destitute persons and the impecunious mission had to support them in addition to supporting their own members. In three years' time, however, the congregation became large enough to need a church, and in the year 1709 funds were raised. Two years later the foundation stone was laid for a church and the first Protestant church in India was built.

The building of the church and feeding of the congregation cost a good deal of money; remittance from home was not coming on time because of the irregular nature of communications, and the charity of local sympathisers proved utterly inadequate for the needs of the community. The civil authorities of Tranquebar, already suspicious of the *bona fides* of the missionaries, were now confirmed in their unbelief of royal patronage of the mission. The Governor acted promptly and with speed. On a trifling pretext he had the impoverished Ziegenbalg thrown into prison. The congregation, poor as it was, raised funds with the help of friends and sympathisers of the missionary and managed to secure his freedom. Soon after, the long awaited remittance came from home together with loyal and devoted workers.

A period of prosperity now ensued and Ziegenbalg who had until now worked among the poor decided to assail the fortress of the mighty. The Brahmins and Rajahs, the hope and despair at once of the European missionary, now claimed his attention. He decided to convert the Brahmin by argument, the most disastrous course of action a European missionary could possibly embark upon. Whatever the superiority of the European in active virtues, in polemics few have proved equal to the Brahmin. The result of Ziegenbalg's enterprise was just what could be expected. In a notable debate held under the auspices of the Dutch in Negapatam, Ziegenbalg disputed with a Brahmin for five hours, and far from converting the Brahmin, the missionary came away with an excessive admiration for the intellectual gifts of his adversary.

The brilliant Brahmin's "quickness in evading logical conclusions, and delivering return thrusts at some weakness in the exposition of the Christian position" evoked Zieganbalg's frank admiration. He derived, he said, very little help from the treatises written by learned men in Europe on how to convert the heathen.

"Well may they write on this subject while they argue with

themselves only, and fetch both the objections and the answers from their own stock. Should they come to closer converse with the Pagans, and hear their shifts and evasions themselves, they would not find them so destitute of arguments as we imagine. They are able to baffle, now and then, one proof alleged for Christianity with ten others brought against it."

It is clear that Ziegenbalg did not have the necessary proficiency in the language and familiarity with the religious literature of the Hindus to make himself a successful disputant. Nor had he the intellectual gifts of some of the learned members of the Society of Jesus. He realized his weakness and gave up all attempts at conversion by argument. He now intensified his efforts to capture the heart rather than the head, and gave wide publicity to the teachings of the Gospel and the simple Christian ideals taught by the Saviour. He translated the New Testament into Tamil. The crudeness of the language elicited derisive remarks by the Roman Brahmin Beschi, but it could be understood and appreciated by the Tamil folk. A catechism for the instruction of the neophytes, a short *Life of Christ*, and the *Danish Liturgy* helped the converts to grasp the fundamentals of Christian doctrine and worship. Other works by Ziegenbalg were *An Elementary Compendium of Theology, A Book of Hymns, A Statement of the Christian, Jewish and Pagan Religions, The Genealogy of the Deities of Malabar* and a *Tamil-German Dictionary* for the use of missionaries. Zeigenbalg was not, however, very strong on the geography of South India and often confused Malabar with Tamil districts. His Tamil dictionary was called by him *Malabarik Dictionary*.

To the delight of Ziegenbalg, a gifted Tamil poet named Kanabadi Vathiar, was converted by him, and the poet rendered into Tamil music the story of Christ and certain incidents from the Bible. Children were taught these songs and the Christian congregations of Tranquebar attracted a large number of Christians and non-Christians. The Tamils are exceptionally amenable to music.

Ziegenbalg was, in short, the originator of those methods of mission work which later Protestant missionaries faithfully followed. His own exemplary life was the main inspiration of his colleagues and congregation.

Ziegenbalg was not only a good missionary but an able publicist. He maintained constant touch with the authorities at home and with other Protestant countries, especially England, and took care to acquaint them of the activities of the Tranquebar mission. "Letters containing full accounts of his doings, and packed with information regarding the country and its people, were regularly transmitted by him to his old teacher and Pietist leader Francks. These were circulated throughout Germany and Denmark, and roused much interest as well as evoking financial help. When translated into English and circulated in England, they proved even more effective as a missionary stimulus." The newly formed Society for the Propagation of the Gospel took immediate notice of the work of Ziegenbalg and remitted to the Tranquebar Mission a token gift of £20. The Society wished to extend its patronage on a permanent basis but its constitution prevented the extending of its activities beyond British colonies. Hence the sister Society for Promoting Christian Knowledge took up the good work and continued to help the mission in many ways.

The favourable impression thus created was taken full advantage of by Ziegenbalg who visited Europe in 1715. He travelled extensively and enlisted support for his mission. The English were particularly helpful. He was well received by the Archbishop of Canterbury and King George I, and the S.P.C.K. presented him an address. He made many friends in Europe and after working in the newly formed Missionary Board of Copenhagen for controlling the activities of missionaries who worked in distant fields, returned to India in August 1715 with his young wife, his marriage having taken place during his stay in Europe.

During his absence, Ziegenbalg's work was carried on by his associates and with the added strength gained from the leader's European tour, the power and prestige of the Tranquebar Mission rose. The hostility of the civil authorities ceased and was replaced by active co-operation. The powerful East India Company of England began to appreciate the work of the Mission, and some of the Chaplains and Presidents of the Company in Madras invited the missionaries to their settlement and gave them considerable financial help. Because of this good relationship between the English and the missionaries, the activities of the Tranquebar Mission, unofficially though, extended to Madras and Cuddalore, and when on February 23rd, 1718, Ziegenbalg died at the comparatively early age of 36, the foundation of Protestant Missions in India had been strongly laid.

During the closing years of his life, Ziegenbalg had considerable trouble with the Missionary Board at home. Wendt, the new President of the Board, was a pious and devoted Christian of extreme views who disapproved of many of the methods of Ziegenbalg. Bovingh, Ziegenbalg's own associate, shared some of Wendt's views. According to these zealots the missionaries were to copy the example of the Apostles in every respect. The missionaries were expected to provide nothing for themselves or their congregation but were to go about preaching to the people eating what chance brought and sleeping wherever they found themselves at night. Churches, schools, orphanages, organized propaganda and requests for contributions had no place in their scheme. Their disapproval of Ziegenbalg's methods burst forth into open hostility when he had to make some reluctant concessions to caste, that despair of early missionaries in India. Though Ziegenbalg did not share the Roman Brahmins' views on caste, he had to recognize a barrier between the Pariah converts and the higher Christians who would not pray with them. Similarly he had to accede to the clamour of the higher converts for precedence in the matter of approaching the Table for Holy Communion.

Though Zeigenbalg had trouble with the Board, it did not assume serious proportions and the first Protestant missionary of India died respected by all. Compared to the work of the early Jesuits, Zeigenbalg had achieved nothing very spectacular. His ambition was not very great either. But he had shown, if nothing else, what a man of average intelligence and capabilities could achieve in the mission field with faith and a willingness to hard work.

The work of the Tranquebar Mission was continued by a band of devoted men of whom Christian Friederich Schwartz was the greatest. When he arrived in Tranquebar on July 30th, 1750, the seed sown by Ziegenbalg had taken root and was growing rapidly. The congregation had increased to 8,000 souls, and the mission had established outposts in Madras, Cuddalore, Tanjore, Trichinopoly and Negapatam. The prestige of the Mission had also risen because of the patronage of the English East India Company which was now recognized as a first rate power able to actively interfere in the affairs of the Indian potentates not only near the coast but farther inland; this no doubt made European Christians more hateful to Hindus and Muslims but India began to view them as a people of superior military strength.

It was in this atmosphere that Schwartz arrived in India. He studied Tamil and generally followed the beaten track of Ziegenbalg. The greatness of Schwartz was not in his intellectual brilliance, nor in his pioneering zeal, but in his devotion to work and exemplary Christian life. His success as a missionary was also due, in some measure, to the active support he received from the English. He worked for some time as the Chaplain of the British garrison in Trichinopoly and it is remarkable that his open association with the English did not adversely affect his reputation for honesty and Christian virtue. The Nawab of Carnatic once told him: "Padre, we had always looked on you, Europeans, as ungodly men who knew not the use of prayers till you came among us."

Schwartz's prayers, however, did not bring about any revolutionary change in the way of life of his countrymen. An interesting incident in this connection is worth narrating. One day the good missionary happened to meet a Hindu friend in the company of a dancing girl and Schwartz, horror-struck, preached to his friend on the sin of associating with dancing girls. The Hindu was warned by the pious Christian that men of such unholy habits would not enter the kingdom of heaven. "In that case," came the quick retort from the dancer, "hardly any European will ever enter it." The dancer knew her Europeans well, and Schwartz could only hold his head down for shame. Schwartz, usually kind and tolerant towards human weaknesses wrote about the Europeans of his time: "It is extremely difficult when describing our situation here to give any one a just conception of it, without adverting to the profligacy of the Europeans. The great among them aim at nothing but to live in pleasure and become rich. If not readily successful in the latter object, they resort to unjust means, the employment of which hardens the mind to so alarming a degree that they will hear nothing of the word of God, and too frequently plunge into the most frightful infidelity."

It is remarkable that when the English approached Hyder Ali with a request for diplomatic relations, he would accept no envoy but Schwartz. The wiliness of the English had made reliable negotiations impossible. "Let them send me the Christian, he will not deceive me;" was the reply the English received from Hyder to their request for opening diplomatic negotiations. The English were not, at that time, in a position to ignore or challenge the power of the Sultan of Mysore or to argue with him. Hence at the personal request of Sir Thomas Rumbold, the Governor of Madras, Schwartz proceeded to Seringapatam as the envoy of the British. The missionary was no cunning diplomat, and he failed in his political mission. But Hyder's esteem for Schwartz only increased by personal contact. It is worth while to mention that during the troublous days that followed, when Hyder's armies scourged the plains of the south, the missionary was permitted to travel unmolested wherever he wished and was allowed to preach and convert. For Hyder had issued his army chief the following order: "Permit the venerable padre Schwartz to pass unmolested and show him respect and kindness; for he is a holy man, and means no harm to my government."

Another political responsibility was bestowed upon Schwartz by the English. The Rajah of Tanjore falling under the evil influence of his minister, the British, who had developed considerable interest in the state, interfered. They deposed the Rajah, dismissed the minister and took over the administration of the state and appointed a council of three ministers to administer the internal affairs of the state; and Schwartz was one of them. The Rajah was an old friend of Schwartz and the new office instead of straining their relations strengthened the bond between them. The Rajah went so far as to entrust Schwartz with the care of his adopted son Serfojee, then ten years of age. On the Rajah's death, his half brother Ameer Singh prevailed upon the British to set aside the adoption and appoint him ruler of the state. Schwartz did not succeed in his efforts to refute the claims of Ameer Singh but he managed to remove Serfojee to Madras and bring him up under his care. He heroically fought for the rights of his protégé and at last the English were obliged to reverse their decision in favour of Serfojee. But the decision came after Schwartz's death.

Schwartz died on February 13th, 1798. All mourned the good man's death. "When the tidings went out, all over the land was heard a great wail that the 'good padre' was no more. Prince and peasant, soldiers and civilians, Christian, Hindu, and Mohammadan alike mourned the friend whom they had lost. Never probably has the death of a Christian missionary been regretted in India by men of so many different races, classes and positions; and certainly no other missionary has been so honoured in his death by the ruling powers. Rajah Serfojee, who had hastened to the death-bed of his revered guardian and had followed his remains to the grave—a most unusual step for a high caste Hindu to take—procured, later from England, for erection in the mission church, a monument in marble on which Flaxman, the eminent sculptor, carved a touching group representing the death of the old missionary. Round the dying saint are gathered his colleague Guericke, some native Christians with their children and the Rajah himself. 'A simple, natural and affecting scene,' said Dr. Duff, fifty years later when deeply moved he gazed upon it, 'and the group who compose it possess an interest to the Christian mind beyond what mere words can express.' A yet further tribute was paid by the Rajah, who himself composed the epitaph engraved on the stone in the church, beneath which rest the mortal remains of the beloved and honoured dead. The lines lack, no doubt, in poetic merit, but that is more than atoned for by the uniqueness of the authorship and the affectionate appreciation of the departed which breath in every word:

'Firm was thou, humble and wise,
Honest, pure, free from disguise,
Father of orphans, the widows' support,
Comfort in sorrow of every sort;
To the benighted, dispenser of light,
Doing and pointing to, that which right:
Blessing to friends, to people, to me,
May I, my Father, be worthy of thee,
Wisheth and prayeth thy Sarabojee.'"

It is considered regrettable by some that Schwartz did not convert the prince. But it shows the liberal views Schwartz held on formal conversion. Though the young Rajah did not become a formal convert, his life and outlook under Schwartz's guidance had become definitely Christian.

After Schwartz, no great missionary worked in the Tranquebar Mision. Kiernander, one of the Tranquebar missionaries, went to Bengal at the invitation of Clive, but he was not comparable to Ziegenbalg or Schwartz. He was wealthy, having married a rich widow, and out of his own private funds he built a church in Calcutta at the expense of Rs. 70,000. But his missionary activities were mainly confined to teaching Protestantism to the Roman Catholics of Bengal. The indifference of the English in Calcutta and his own want of resourcefulness impoverished him, and the Sheriff of Calcutta laid hold of his church which was appraised at a value of Rs. 10,000. The charity of some well-meaning Englishmen just saved the church.

After Schwartz the decay of the Tranquebar Mission set in. The help from home became scant, missionaries with the necessary zeal and skill for organizing were few, and old Hinduism took back her prodigals. During the heyday of the Mission under Schwartz, it had a congregation of 20,000 souls which soon after Schwartz's death dwindled into an insignificant community of 5,000 Christians scattered in Tranquebar, Trichinopoly, Madras, Cuddalore and Tinnevelly.

WILLIAM CAREY AND THE SERAMPORE MISSION

The East India Company had officially banned missionary activities in the regions under its influence, but there were individuals in the service of the Company who wished to propagate the Gospel in India. One such individual was Dr. John Thomas, the Company's surgeon in Calcutta. Of Dr. Thomas' skill as a surgeon we know very little, but of his missionary activities we have some account. He was a peculiar individual whose life was marked by periodical outbursts of missionary zeal relieved by intense commercial speculation. He had active supporters in his missionary work of whom Charles Grant who was later to become the Chairman of the Court of Directors of the East India Company was one. Mr. Grant entrusted Dr. Thomas with some money for promoting Gospel work but the Doctor invested it in some commercial enterprise and this was all that was known of this fund. Dr. Thomas made some effort to retrieve his lost ground in commerce by borrowing lavishly and speculating heavily. For the satisfaction of his creditors and patrons he translated some portions of the New Testament in a language which he claimed to be Bengali. But neither the creditors nor the patrons were satisfied. The latter stopped their contributions and the former threatened legal action. This shook the Doctor's faith in his countrymen in India and confirmed his conviction that his genius would be appreciated only at home. Accordingly he sailed for England, but the people at home proved no better. He was heavily involved in debts at home and became anxious to return to Malda, his mission field, but had not enough money for the passage. In this predicament his thoughts turned to God.

This was the time when William Carey, a cobbler in an insignificant village in Northamptonshire, had left cobbling and turned his thoughts to strange lands that had not heard the name of Christ. His first attempts at interesting the English public in Gospel work were disappointing. As mentioned elsewhere, Mr. Ryland thought the work of conversion of the heathen was God's and not of Englishmen. Carey, however, did not give up hope. He persisted and some Englishmen of note were converted to his way of thinking and the Baptist Missionary Society was formed in 1792, with Mr. Fuller as the secretary. The Society had not much funds to start with. But Carey was willing to undertake mission work anywhere in the world without funds from the Society. He had no funds of his own either, but had an indomitable will and an infinite faith in Christ. The only decision he had to make was about the field of his mission. Dr. Thomas now came to his aid. He described to Carey in vivid detail the condition of India and the extreme need of the country, and the Doctor's passionate pleadings had the desired effect and Carey decided to go to India with Dr. Thomas.

Carey and his family consisting of his wife, sister and five children with Dr. Thomas and his wife had hardly boarded a ship bound for India when the Doctor's creditors appeared on the scene. Suspecting that he was trying to escape, they threatened to inform against the captain of the ship for taking missionaries to India without licence; the punishment for such an offence was severe at the time and Carey and his party were promptly ejected out of the ship. Before, however, Dr. Thomas' creditors could give effect to the writ for his arrest which they had obtained, the missionaries managed to board a Danish ship, and sailed away to India.

Carey and his ill-assorted company landed in Calcutta on November 10th, 1793. They had serious apprehensions about the kind of reception they were to meet with because of the absence of licences, but were considerably relieved to find that Calcutta was too busy with its own affairs to take any notice of the miserable party.

No man had ever embarked upon an evangelical mission to India so poorly equipped and badly handicapped as Carey. Xavier and Ziegenbalg had the support of royalty. The Jesuits, the Franciscans and Augustinians had the powerful backing of their organizations, and in some cases of civil authorities; further, they were all unmarried people free to go where the spirit moved them. But poor Carey had little money and a large family and the Baptist Mission itself was financially hard up at the time. At the suggestion of Dr. Thomas, Carey had, however, brought some merchandise with him which he hoped to sell at a profit in India to equip himself with the necessary funds for the prosecution of his plans. Dr. Thomas had charge of these goods; he sold the goods as soon as he landed in Calcutta but got no money out of it. And Carey and his family were reduced to starvation. He would have received some money from his countrymen, for Calcutta with all its faults was not completely devoid of earnest and helpful Englishmen; but Carey's association with the notorious pauper of Malda closed the door of every decent Englishman against him. Carey and his family were stranded in Calcutta but a well-to-do Hindu gentleman took pity on them and gave them shelter. Unable to do anything in Calcutta where the English lived in luxury and the missionary as a beggar, Carey migrated to the Sunderbans, notorious for its wild beasts and pestilential climate. Here he lived by hunting wild game, obviously a mad thing for an Englishman to do at the time. Whenever Carey got a chance he preached to the farmers and to his fellow huntsmen. The reproach of his wife and sister who had, from the very beginning, discouraged him in his wild missionary enterprise and had come with him almost under compulsion, became unbearable and poor Carey's life in the Sunderbans became a veritable hell on earth.

And then Dr. Thomas proved his mettle. He had one friend left in the world in a Mr. Udny, a sincere Christian in the employ of the East India Company. Mr. Udny had just established an indigo factory in the Malda district where Dr. Thomas was supposed to be doing missionary work, and learning from the Doctor the plight of Carey offered him the post of manager of the factory, on a salary of Rs.200 a month, a princely sum to the impoverished Carey; more than this, Mr. Udny was a missionary at heart and he gave Carey full permission to preach and convert. Without impairing his efficiency as manager of the indigo factory, Carey did a good deal of missionary work and studied Bengali and the literature of the Hindus.

In 1799 Mr. Udny sold his factory, but Carey had by then saved enough to buy a factory of his own at Kidderpore, not far away, and from the profits of this business hoped to build a sound missionary base at Malda. The business prospered and Carey was able to report to his headquarters that he had started making progress and he asked for some workers from England.

The missionary spirit was by now kindled in England and four Englishmen responded to Carey's call. They sailed from England in an American ship but as the ship arrived in the Hoogly, Calcutta took alarm and refused permission for the missionaries to land. This eventuality was not altogether unforeseen and the missionaries hired a boat and slipped off to the Danish settlement of Serampore close by. But the presence of these four desperate men so near Calcutta only increased the suspicion of the authorities, and Lord Wellesly, the then Governor-General, demanded the surrender of the fugitives in order to deport them to England. But Col. Bie, the Danish Governor of Serampore, had been a close friend of Schwartz and thought there was some good in missionary work and refused to surrender the missionaries. Wellesly, though he had to take some notice of the popular objection to missionaries in his official capacity, probably held the same personal views as Col. Bie and let the matter drop.

The difficulty of the four workers reaching Malda becoming plain to Carey, he decided to transfer his missionary activities to Serampore. The hostility of the British authorities to organized mission work and the patronage accorded by the Danes also influenced the decision. Accordingly Carey migrated to Serampore and joined the four. Of these, Grant and Brunsdon succumbed to the climate before realizing their ambition. With the remaining two, William Ward and Joshua Marshman, Carey built up the famous Serampore Mission which has done such splendid work in India.

Printing had now been discovered and afforded scope for a wide dissemination of knowledge and the missionaries took full advantage of it. Indian languages were studied in feverish haste and the translation of the Bible in the principal languages was undertaken. Carey was a gifted linguist and as soon as he translated the Bible Ward, who was a professional printer, printed them. The Serampore pioneers translated the Bible into thirty-six languages the principal being Hindi, Marathi, Sanskrit, Gujerati, Ooriya, Telegu, Canarese and Malayalam. They tried a hand at Chinese and Burmese too. The excessive enthusiasm and speed did affect the quality of the Translations, but all were readable and this was the main aim of the missionaries.

The converts, however, were not many. Carey laboured in India for seven years without making a single convert. In the year 1800 the first conversion took place. The neophyte was a carpenter, Krishna Chandra Pal by name, who happened to dislocate an arm in an accident and come to Dr. Thomas for treatment. There was great rejoicing all over the mission field on the occasion of his baptism. Dr. Thomas went literally mad with joy. He started raving and had to be kept in confinement.

The Serampore missionaries were the pioneers in the field of education in India. Most of the social evils of the country, the missionaries rightly concluded, were the result of ignorance or improper education. Hence they devoted themselves wholeheartedly to the dissemination of knowledge in general and Christian knowledge in particular. The ban on missions was removed in 1814 and the activities of the Serampore mission spread to wider fields. The main centres were Bengal, Burma, Orissa, Bhutan and Hindustan proper, these five centres constituting what was known as the 'United Missions of India'. The ministers in 1817 numbered thirty of whom eighteen were Europeans and twelve Indians. "By the year 1818 the mission possessed 126 vernacular schools with 10,000 pupils, all receiving elementary education and also simple continuous instruction in the Christian religion!" Carey's educational activities were not confined to elementary schools. In 1821 was established the famous Serampore College for the study of English and Oriental classics. Science, History, Philosophy and Medicine were later on added and the College was raised to the rank of a University. Carey was a protagonist of instruction in Indian languages. Later, Alexander Duff in his college introduced English as the medium of instruction and brought about a revolutionary change in the educational system in India which had far reaching consequences in the matter of spreading Western religious and political ideas in the East.

The success of the Serampore Mission was in no small measure due to its financial soundness. Although Carey started as a pauper, on his death on June 9th, 1834, the Serampore Mission was the wealthiest of such organisations in India. For this Carey's forethought and introduction of new methods in the daily life of the missionaries were solely responsible. The Serampore missionaries lived on the lines of the Moravian brotherhood, forming a community of their own with a common kitchen and common fund each bringing to the mission what he got and receiving what he needed. According to Carey self reliance was the prime virtue of the missionary and a missionary should live by his own labour and not be thrown on the charity of either his patrons or his congregation.

Soon after coming to Serampore, Carey started a boarding school for European children and it proved so popular that the annual profits from this enterprise alone ran into more than £1,000. This amount was further augmented by the salary of £1,000 Carey received for taking up the professorship of Bengali in the new College Wellesly had started in Calcutta for instructing young Englishmen who sought service under the widely expanding East India Company. The common kitchen and the communistic way of life saved many unnecessary items of expenditure and left the mission with a handsome balance for God's work. This, apart from the zeal of the missionaries, was mainly responsible for the long life and continued prosperity of the mission.

CHAPTER X

CRUSADE ON THE NABOABS

WE have seen in a previous chapter that the English had successfully challenged the supremacy of the Portuguese on the Indian seas and obtained trading settlements in all the important ports of India. These settlements attracted a good many English and other adventurers whose want of religious zeal did not impair their efficiency as traders. Profit was the god of the English settlers of the time and they flourished by the worship of Mammon. They were not concerned about conversions. Some conversions were, however, reported. For instance a son of Sir Heneage Finch, who had been Attorney-General and Lord Keeper in the reign of James II, was irresistibly attracted to Islam and embraced this religion in Bombay. "The grief occasioned by the fall of this misguided young gentleman was nothing in comparison with that resulting from the occasional apostasy of some of our people who were attracted by the conveniences and enticements of the Muhammadan religion. One example of this may be especially noted. In 1691 a man rejoicing in a name which afterwards grew into better odour, vexed the spirits of the factors at Surat by openly embracing Muhammadanism." Again, "there is one of our wicked Englishmen, by name John Newton, that came out in the *Royal James and Mary*, and came from Umboor yesterday, and went immediately to the Cossys and declared his intention to turn Moor, and before we possibly could have an opportunity to send to the Governor, the business was done and he circumcised, which was past our remedy of our retrieving his wicked soul."

The English elsewhere were little better. Of Job Charnock, a notable servant of the Company in Chuttanutty (old name for Calcutta) who died in the last decade of the 17th century, it is written that he married a Hindu lady and "instead of converting her to Christianity she made him a proselyte to Paganism; and the only part of Christianity that was remarkable in him was burying her decently and he built a tomb over her, where all his life after her death he kept the anniversary day of her death by sacrificing a cock on her tomb after the heathen fashion."

Some religious activity was reported from Bengal too. Sir John Gouldsborough was grieved to note the hold Roman Catholics had got over the Christians of Chuttanutty and took vigorous measures to combat it. In his own words, "I turned their priests from hence, and their mass-house was to be pulled down to make way for the factorie, when it shall be thought convenient to build it; and I disbanded all black Christian soldiers and lowered their wages from five to four rupees a month and made them entreat to be received again so." It is, however, some comfort to note that the murderous quarrels between Catholics and Protestants that shook Europe at the time were, in India, confined to such isolated instances and did not break out into open hostility.

Though the English settlers of the time generally held Indians in contempt, some of the Indian customs were considered worthy of emulation. Concubinage was one of them. The Harem became fashionable among the 'Naboabs', and some of them at least as a mark of honour to a distinguished guest sent out troops of slave girls and dancers to receive them at the gate. While the concubinage that was common among European settlers can rightly be attributed to the dearth of European women in India, the Harem life can be excused on no grounds whatsoever. The East India Company did make an effort to equalize the male and female population of their settlement in Calcutta. For complaints reaching the authorities of the profligacy and concubinage in the settlement, the Company took upon itself the task of supplying women to their servants. A shipload of European women were landed in Calcutta to the delight of the settlers. But the demand proved so far in excess of the supply that the gay ladies, following strict economic laws, took to prostitution as more profitable and pleasant than marriage. They were so prodigal of their charms and lightly-earned money that most of them soon lost their attractions and had to ask the Company for maintenance. After this bitter experience, the Company left their servants to find women for themselves.

Complaints about the Godless life of the English in India became too numerous to be overlooked by the management of the East India Company at home and the need for Christian ministers was pressed home by well-meaning members of the Company's staff. From Bombay went a request to the Governors of the Company to supply them with two good ministers together with 'a little good English beer, called stout; and a little wine.' The demand for the ministers was probably an indication of a guarantee that the beer and the wine would be sparingly used. Anyway, the new charter granted to the second East India Company had a clause in it which compelled every garrison and important factory to maintain a minister. The minister had an obligation to learn Portuguese, the then *lingua franca* of the coastal regions of India, and the necessary Indian language for the instruction of the Indian Christian population of the settlement.

But far from improving the standard of the European settlements, the ministers seem to have fallen into line with the ways of the settlers. We know very little about the religious activities of these early Christian ministers, and their spiritual gains were negligible. It was otherwise with their material gains. "From an entry in Kiernander's journal we learn that Mr. Blanshard, who was chaplain on the establishment during the administration of Warren Hastings and Lord Cornwallis, carried to England, after a service of little more than two years, a fortune of £50,000. Another chaplain, Mr. Johnson, after 13 year's service took with him from Calcutta £35,000; and Mr. Owen, after ten years' service, £25,000. Unless they performed a vast number more burial and baptismal services, and married more Christian couples than there is any good reason to believe and unless the fees received for such offices were exorbitantly high, it is not clear how such fortunes could have been accumulated from the ordinary wages of clerical labour. A slight suspicion of profitable trade must therefore disturb the reflection even of the most charitable."

All the chaplains of the Company were not, however, of this type. There were some who had a keen sense of their duty and responsibility and did what they could to improve the lot of their countrymen and of Indians. Of such worthy ministers mention may be made of David Brown, Claudius Buchanan and Henry Martyn. These men were heavily handicapped, because of their official position, in their missionary activities, but they did good work among their own countrymen. Henry Martyn, the greatest of the Chaplains of the period, deserves some detailed mention.

Martyn was a peculiar man with a Hebrew Prophet's horror of the wickedness of man. He was a brilliant scholar who had distinguished himself in St. John's College, Cambridge. His father's death turned his mind to spiritual matters. It was his intention to come to India as a missionary, the work of the Tranquebar pioneers having fired his imagination. But Martyn had considerable responsibilities and accepted the post of Chaplain to the Calcutta settlement which carried with it a salary of £1,000. He set out to India on board the *Union*, on August 31st, 1805. The experience on board the *Union* gave him an inkling of what was in store for him in Calcutta. "With him travelled H.M. 59th regiment, and officers and men alike reflected only too truly the callous, even hostile attitude to religion which Martyn was to face among his own countrymen in India. His mere presence on board their ship—the only chaplain in the whole fleet—was felt to be an infliction and the captain of the vessel shared the feeling. One service on Sundays, he was permitted to hold, but nothing more, and to show their contempt for him and his work, the officers, though not attending the service, would sit near at hand, smoking, drinking, talking and laughing while the service was proceeding."

The soul of the sensitive young minister revolted and he bided his opportunity. And soon after landing in Calcutta, the opportunity presented itself. In his first sermon to the seasoned sinners of Calcutta he told them that but for the mercy of the ever-patient

Saviour they would all have been now in a place quite different from the one the Son of Man had prepared for the righteous. "Tremble ye," he thundered, "at your state, all ye that from self-righteousness or pride or unwillingness to follow Him in the regeneration disregard Christ! Nothing keeps you one moment from perdition but the sovereign pleasure of God. Yet suppose not that we take pleasure in contradicting your natural sentiments on religion, or in giving pain by forcing offensive truth upon your attention—no! as the ministers of joy and peace we rise up at the command of God, to preach Christ crucified to you all!"

And many did tremble, for the passionate sincerity of the young zealot and his force of expression were irresistible. Martyn, very often after his sermons repaired to his private apartment to weep over the sins of his countrymen and beg the Almighty pardon for the failings of his brethren.

Martyn was an impetuous zealot. He was impatient of the weaknesses of men. The foul atmosphere of this sinful world choked him. His countrymen in India were bad enough, but the Indians were worse. The idols struck him with horror. The iniquities of caste appalled him. One day he saw a widow being conducted to her husband's funeral pyre, and the frail man rushed to save her but before he reached the spot the flames consumed her. His dread of the Hindu temple was truly Hebraic. On visiting one he wrote: "I shivered at being in the neighbourhood of hell; my heart was ready to burst at the dreadful state to which the devil had brought my poor fellow creatures. I would have given the world to have known the language and to have preached to them."

He was like a man in a hurry who thought one life too short for the great work he had to do. He worked day and night and crowded into six years of active life the labours of a lifetime. He studied Hindustani with enthusiasm and as soon as he gained some knowledge of it preached to the Hindus. But the Hindus did not show an over-enthusiasm to accept Christianity. As his superficial knowledge of the Hindus and their way of life increased, he abandoned them as a people lost beyond redemption. "Truly, if ever I see a Hindu a real believer in Jesus, I shall see something more nearly approaching the resurrection of a dead body than anything I have ever seen."

From Calcutta Martyn was sent to Dinapore, but the people he met here were no better than those of Calcutta. His fame had probably preceded him and the sinners of Dinapore avoided him like the plague. The dread of the minister was universal. "A more wicked set of men were, I suppose, never seen;" he wrote to Corrie his friend in Calcutta. Martyn did not spare even the sick. "At the hospital when I visit, some go to a corner and invoke blasphemies upon me because, as they now believe, the man I speak to dies of a certainty."

It was impossible for Martyn to understand the Hindus. Their religion and way of life were so strange that he found it difficult to reconcile them with his notions of a civilized community. But the Muslims, he thought, were better. He had a good knowledge of the background of their religion, and he now diverted his attention to the study of Arabic and Persian in addition to that of Hindustani of which he had already gained a working knowledge. His intention was not only to preach in but to translate the Bible into these languages. With the help of able Indian assistants, he undertook the work of translation and the progress in Hindustani and Persian was smooth; but the same was not the case with the Arabic branch. In this work he was assisted by Sabat, a half converted Arab, fierce and self complacent, who had a very high opinion of his literary accomplishments. Sabat gave a good deal of trouble to the English enthusiast; he did not have a very high opinion of Martyn's Arabic and between the two the work of translation suffered badly. An entry in Martyn's journal shows his tribulation in respect of Sabat:

"Sabat had been tolerably quiet this week; but think of the keeper of a lunatic and you see me. A war of words broke out the beginning of last week, but it ended in an honourable peace. After he got home at night he sent a letter, complaining of a high crime and misdemeanour in some servant; I sent him a soothing letter and the wild beast fell asleep."

By working day and night during his ministry in Kanpur, Dinapore, and Berhampore, Henry Martyn at last realized his cherished ambition of translating the New Testament into the three main Muslim languages of Asia. He had also kept touch with the Serampore translators. Martyn's translations were not, however, received with universal applause. Sabat not only claimed unquestionable proficiency in Arabic but thought himself competent to handle the Persian translation and form an opinion of the Hindustani work. He declared Martyn's Hindustani to be vulgar and the critics at Calcutta and Serampore considered the Persian and Arabic too high flown to be understood by general readers. Martyn appreciated the criticism of the Persian and Arabic works as he had his own doubts about them, though constantly harassed by Sabat he had surrendered his common sense to the vanity of the Arab. Anyway, to retrieve the situation the only thing Martyn could think of was to render the Persian translation in Persia and the Arabic in Arabia. With this end in view he left India for Persia on January 7th, 1811.

He finished his Persian work but was prevented from undertaking the journey to Arabia by ill health. In order to regain his health he wished to go home, and set out for England by way of Constantinople. He took seriously ill in a little village near Tokat, and in October 1812 (the exact date is not known) died at the early age of 31 and was buried in the Armenian churchyard of Tokat. The last entry in his diary is dated October 6th, 1812 and reads as follows:

"No horses to be had, I had an unexpected repose. I sat in the orchard and thought with sweet comfort and peace of my God, in solitude my Company, my Friend and Comforter. Oh, when shall time give place to eternity! When shall appear that new heaven and new earth wherein dwelleth righteousness! There, there shall in no wise enter anything that defileth: none of that wickedness which has made men worse than wild beasts, none of those corruptions which add still more to the miseries of mortality shall be seen or heard of any more."

Henry Martyn is not to be judged by the number of converts

he made; these were not more than five during the six years of his ministry in India. He must be judged by his abounding zeal for Gospel work and righteous living which inspired many of his countrymen in England and India.

Martyn and other chaplains of his way of thinking were considerably handicapped in Gospel work by their official position as the paid men of the Company. The civil authorities rigidly enforced the missionary clause of their 1793 Charter throughout their dominions and the chaplains were debarred from embarking upon any missionary activities but had to confine themselves strictly to their official duties.

That the Christian English should ban the spread of the Gospel in their territories could only be attributed by missionaries and their partisans to the perversity of the Directors of the Company and their employees. That these gentlemen were more concerned with the spread of their power in the East than that of the Gospel is no doubt true. But we must pause in our judgement when we consider the fact that even men of the calibre of Lord Cornwallis subscribed to these views, and enforced the instructions of the Board of Directors. There were both in India and England responsible officials of the Company, very good Christians, who recognized the need for exercising extreme caution in the matter of letting the missionaries run wild in their dominions. The territorial acquisitions of the Company were rapidly increasing and the Directors of the Company very naturally considered it their prime duty to consolidate and hold these possessions. British statesmen knew that it was impossible to hold a vast country like India by a few British soldiers. The mainstay of British power in India then as in later years was the indigenous army; and this army was at the time constituted mainly of Hindus and Muslims who found in the growing power of the British some security of person and property and a desirable salary. It was of the utmost importance that the loyalty of the Indian Army should in no way be jeopardized.

Most of the European missionaries of the time were inclined to treat the Hindus as an abandoned race of barbarians little better than the cannibals of Africa; we have already noticed Henry

Martyn's opinion of the Hindus. Of the mission of Muhammad too they had fixed notions. The English civilians who brought an open mind and studied the religion and literature of the Hindus found, on the other hand, that though their practices were not at their best at the time, the Hindus were heirs to an ancient civilisation of much spiritual value. They realized, above all, that both the Hindu and Muslim were passionately attached to their religions, and those who belittled their beliefs were not likely to be viewed with favour or treated as their saviours. The state aid the Portuguese extended to missionary work in India often led to abuses and forcible conversions, and this was one of the reasons why the Portuguese came to be hated by Indians, and the experience of the Portuguese was fresh in the minds of the early British.

Considering all these, the Parliament had given full powers, in the Charter of 1793, to the East India Company to regulate the migration of Englishmen to India and refuse licence to persons who, by their religious or other activities were likely to create trouble for the Company. The result of this privilege was that while common rogues easily got licence to migrate to India, the preachers of the Gospel were all refused licences.

As long as Englishmen at home remained indifferent to missionary activities, the ban on missionaries did not seriously inconvenience anybody. But the later half of the eighteenth century was marked by considerable religious activity in the United Kingdom. The inevitable reaction to the licence of the Restoration set in and people began to feel that life had a higher aim than eating, drinking and love-making. The official church was established on a sound footing, and the travels of Englishmen in many lands brought home to the English the need for propagating the Gospel among strange people inhabiting distant lands. Several societies were now formed for spreading the Gospel, and individuals began to burn with missionary zeal. The Baptist Missionary Society was formed in 1792; the London Mission in 1795, and the Church Missionary Society in 1799.

And then the ardent missionaries woke up to the fact that

missionary activities were banned in countries ruled by Englishmen who professed to be Christians!

It is but natural that these zealous pioneers should have thought it preposterous that when non-Christian rulers in Asia often gave the missionary permission to preach the Gospel in their kingdoms the Christian British should deny this elementary human right to the missionary. Not only preaching but even the very presence of the missionary was obnoxious to the Englishman in India. This had to be fought out, and in the beginning of the nineteenth century war was declared on the Naboab by the missionaries. They fought their case in the pulpit, in the press and in the Parliament. Pamphlet after pamphlet issued forth from the press describing in vivid detail the Godless life of Anglo-Indians; how they had converted India into a profligate's Paradise, how they were actively aiding Paganism for profit and how they were serving as bodyguards to the idols. The Naboab was painted in lurid colours, and strange tales of his extortions, of his harem life, of his power of communicating with the devil and of weird midnight mysteries in his lonesome house got wide circulation. And honest Englishmen were warned that if the power of the Naboab was not checked in time and he himself reclaimed from the devil, they could very well look forward to an England in the near future completely paganised.

The Naboabs took up the challenge. They maintained that the missionaries' raillery was born out of ignorance of India and her people. As very often happens in such heated controversies, the real intentions of the parties were lost in a maze of evidence factual and fabricated, and in wild exaggerations that clouded the main issue. The Naboabs maintained that while England had a divinely appointed right to India and her trade, she had no responsibility to convert the Indians. A Mr. Twining, who had considerable interest in the tea trade, addressed a lengthy letter to the Chairman of the East India Company in which he vigorously attacked the missionaries and their propaganda. Of this letter a missionary wrote that "no such letter was ever before written in a Christian country, under a Christian king by a man professed to be a Christian". That Mr. Twining was inspired not merely by a fear of the threat to his tea trade but a real sense of danger to his life is evident from the tone of the letter. The originators of the Church Mission Society and the Chairman of the East India Company were in England, but Mr. Twining had to live the major part of his life in India and he had, he said, a right to say what he thought of Christian missions to India. The concluding paragraph of his letter, reproduced below, shows him up as a man who had no desire to court martyrdom for the sake of his religion:

"As long as we continue to govern India in the mild, tolerant spirit of Christianity, we may govern it with ease; but if ever the fatal day should arrive, when religious innovation shall set her foot in that country, indignation will spread from one end of Hindustan to the other, and the arms of fifty millions of people will drive us from that portion of the globe, with as much ease as the sand of the desert is scattered by the wind. But I still hope, Sir, that a perseverance in the indiscreet measures I have described, will not be allowed to expose our countrymen in India to the horrors of that dreadful day: but that our native subjects in every part of the East will be permitted quietly to follow their own religious opinions, their own religious prejudices and absurdities, until it shall please the Omnipotent Power of Heaven to lead them to the paths of light and truth."

The letter of Mr. Twining, tea-dealer, stirred up a hornets' nest, and pamphlet after pamphlet poured forth from mission presses refuting his arguments. Another sensational letter on the lines of Twining's letter was published by Rev. Sydney Smith in the *Edinburgh Review* in 1808. The controversy raged with unabated fury and the climax was reached in 1813 when the question of renewing the Charter of the East India Company came up before the Parliament. The missionaries valiantly fought for the deletion of the obnoxious clause and substitution of a new one giving full permission to Evangelists of all denominations to preach the Gospel wherever they pleased in the Company's dominions. Both parties closed in for mortal combat by word of mouth, and speech after speech was made, and important witnesses examined. Claudius Buchanan's interesting report on the religions of India stirred many a zealot to denounce the Naboabs as a Godless set of reprobates and to call upon the Parliament to compel the East India Company to take some positive interest in the moral welfare of their subjects. To this Sir Henry Montgomery, who had lived long enough in India to know the Hindus, replied that Buchanan's account of the Hindus was "an imposition upon England and a libel upon India". He declared that Christianity had nothing to teach Hinduism, and no missionary ever made a really good Christian convert in India. He too, like the tea-dealer, had a sound respect for the martial powers of the Indian, and concluded that he "was more anxious to save the 30,000 of his countrymen in India than to save the souls of all the Hindus by making them Christians at so dreadful a price."

The then recent Vellore Mutiny, though actually engendered by the descendants of Tippoo from political motives, was given a religious colour, and lent a sense of reality to Sir Henry's fear of the impending massacre of 30,000 Englishmen in India through the folly of the missionaries.

Mr. Marsh, an able lawyer who had lived many years in Madras, asked the missionaries to learn at the feet of the Hindus instead of trying to teach them. In fact the picture he painted of the Hindus and their religion was one which the most enthusiastic Hindu would have loved to emulate:

"Indeed, when I turn my eyes either to the present condition or ancient grandeur of that country; when I contemplate the magnificence of her structures, her spacious reservoirs, constructed at an immense expense, pouring fertility and plenty over the land, the monuments of a benevolence expanding its cares over remote ages; when I survey the solid and embellished architecture of her temples, the elaborate and exquisite skill of her manufactures and fabrics, her literature sacred and profane, her gaudy and enamelled poetry on which a wild and prodigal fancy has lavished all its opulence; when I turn to the philosophers, lawyers and moralists who have left the oracles of political and ethical wisdom to restrain the passions and to awe the vices which disturb the commonwealth; when I look at the peaceful and harmonious alliances of families, guarded and secured by the household virtues; when I see amongst a cheerful and well-ordered society, the benignant and softening influence of religion and morality, a system of manners founded on a mild and polished obeisance, and preserving the surface of social life smooth and unruffled —I cannot bear without surprise, mingled with horror, of sending out Baptists and Anabaptists to civilize or convert such a people at the hazard of disturbing or deforming institutions which appear to have hitherto been the means ordained by Providence of making them virtuous and happy."

Wilberforce, Forbes, William Smith, Whitbread and a host of other speakers refuted the arguments of the eloquent Mr. Marsh, and painted the other side of the picture. Much was made of Sati, infanticide, idolatry, religious suicide, and the victims of Mother Ganges at Saugar. Descriptions of wild scenes at Jagannath during the pilgrim season were given in vivid detail, and the Baptists, corroborating Buchanan's account, put down the number of victims that perished annually at the shrine to not less than 120,000; when challenged they admitted that they did not actually count the dead bodies, but arrived at the figure by an ingenious calculation.

To cut a long story short, in the wordy warfare the missionaries won and in the new Charter of 1814, not only were they given full liberty to spread Christian knowledge in India, but the Indian episcopal problem was also taken up and a Bishop was appointed who had his headquarters at Calcutta with jurisdiction over all the dominions of the East India Company.

The long controversy and stiff opposition made the missionaries realize, if nothing else, the need for restraint and moderation in their activities. They were anxious to show that the Naboabs were wrong in supposing that the removal of the missionary clause would lead to the immediate massacre of 30,000 Englishmen in India. As a matter of fact, nothing happened. The missionaries went about their business quietly and the official visitations of the

7. St. Thomas Mount, Mylapore
Traditional site of the Apostle's Martyrdom
(Photo : *Mount Photo House, Madras*)

8. The Palace of Begum Samru, at present St. John's College, Sardhana
(Courtesy : *Rev. Mark, Sardhana*)

9. St. Thomas Cathedral, Mylapore

10. Christian Medical College Hospital, Vellore

Popularly known as the American Hospital, this is one of the best hospitals in India

first two Bishops, Middleton and Heber, excited nothing more murderous than a mild curiosity on the part of Indians in the picturesque costumes of Anglican Bishops.

The removal of the missionary clause from the charter was but the first round in the fight between the missionary and the Naboab. With the removal of the ban, several missions started their activities in India, and they began to study carefully the relationship between Hinduism and the East India Company. The Company, as the ruling power, had taken over some of the responsibilities of their Hindu predecessors which included protection of temples and their vast property and control of pilgrims to the great Hindu shrines. The pilgrim taxes yielded a handsome revenue to the government, and in return the officers of the government had to supervise the activities of the temple, regulate traffic and generally behave in a way that suggested active government support to idolatry.

As the natural patron of the temples, the Company had other duties as well which in the case of the larger and more important temples took the form of directly or indirectly supervising the temple establishment, appointing trustees when disputes arose, carrying out repairs to temples that had fallen into ruins, etc. In short, according to the missionaries, the Company "took upon itself the office of dry nurse to Vishnu. . . . Nor was it merely in the administration of the revenue of idolatry and the superintendence of its establishments that our tender regard for the heathenism of the people evinced itself. We made much open display of our reverence for their institutions by attendance at their festivals; turning out our troops to give additional effect to the show; firing salutes in honour of their highdays and holidays; and sanctioning, nay promoting, the prayers, and invocations of the Brahmins to propitiate the deity for a good harvest or a good trade."

When the affairs of a temple fell into a bad way due to the mis-management or rapacity of the trustees, the Company took over the management and applying British efficiency in the administration of revenue and expenses, put the temple on a sound financial basis. The Naboabs were neither Hindus nor Christians, nor even Muslims as the name seems to suggest, but ardent students of politics and commerce and were, by these means, merely courting the goodwill of their Hindu subjects and soldiers.

The missionaries very naturally objected to these activities. They did not, of course, want the East India Company to destroy the Hindu temples as some of the early Muslims and Portuguese did; but they expected that when the affairs of a temple fell in a bad way the British should, as good Christians, take a secret pleasure and leave it to die a natural death. The missionaries were thoroughly dissatisfied with the attitude of the Company towards idolatry, and in a memorial they submitted to the Government of Bombay in 1837, some of the anti-Christian practices of the Company pointed out were:

"1. The employment of Brahmins and others for the purpose of making heathen invocations for rain and fair weather.
2. The inscription of 'Sri' on public documents, and the dedication of Government records to Ganesh and other gods.
3. The entertainment in courts of justice of questions of a purely idolatrous nature with no civil rights involved.
4. The degradation of certain castes by excluding them from particular offices and benefits not connected with religion.
5. The attendance of Government servants, civil and military, in their official capacity at Hindu and Muslim festivals, with a view to participate in their rites and ceremonies or in the joining of troops and the use of regimental bands in the processions of Hindu and Muslim festivals or their attendance in any other capacity than that of police for the preservation of peace.
6. The firing of salutes by the troops or by vessels of the Indian Navy, in intimation and honour of Hindu festivals."

The Christian Knowledge Society was particularly vehement in its denunciation of the Company's connection with idolatry, but when the question of the Pilgrim Tax came up, the members of the Society found themselves on the horns of a dilemma. The tax yielded considerable revenue to the Company and good Christians thought it ill-gotten wealth. On the other hand, the removal of the tax was likely to encourage pilgrimage as this activity would then become less expensive by comparison. The Muslims had, in fact, imposed it as a deterrent to Hindu pilgrimage, but the collections were found so substantial that even Hindu kings introduced it and the East India Company continued the practice. The missionaries, however, after much deliberation decided in favour of its removal.

As a result of petitions from responsible individuals and organisations and continued agitation in England, the Court of Directors under the influence of Charles Grant issued instructions to the authorities in India for the complete severance of Government connection from the religious activities of their subjects. The local authorities were given discretionary powers in giving effect to the directions of the Court, and most of them used these powers with much wisdom. A few disregarding the orders completely, complaints reached the highest quarters and the Parliament had to interfere. On the whole the directions were given effect to in the spirit if not to the letter. The salute to the gods was stopped; pilgrim taxes were abolished; the superintendence of religious festivals by the officials of the Company ceased and their function was confined to policing of the vast gatherings; temple lands were made over to Trusts and the Trustees were elected either by the congregation or nominated by British authorities from among respectable Hindus. Thus a good deal of neutrality was obtained. All told, the East India Company and the missionaries exercised a wholesome check on each other which helped the smooth progress of both Christianity and British rule in India.

Pious Christians, however, often took offence at perfectly innocent happenings. For instance, the casual mention in a court of law by a lawyer that Bishop Middleton had attended a Nautch in the Government House at Calcutta created quite a sensation in

England. The worthy Bishop emphatically denied the allegation but vaguely referred to an invitation he had received from the Governor-General to attend a party; he did not attend the party, he stated, but the ladies of his household did. It was now up to the Governor-General to say what happened further. Lord Hastings in a letter to the Lord Chancellor admitted there was a party at the Government House and the ladies of the Bishop's House attended it. There was, however, no Nautch. A woman sang, he confessed, but she did not dance—"the mere movement of her feet, while she was singing, not deserving the name."

This amusing incident throws much light on the state of society at the time. The days of Clive and Warren Hastings were gone for good. The very fact that the ladies of the Bishop's House attended the party shows that Government House parties had definitely risen in standard. There was probably some Indian music which wagging tongues exaggerated into a Nautch; a Nautch at that time meant a good many dancing girls and more drunkards. Anyway the incident shows the watchful eye good Christians kept on Anglo-Indians and their activities.

CHAPTER XI

PROGRESS OF CHRISTIANITY UNDER THE BRITISH

THE East India Company, started in 1600, had, by the middle of the 18th century, become the dominant political power in India. The historic battle of Plassey in which Clive defeated the Nawab of Bengal opened for the British the way to the plains of Hindustan. The anarchical conditions then prevailing in northern India made advance easy and by the end of the eighteenth century they were the virtual rulers of India, and it was plain to the discerning that the fall of the few independent kingdoms would be a matter of decades. In 1849 the Punjab, the most powerful of the independent kingdoms fell, and the turbulent Sikhs acknowledged the suzerainty of the British. From that time till August 15, 1947, the British were the rulers of India, the first Christian power to attain this distinguished position. Political suzerainty has obvious powers to enhance the spread of the religion of the rulers, and the gains to Christianity during the British period were the most remarkable.

After the removal of the missionary clause, there was an influx of missionaries into India both from England and America. The severance of the Company's connection from Hinduism appears to have been followed by an active campaign by the servants of the Company to Christianize India, and an interference with Hinduism was reported. For in a despatch of the Court of Directors we find that strict instructions were issued to the Governor-General to impress upon the servants of the Company the need for neutrality and non-interference. The nature and extent of the interference are not known in detail but if there was any, it was but short-lived and led to no serious consequences.

While the early Catholic missions gave greater importance to formal conversion, the new Protestant missions were more concerned with the dissemination of Christian knowledge. Street preachings, circulation of the Bible and pamphlets and active humanitarian work among the needy were given greater importance in their programme than formal baptism. Some of the missions did splendid work among the aboriginals, and here mass conversions were frequent.

The nineteenth century was marked by the arrival of the first batch of American missionaries. The American missions that have done splendid work in India had, like many another missionary enterprise, a very modest beginning. The American Protestants, like their brethren in Europe, were at first more concerned with organizing their own churches than mission work among non-Christians. The colonists were busy consolidating their own position and exploring the vast and unknown New Continent. Soon, however, the spirit that had moved England and Scotland to send out missions to the East spread to America too.

"It was beside a haystack that the foreign missionary movement in America was born. In the year 1806 in Massachusetts a little group of students met under a cluster of trees near their college for their usual prayer meeting. An impending thunderstorm drove them to a safer place, and beside a haystack they began to speak about the subject that was absorbing more and more of their attention, the need for proclaiming the good news of the Lord Christ in the lands of the Orient. One of the students, Manuel Mills, made the proposal that they send the Gospel to Asia. 'We could do it if we would', he said. Sheltering from the storm they discussed the matter; as the sky began to clear, Mills said, 'Let us make it a subject of prayer under this haystack, while the dark clouds are going and the clear sky is coming'."

America then, it must be remembered, was not the Dollar Land it is now, and to the early pioneers who needed on a modest estimate 60,000 dollars for their enterprise, the amount appeared almost impossible of realisation. They tried to interest rich Englishmen and the newly formed mission societies of England and Scotland, but while they proved very courteous sympathisers the zealots were given to understand that America had to support her own missionaries. After much propaganda among a sceptic population, the enthusiasts were, however, able to interest enough Americans to donate the amount.

The first American Missionaries to arrive in India were Gordon Hall and Mr. and Mrs. Nott. They reached Calcutta in November 1812 when the ban on missionaries was still in force. With Hall and the Notts had come Mr. Rice and Mr. and Mrs. Judson, but these three on arrival in Calcutta broke off from the American Board and joined the Baptists of Serampore. Hall and the Notts were not allowed to land in Calcutta but were told that if they were wise they would sail for Mauritius like the Newells who had departed four days before their arrival. The missionaries refused to be wise. The authorities in Calcutta decided to deport them to England. Hall, however, came to know that Sir Evans Napean, the then Governor of Bombay, was a devout Christian favourably disposed towards mission work, and the missionaries managed to board a ship bound for Bombay and reach this port on February 11, 1813.

Sir Evans was, no doubt, a good Christian but he was an official of the East India Company and had to respect the Missionary Clause. Besides, information was received by him from Calcutta that the Americans were absconders. Hence the Bombay authorities asked the missionaries to sail for England by the next boat. Hall wrote a long letter to Sir Evans in which he politely pointed out that he had a duty towards God to preach the Gospel in India and gave more than a hint that he would not go to England unless removed to the ship by force. He also explained that he had moved authorities in England through the American Board for permission for the missionaries to stay in India, and a reply would be received soon.

News of the declaration of war between Great Britain and America now reached India, and Sir Evans' position became difficult. While he was unhappily pondering over what to do with the missionaries, the latter secretly boarded a vessel bound, as they thought, for Ceylon. The ship was actually sailing to Quilon which they mistook for Ceylon and as they landed in Cochin on their way and were anxiously waiting for the departure of the boat from the port, a ship arrived from Bombay with a warrant for the arrest of the missionaries. The order was promptly executed and the missionaries were sent back to Bombay. Sir Evans had been considerably upset over the secret departure of the missionaries and it was his intention to send them to England. Hall, however, prevailed upon him to detain them at Bombay till the receipt of instructions from England. This was fortunate, for before long orders were received to allow the missionaries to stay in India.

Hall did a good deal of street preaching and became a familiar figure in the streets of Bombay but was not very successful at making converts. He did much humanitarian work in the Province, and died of cholera in Nasik in the year 1826 while doing relief work during the epidemic.

A great impetus to the spread of Christian knowledge was given by the adoption of the English language as the medium of instruction in India. The pioneer in this move was the Scottish missionary Alexander Duff. He realized that Christian knowledge could not be effectively imparted to Indians without opening to them the treasures of Christian literature through the medium of the English language. As an experimental measure he started a course of instruction in English which proved exceedingly popular in Calcutta. This encouraged the British authorities to adopt a favourable view to the question of adopting English as the medium of instruction which had been broached by many responsible Indians and Englishmen. After much deliberation and a heated controversy the British, under the directions of Macaulay, decided to adopt English as the medium of instruction in India.

By now the old prejudice against Christians had been sufficiently overcome to make the innovation acceptable to Indians. In fact, Indians like Raja Ram Mohan Roy actively agitated for adopting English against the protagonists of Sanskrit and other Indian languages. The following extract from a letter he wrote to Lord Amherst is of interest in this connection:

"If it had been intended to keep the British nation in ignorance of real knowledge, the Baconian philosophy would not have been allowed to displace the system of Schoolmen, which was best calculated to perpetuate ignorance. In the same manner the Sanskrit system of education would be the best calculated to perpetuate ignorance if such had been the policy of the British legislature. But as the improvement of the native population is the object of the Government it will consequently promote a more liberal and enlightened policy of instruction."

The British settlements that had by now sprung up all over India were quite different from the old settlements of the ports which had been dreaded by Indians as social plague spots. The Godless society which had earned for Christianity the name of 'devil religion' among Indians was replaced by a highly respectable society controlled by clergymen, honest and upright civilians, and the vigilant missionaries. That sound, healthy, liberal outlook which in the aggregate is known as the 'British character' had also been built up at home, and the men who filled responsible positions in India were highly respectable and fair-minded, and the British as a race began to be looked upon by Indians as a superior people. Their efficient system of administration, their way of life and worship attracted intelligent Hindus who began to ponder over what constituted their apparent superiority. In physique, Indians, especially the hardy races of the north, were not much inferior to the British; in intelligence the higher classes among the Hindus were equal if not superior; in numerical strength Indians were definitely superior. Then remained religion and social organisation.

Some intelligent, bold Indians discarding their age old notions of self-importance began to take an active interest in their foreign masters and study the religion and social institutions of Europe. Curiosity was sufficiently roused to prompt the bolder individuals to challenge caste rules against undertaking sea-voyage and travel abroad to study the institutions of the West at first hand. The casteless society of Europe, their democratic institutions, monogamy, monotheism, the freedom of European women, and the general emancipation of the West from the superstitions and ignorance of the dark ages immensely impressed these inquirers.

G*

With knowledge came understanding, with understanding appreciation and with appreciation enthusiasm.

The large number of Indians who received instruction in English got easy access to Western religious and political ideas and were greatly influenced by these. The indifferent language of the translations of the Bible had made them contemptible for the cultured, and the better class of Hindus seldom cared to read them. But their newly acquired ability to read the scripture in English made them ardent students of the Bible. The teachings of Christ, especially the Sermon on the Mount, struck Indians, always keen students of religion, as superb and they had no difficulty in accepting Jesus as one of the greatest of religious teachers. Whatever the objections Hindus or Muslims had to the way of life of some of the Christians, of Jesus all had the most profound respect. This admiration for Jesus and His teachings has continued to the present day and His name and gentle message has penetrated the remotest corners of India.

The new ideas worked like magic, and the whole country began to vibrate with a fresh energy. The first reaction was of revolutionary zeal. A horror of caste and idolatry seized young India. Sati, religious suicide, cow worship, seclusion of women, etc. came up for severe criticism and young India decided to break away, once for all, from the old order. The reaction at times took a particularly violent turn.

The revolt against the old order started from Bengal. Here the British had their headquarters and had their influence most effectively felt. The missionaries in Bengal, unlike their brethren in the South, were uncompromising opponents of caste and had repeatedly driven home to Indians the iniquity of this institution. Young Bengal, always emotional, registered its opposition to caste in a most determined manner. A band of revolutionaries who had listened to Corrie and Duff decided to put a speedy end to caste. They collected in the house of Babu Krishna Mohan Bannerjee, a Kulin Brahmin, and cooked and ate beef and shouted to all the neighbours what they had done. Not content with this they threw cooked and uncooked beef into the houses of respectable caste Hindus nearby and ran about the streets proclaiming that the best Brahmins of Calcutta had all lost caste.

This method of emancipating India from the bonds of caste had the inevitable result. The whole of Calcutta rose in revolt and responsible social reformers declared that this was not at all what they had advocated. The missionaries also denounced the action. Krishna Mohan Bannerjee was not in his house when the incident took place but his absence did not save him. Orthodoxy punished him severely and he was hounded out of home and society and had to wander about till Duff gave him asylum.

In Bombay the commotions were of a different type. Under John Wilson, George Bowen and others, educational activities were taken in hand by the missionaries and where years of street preaching yielded nothing, the English schools began to show astounding results. The earliest converts were some well-to-do Parsi young men and their baptism caused a sensation in the city, the whole community rising against the missionaries. The neophytes were persecuted, the case was taken to law courts and the whole city had to be guarded against riots. But with the determined stand of the neophytes and the missionaries, opposition died down.

The next sensation in Bombay was created by the conversion of Narayan Sheshadari, a Brahmin who did splendid work in the mission field. Close on Sheshadari's baptism, his twelve-year-old brother Shripat declared his intention to become a Christian. Shripat caused much sorrow and heartache to many. The boy was a minor and he could not be baptized without his guardian's permission, and the missionaries asked him to wait. But the impatient lad, to break down opposition, ate forbidden food and thus voluntarily lost caste. This desperate method of wearing down opposition had unexpected results. A section of the Hindus maintained that the boy could be taken back to his caste after proper purification but the orthodox thought otherwise. Regardless of the opposition of the latter, a priest in the presence of certain witnesses took back the boy after performing certain purificatory ceremonies. Thereupon the orthodox excommunicated the priest and all those who took part in the proceedings. The offenders repented and after paying a severe penalty were taken back into the Hindu fold.

These were not isolated instances. All over the country such happenings became frequent, and as time went on the incidents became too numerous to be taken notice of. For the first time in the long history of India Christianity became a force to be counted with. It was no more the religion of the downtrodden and of outcasts but worthy of the attention of Brahmins and noblemen. The old prejudice against the Parangi was also gone. European Christians far from being contemptible began to be looked upon as worthy of imitation and it became fashionable among the English-educated higher classes of Indians to affect the customs, manners and dress of Englishmen. De Nobili's arguments were advanced in reverse by these emulators of Westernism. They maintained that Hindus could dress like Europeans, use knives and forks, sit on chairs and crop their hair short, and even eat any food in the company of any one without losing their religion.

Nor was it the Hindu alone who was affected. Muslims, Parsis, Sikhs, in fact all races from the tribesmen on the frontier to the Kulins of Bengal began to feel the impact of Christianity. The Gospel also reached the kingdom of old Gundaphoros of Christian legend and the complacent missionaries began to dream great dreams about the whole sub-continent turning Christian.

And then came the Mutiny. Both European and Indian Christians suffered heavily, especially in the north, and the British were well nigh driven out of India. Incidents of extreme cruelty and excesses were reported from both sides. But the Europeans were more impressed by the cruelty of Indians than of their own, and it was wondered by many men in England and Scotland how human beings could have perpetrated the reported brutalities. Bitter were the comments made on this most unfortunate incident in Indo-British history. The Naboabs attributed the mutiny to the activities of the missionaries which, they said, had alarmed the people, and pointed out that they and their forefathers had prophesied it. The missionaries, on the other

CHRISTIANITY UNDER THE BRITISH

hand, maintained that the catastrophe was a well-deserved visitation of God's wrath on the British for their criminal neglect of a people who had been placed by Him under their care; they had more than 100 years at their disposal, the missionaries pointed out, to make human beings of Indians if not Christians but they had not only wasted their opportunity but actively hindered all attempts of sincere Christians to Christianize India. And there the dispute stood.

We need not go into details of this unhappy controversy. The real cause of the mutiny, as is now admitted by all, was political and not religious. The British had no greater right to rule India than the Moguls and the Maharathas to rule Great Britain, and Indians had made a desperate attempt to assert their natural right to rule or misrule themselves. Anyway, the mutiny was put down and the administration of India passed directly under the Crown and the Parliament, and Queen Victoria by her famous proclamation of 1858 ushered in a new era in the history of India.

The mutiny did not cause any serious setback to the work of the missionaries. There was, it is true, some violence against the missionaries, churches and Christians in general, but this was the work of fanatical individuals and not of responsible leaders. In the benevolent and prosperous reign that followed, these unfortunate incidents were soon forgotten and forgiven.

With the rapid spread of English education, the security of person and property the new era ensured, and the general favour and esteem the missionary enjoyed brought in a glorious period of Christian expansion in India. Throughout the length and breadth of the country churches, chapels and steeples began to appear and every city and town of importance could claim a respectable church and an indigenous congregation.

All this, however, made mission work somewhat prosaic. The old pioneers had to often contend with hostile elements and work in unfamiliar ground. They had to study the languages of the country for several years before being able to make themselves understood to the people. The new missionary had none of these handicaps. The moment he set foot in India he could start work wherever he found himself, the advance of English education having given him this advantage. Though the old hazards were gone, India was still a vast land and its remote villages and hilly regions gave the missionary some sense of strangeness, and mission work was not altogether uninteresting.

Nor was the element of persecution completely absent even after Queen Victoria's proclamation. In 1882 when Bombay, for instance, was invaded by the Salvation Army, there was considerable stir in the city and the civil authorities were greatly perturbed. News of the invasion reached India before the forces landed, and almost all Indian journals published the exciting news. Even the *London Times* expressed its apprehension. When the Army landed in Apollo Bunder every one, however, heaved a sigh of relief for it consisted of four soldiers only i.e. Major Tucker and two men and one woman under him. Soon the war on India began. A procession of war chariots was taken; the chariots were bullock carts and the battle cry was sounded by the cornet player, Lt. Norman. Now the sounding of this instrument was in defiance of a police ban and Norman was promptly arrested and removed to the police station. Next morning he was produced before the Magistrate and fined Rs.20.

The veto on music was resented by the Army as it was "a great handicap in a city where the bazaar noises were often deafening, and all religious and marriage ceremonies are accompanied with the beating of drums and clanging of cymbals." The personnel of the Army was strengthened by new arrivals from the Headquarters, and several of them were arrested for various offences connected with the Police Commissioner's inconvenient orders which seemed to retard the progress of the war. After a year of hostilities truce, however, was declared in 1883, the police and the Army accepting certain terms. The main idea of the Salvationists was to create some public interest in their activities and in this they were eminently successful. Where other missions came and went without any one knowing anything about them, the soldiers of the Salvation Army heralded their arrival by forcing the attention of all India by their novel methods of propaganda. The excellent humanitarian work the Army has since done to alleviate human suffering in India is too well known to be given in detail here.

The missionaries were the pioneers in the field of women's emancipation in India. The condition of Hindu women during the middle ages was one of abject misery and dependence on man. Medieval Hindu law givers were quite definite on this point. A woman, according to them, was to be dependent upon her father in childhood, on her husband in youth and on her sons in old age. "A woman is never free." Agreeable to these notions everything had been done to curb her intellectually and physically. A respectable woman lived in seclusion and knowledge of letters was denied her. She was married in childhood and as a widow mounted the funeral pyre of her husband or suffered a worse fate.* With the arrival of the Muslims, the lot of Hindu women became even worse.

It was in this atmosphere that the missionaries began to work for the education of girls. Initial difficulties were many, and the mission schools for girls were at first shunned by the respectable; only Indian Christian girls could be persuaded to attend them. With the increase in the European female population in India, their example and social standards gradually began to influence the better classes and tendencies set in which viewed female education with less hostility. The Parsis who were happily free from many prejudices of their Hindu and Muslim brethren were first attracted to the mission girls' schools. Soon the bolder spirits among the Hindus and Muslims followed suit.

Pioneer work in the field of women's emancipation was done by Pandita Ramabai, a remarkable daughter of India. A short account of the life of this great Indian Christian lady would be of interest to the reader.

Ramabai was born in 1853 in the forest of Gangamula. Her father Ananta Sastri, was a wandering pilgrim and Rama was born in the forest during one of his wanderings. The pilgrimage continued and Rama's parents visited several Hindu shrines

* Those interested in the subjection of Indian women are advised to read the author's book *Women and Marriage in India* (Allen & Unwin).

and from the very childhood she was imbued with the teachings of Hinduism. Her parents and a sister died of starvation in the terrible famine years 1876–77. One of her brothers, Srinivas, died in 1880 and her husband in 1882. The loss of so many dear ones within such a short period made a deep impression on young Ramabai's mind and she began to seek solace away from the world she lived in. After visiting many cities in India she came with her little daughter to Poona. She had, by now been attracted by the activities of the missionaries and by the preachings of Father Gore, a high caste Brahmin of Maharashtra who had embraced Christianity. The education and uplift of widows became her special care. Though Sati was abolished in British India in 1829, the plight of widows was most miserable and Ramabai herself was a victim of the social codes of the time.

She needed training and for this purpose went to England. Here in the company of the Wantage Sisters she found many solutions to her spiritual riddles and in 1883 was baptized along with her daughter. From England she went to America and evoked considerable interest in Indian affairs. While in America she published her sensational work *The High Caste Hindu Woman*, and many Americans actively interested themselves in Indian social reforms. Ramabai herself was a living argument in favour of women's emancipation in India, for she was a woman of great charm and force of character.

After making many friends in England and America, Ramabai returned to India. On March 1, 1889 the Sarda Sadan (Home of Wisdom) was opened in Bombay for the education of girls in general and of widows in particular. Ramabai, like all pioneers, suffered many handicaps. Her conversion brought much opposition from Hindus and her educational activities from the orthodox of all persuasions. The prayer meetings in the Sadan brought forth the old cry of forcible conversions.

In 1890 the Sadan was transferred to Poona because of the rising cost of living in Bombay. Ramabai worked indefatigably for the progress of female education, and founded the Home of Salvation the inmates of which by the year 1900 swelled to two thousand, all engaged in educational or Gospel work. As years passed on and her fame spread opposition gave place to admiration and till her death in 1922, this great pioneer and devout Christian lady worked incessantly for the emancipation of her sisters and for the spread of the message of the Master in whom she had found peace. By the time she breathed her last, India's emancipated womanhood was working in all fields of public activities, even in politics.

The latter half of the nineteenth century and the twentieth century were marked in the mission field by the growth of organisations and an absence of outstanding personalities. The various missions, no doubt, did active work all over India preaching, converting, distributing tracts and building churches, but men of the calibre of Schwartz, William Carey and Henry Martyn were wanting. Even the Jesuits, who after their expulsion in 1803 had come back and started work, failed to produce men like Francis Xavier and de Nobili. The reason for this is not far to seek. The passing of India under the British crown and the freedom with which mission work was allowed to proceed in India, and the familiarity of Indians with Christians and Christianity made the country less attractive for bolder spirits who pined for martyrdom and adventure. But quantity more than compensated for quality, and the various missions worked steadily and quietly and built up large congregations all over India.

During this period oriental scholarship advanced in Europe and both missionaries and savants began to take a lively interest in the religious and secular literature of India and as a result a better appreciation of Hindus and Muslims began to gain ground among Europeans. The old horror of the 'heathen' vanished and even idolatry was viewed as a concession to human nature. Sanskrit literature was studied as a classic comparable to Latin and Greek.

With a better understanding of the Hindus greater stress was laid by the missionaries on Christian work as distinguished from conversions. The dissemination of knowledge in general and

Christian knowledge in particular, humanitarian work and educational activities were given greater prominence in their programme than formal conversions. The work of the Medical Missions deserves particular mention. Hospitals and dispensaries mainly manned by the missionaries were established in several parts of the country. Institutions for the training of nurses, and Medical schools and colleges were also founded by the Missions and supported by foreign and indigenous munificence. The Christian Medical College Hospital, Vellore, founded by Dr. Miss Scudder, has, under the able directorship of the well-known Dr. Miss H. M. Lazarus, the first Indian lady to be appointed Chief of the W.M.S., risen to be one of the foremost institutions of its kind in Asia.

We may now divert our attention to the political consequences of British rule and the spread of English education in India. For the political struggle that culminated in Indian independence in 1947 had none of the undesirable elements of the mutiny of 1857 and was conducted on both sides in a truly Christian spirit.

Together with Christian knowledge, revolutionary theories in politics and religion reached India through the medium of English instruction. The irreligion of some of the Western schools of thought did not make any lasting impression on India, but it was otherwise with the political theories. As Indians travelled abroad and got higher education in England and America, they woke up to the fact of the humiliating political subjection of their country to foreigners and were naturally anxious to free India from British rule and apply the democratic principles of government to India too.

It is good to remember that democracy and political liberalism are essentially offshoots of Christianity. It is true that early Christians believed only in the spiritual equality of man and not in political and economic equality. It is also true that the Buddha had made some effort to establish the equality of man, but his acceptance of the dogma of transmigration made the effort ineffective. On the other hand, early Christian theologians firmly established the equality of man on the ground of every one possessing an equal imperishable soul created by God and infused into the embryo. During the middle ages this equality was in practice confined to the spiritual sphere but with the Reformation and the bold schools of thought it gave rise to, the principle of equality was extended to material spheres to include the political theory of democracy and economic theory of socialism.

When Indians first began to agitate for democracy and independence the British were considerably surprised. They put it down to gross ingratitude on the part of Indians and pointed out all the great things they had done for the country, the thousands of miles of railways they had built up, the peace, prosperity and solidarity they had given etc. etc. But Indians were not convinced, and argued that all this was done not for the benefit of Indians but for exploiting the country for the benefit of the British. When the charge of ingratitude failed, the British pointed out that Indians were not yet ready to rule themselves; the caste, untouchability, unapproachability, poverty, illiteracy and the stock-in-trade arguments familiar to all students of the Indian struggle for freedom were made much of. The Indians on the other hand, thought that these evils were inherent in subjection and could be overcome only through freedom; besides according to the theories of Englishmen themselves every nation had a right to misrule themselves. These undecided arguments naturally led to blows, and Indians who had looked upon the British as benefactors, especially after the country had come under the Crown and the Parliament, began to treat them as oppressors and tyrants. Feelings ran high and it looked as if the bad old days of the mutiny were coming again.

At this crucial moment in the history of the country, the leadership of the struggle passed into the hands of a man who saved both Britain and India from the grim tragedy the countries were drifting into. For Mahatma Gandhi, whatever his differences with the British, steadfastly advocated a non-violent fight against the British and the freedom movement under his able guidance was a peaceful war with but isolated outbursts of violence which never marred the general effect of the struggle as a whole.

The history of the political struggle is outside the scope of this book but not its Christian aspect. For Gandhiji was the first leader in a political struggle who applied the principles of the Sermon on the Mount on a national scale. He himself had his higher education in England and his spiritual leanings made him an ardent student of the Bible, and his political and social activities were not a little influenced by the teachings of Christ. "Turn the other cheek also," was his constant command to his followers even in the most provocative situations. In his prayer meetings the Bible was read along with other sacred books. He was not a formal convert, but was certainly a member of the Universal Church of Christ.

The political struggle under Gandhiji's leadership destroyed many old loyalties and had its repercussions on the Christian community in India. The position of the missionaries was particularly unenviable; most of those who came from the United Kindom had some connection with the official Church of England or institutions allied to it and it was difficult for them to actively side with the national movement against the British. The plight of the American missionaries was worse. The American missionary in India was more or less a guest of the British Indian government as the missionary before entering India had to sign a declaration of neutrality in the political affairs of the country. The position of Indian Christians was also difficult. As Indian nationals they had their loyalty to the country and could not afford to be passive spectators in a struggle of such momentous national importance as the Civil Disobedience Movement; further there was a tendency among Hindus and Muslims to look upon Indian Christians as denationalized and drawing inspiration from Europe in spite of the fact that Jesus was an Asian. Hence while many distinguished Hindus and Muslims condemned the Civil Disobedience Movement as a force of anarchy, any such pronouncement by a responsible Indian Christian was likely to be misconstrued. And the whole question was complicated for all Christians by the method of the movement which eschewed all violence and preached success through suffering and tribulation.

The *Indian Witness*, a journal published from Lucknow was probably the only party that had no doubts as to the conduct to be followed by good Christians in this situation. The journal held that the non-violent activities of Gandhiji and his followers were as bad as those of cheque forgers and smugglers and declared that what influence it had would be 'upon the side of law and order'. But all Christians were not quite sure of this. Law breaking could not always be condemned by Christians since Jesus Himself broke some of the laws of His community and had to suffer for it. Father Verrier Elwin of the Chista Seva Sangh Ashram was of opinion that it was the duty of Christians to break the laws of a state when these conflicted with the higher law of God, and in a pamphlet entitled *Christ and Satyagraha* enumerated several conditions under which the authority of a state could be challenged by its citizens, and concluded: "There is nothing either in the teaching of Christ or in the dominant philosophical tradition of Christendom to prevent a conscientious Christian, if he feels the above conditions apply to India, from giving his wholehearted support to the noblest ideals of Indian nationalism as expressed by Mahatma Gandhi. . . . The real conflict today is not between nations, but between principles; not between England and India but between violence and non-violence; so surely it is the duty of Christians to throw their whole weight on the side of non-violence."

Mr. J. C. Kumarappa, an Indian follower of Mahatma Gandhi who was then living in his Ashram, wrote when the historic Civil Disobedience Campaign of 1930 was started by Gandhiji:

"Amongst Christians, there are Indians and foreigners who see eye to eye with national movement and those who honestly believe that the Nationalists are misled. But there can be no difference of opinion regarding non-violence amongst those who were enjoined by their Master to turn to 'whosoever shall smite thee on the right cheek the other also' and to return good for evil. Before our very eyes, Gandhiji is substituting for warfare the gospel of love in a practical way. . . . What is going to be the contribution of those who profess to follow the Prince of Peace whose banner is love? . . . Here is an opportunity at our very door the like of which Christendom has never faced before. Do we not hear the Man of Sorrows say, 'He that taketh not his cross and followeth after me is not worthy of me'. The choice is imminent."

On the eve of convening the Round Table Conference, a statement signed by 200 missionaries of British birth was issued in which they emphasized the need for sympathetic attitude towards India's political aspirations. "We therefore urge that the principle should be fully and frankly recognised that the determining factor in laying down the lines of India's future constitution should be the wishes of the people of India. This principle is held by politicians of all schools and it is one that accords with our deepest Christian convictions. Its acceptance by the suzerain power would go far to ensure the success of the Round Table Conference."

All told, religious organisations remained neutral and individuals were left to their own light. Politically minded Indians generally felt that their duty was towards the National Movement and a large number of them took active part in the Civil Disobedience Movement and suffered the consequences with their Hindu and Muslim countrymen.

What organized political voice the Indian Christians as a community had at the time was on the side of the Congress. The Nationalist Christian Party of Bombay declared itself with the Congress. The Council of the All India Conference of Indian Christians, in a meeting held at Lucknow on July 11, 1930 condemned the repressive measures of the Government. "The more powerful and organized a Government is," they pointed out, "the more does it stand condemned for employing methods which cannot bear the scrutiny of the highest principles of the Christian civilisation."

We need not go into the details of the Indian struggle for freedom. Suffice to say that the outbreak of the war in 1939 pushed the Indian question into the background, but with the termination of the war events moved faster than anybody had expected. The first thing the Labour Government on coming to power did was to solve the Indian problem. They cut the Gordian

Knot and divided India on a hastily agreed plan between the Congress and the Muslim League. In the division the majority of Christians found themselves in the Indian Union as Pakistan had but a negligible percentage of Christians.

In our praise for Mahatma Gandhi's Christian virtues and his victory in the non-violent war, we must not lose sight of the fact that he was fighting a Christian foe. Gandhiji himself had admitted that non-violence is ineffective against an insane or hardened foe. The stories of Christian martyrs and the crucifixion of Jesus himself prove this. Why, the Apostle of non-violence himself fell by violence. In the British he had a humane opponent prone to persuasion and endowed with Christian charity. And this was mainly responsible for Gandhiji's success. For in the whole history of imperialism we look in vain for a precedent to the British granting of independence to India. The attachment to possessions is more developed in nations than in individuals and no nation has ever voluntarily relinquished control over a vast land that yielded much profit and more prestige. Truly the granting of independence to India by Britain was renunciation on a national scale.

Apart from the Christian influence which was everywhere felt under British rule in India, the numerical gains from a proselytizer's point of view were also considerable. By the end of the British period the number of Christians in undivided India was computed at over 8,000,000, outnumbering the Sikhs by about 2,000,000.

CHAPTER XII

THE INFLUENCE OF CHRISTIANITY ON HINDUISM

WE have seen that Christianity had firmly established itself in India in the first century of the Christian era, and in the South powerful Christian communities had even disputed with the Hindus political and economic dominance. But we find very little reference to Christ, His teachings or even about the Christian communities, in the religious literature of the Hindus. In fact, till the British came to India as their masters, the Hindus seem to have remained completely indifferent to Christianity.

This is mainly due to the fact that ancient and medieval Hindus generally considered all races except themselves as barbarians beneath their notice. Hindus, especially of the South, had in ancient times travelled abroad for trade and in search of colonies, but none of them took the trouble of studying the people or places they came in contact with. Even Indian Buddhists who had been responsible for the conversion of many nations outside their country were victims of this prejudice. They considered it their duty to teach and not to learn. Hence we have no Hindu work comparable to the delightful travel accounts of Hiuen Tsang, Fa Hian, Ibn Batuta or Marco Polo.

During the middle ages even the little interest the ancients had in foreigners ceased. A rigid social code made contact with others taboo, and no respectable Indian was allowed to leave the country for lands overseas. Those who did were promptly excommunicated. These restrictions made the Hindus one of the most self-centred and conservative people in the world. The Muslim scholar Alberuni wrote of medieval Hindus: "They are by nature niggardly in communicating that which they know and they take the greatest possible care to withold it from men of another caste among their own people; still much more, of course, from any foreigner. According to their beliefs, there is no country on earth but theirs, and no created being beside them has any knowledge of science whatever. Their haughtiness is such that if you tell them of any science or knowledge in Khorasan or Persia they will think you both an ignoramus and a liar. If they travelled and mixed with other nations, they would soon change their minds, for their ancestors were not so narrow-minded as the present generation."

These tendencies continued till the British through their educational system forced the Hindus to take some notice of other people.

Further, an old Hindu literary practice makes the discovery of the real source of a religious innovation difficult when the ideas behind it were actually borrowed. A Hindu writer seldom recognized any source of inspiration except that of a god or of his Guru. That he borrowed freely from his fellow men and even his opponents is quite apparent from Hindu religious literature. The introduction in unexpected places of some hoary sage or god who starts a long sermon which has no connection with the text is a regular feature of works like the *Mahabharata*, *Ramayana* and the *Puranas*. When a Hindu writer found that his own authority or that of his Guru was not sufficient to compel conviction, he made no scruples of putting his novel ideas in the mouth of some sage or god whose authority was indisputable. Interpolation was the besetting sin of all Hindu writers, and any Christian ideas that might have been borrowed were incorporated in the Hindu system with no acknowledgements. Hence though Christian legends and teachings are discernible in ancient and medieval Hindu literature, there is no positive evidence to show the source.

There is a passage in the *Mahabharata* which is believed to be an account of a eucharistic celebration in a Christian church probably in Persia or farther west. Three Hindu pilgrims had travelled from their homeland to the "White Country," and here they beheld the impressive ceremony:

"Then we beheld glistening men, white, appearing like the

moon adorned with all the auspicious marks, with their palms ever joined in supplication, praying to the Supreme Being, with their faces turned to the East: the prayer which is offered by these great hearted ones is called the mental prayer.

"Then we suddenly saw a glory diffused, like that of a thousand suns shining at once, and those men quickly advanced towards that glory joyfully exclaiming, 'Hail to thee!' We heard the loud sound of them exclaiming, and knew that these men were offering the oblation to God, but we were rendered suddenly unconscious by this splendour and saw nothing, deprived of the use of our eyes, void of strength and senseless. But we only heard a loud cry uttered: 'Thou art victorious, O Lotus-eyed. Hail to thee, O creator of the Universe! Hail to thee, the Eldest Son of the Supreme Soul!' Such was the sound heard by us, accompanied with teaching. In the meanwhile a pure wind laden with perfumes, brought heavenly flowers and healing drugs."

This, it is true, need not necessarily have been a Christian service. The Manichees had similar celebrations and the pilgrims were probably witnessing one of these.

But Christian influence is clearly traceable in the great theistic movements that arose in Hinduism. The fact that these movements originated from the South, where Christianity had strongly established itself from very early times, is indicative of their Christian origin.

Prior to Sankara, Buddhism was the dominant religion of India. The philosophy of pure Buddhism is non-Theistic if not atheistic. The Buddha 'passed the gods by' and in his system there is no place for a Creator of the Universe; the Law is supreme and personality subordinate to it. Every sin has to be lived down in numerous rebirths till the ego is destroyed by the accumulated virtue of good deeds. Buddhism viewed life as an exotic growth in the grand immeasurable expanse of annihilation. It was this dry philosophy that Sankara successfully challenged.

Sankara was born in Kalady, a village two miles away from Angamali in the Serra, the ancient Syrian Christian stronghold. His date is uncertain but he is believed to have lived in the eighth century of the Christian era. Though his contact with Christianity cannot be positively established, it is quite unlikely that so bold an enquirer as Sankara failed to take notice of a powerful community of Christians living near his native village. Sankara was quite unconventional in his religious leanings and was excommunicated by the Nambudiri Brahmins among whom he was born and educated. He travelled throughout the length and breadth of India, mainly refuting Buddhist beliefs and eventually driving Buddhism out of India.

Sankara's intellectualism drove him to the conception of ultimate reality as Nirguna Brahmam (God without attributes), but in his system considerable importance is given to Isvara, the Personal God, who is to be worshipped, prayed to and propitiated. "Having created the world," says Sankara in his commentary on the *Gita*, "the Bhagavat (God) with a view to its maintenance and well-being first caused the form of religion known as pravritti to be established among men." Bhagavat or Isvara "creates, upholds, and destroys universe. He pervades all things as their *antaryamin*, their 'Inner Ruler', controller, director, guide. He ordains the courses of Time, and determines the conditions of souls from birth to birth in accordance with the Law of the Deed. He is everywhere present, all-knowing and almighty. Presiding over all human destinies, he is the object of men's worship, and he bestows rewards and metes out punishments."

This is theism and not pantheism and is the beginning of the theistic movement in Hinduism that started from the South. Sankara though a theist for practical purposes, was an ardent protagonist of salvation through knowledge. His idea of salvation was not release (Mukti) but self realisation through knowledge. Devotion, pilgrimage and other well-known religious exercises were only stepping stones to the higher knowledge in which the ego realizes its fundamental unity with the Universal Soul. As such his philosophy was permeated by an intellectualism too lofty to be understood by the generality of men.

Further Sankara had spent the better part of his life combating Buddhism and had neither time nor inclination to reform existing

Hindu practices. Hence he absorbed the existing Shaivism, the dominant Hindu cult of the time, in his system. Shaiva doctrines were largely connected with power worship and asceticism. The worship of Shiva is as old as India and most of the great ancient Hindu kings were Shaivas. His temples were the richest and most widely known. Though Shaivism suffered a setback during the ascendency of Buddhism, Sankara revived the old religion which now ousted Buddhism and established itself firmly in India.

Soon after Sankara's revival of Hinduism, we find rising from the South a movement glorifying a new aspect of Shiva. The devotees of the new cult were not impressed by the terrific power or severity of asceticism of Shiva, but by his love and grace. These Shaiva saints filled South India with hymns in praise of these newly discovered virtues of the god, and *Devaram* the first collection of Shaiva hymns was composed in the 11th century of the Christian era. Tiru Mular thus summarises the newly discovered aspect of Shiva:

> The ignorant say that Love and God are different;
> None knows that Love and God are the same.
> When they know that Love and God are the same,
> They rest in God's Love.

Further,

> They have no love for God who have no love for all mankind.

Appar, another Shaiva saint, definitely turns his face away from conventional ideas of propitiating Shiva by penances. Says he:

> Freedom from sin and corruption is to those only who see him in all things
> And not to those who see him only in particular places,
> Not to those who merely chant the Vedas or hear the Sastras expounded.
> It is to those only who crave for atonement
> With omnipresent and all powerful Lord
> And not to those who bathe at dawn,
> Nor to those who make daily offering to the Devas.

> It is to those only who know the Lord to be boundless in love and light
> And not to those who roam in search of holy shrines,
> Nor to those who practise severe austerities or abstain from meat.
> No gain of spiritual freedom is there to those who display the robes
> And other insignia of Yogins and Sanyasins or who mortify the flesh.
> That gain is only for those who glorify him as the Being
> Who vibrates throughout the universe and in every soul.

Of particular interest in this connection is the Shaiva saint and poet Manikka Vasagar. The Christian tradition in South India and Malabar attributes the disappearance of St. Thomas Christians in the Tamil country to the activities of Manikka Vasagar. He is believed to have re-converted a vast number of Christians to Hinduism; those who refused to go back to Hinduism were driven over the Ghats to Malabar. These Tamil Christians remained a separate community known as Manigramakkar for a long time till they were absorbed by the Syrians.

Manikka Vasagar was a sinner-converted saint. In his youth he was indifferent to the needs of his soul and a brilliant career under royal patronage opened for him all the pleasures of the world. It was while he was wallowing in luxury that he was arrested in mid-career by a power that seized him by the throat. "He laid his hand on me;" said Manikka Vasagar. The experience was indescribable:

> My inmost self in strong desire dissolved, I yearned;
> Love's river overflowed its banks;
> My senses all in him were centred; 'Lord', I cried,
> With stammering speech and quivering frame
> I clasped adoring hands; my heart expanding like a flower.

From now on he turned his face away from the world and its pleasures and lived an intensely active religious life. Some of his hymns in humility, devotion, love and deep sense of sin could have been very well composed by Christian saints. He sang:

> I know thee, I, lowest of men that live,
> I know, and see myself a very cur,
> Yet, Lord, I'll say I am thy loving one!
> Though such I was, thou took'st me for thine own.
> The wonder this! Say is there aught like this?
> He made me servant of his loving saints!
> Dispelled my fear; ambrosia pouring forth he came,
> And while my soul dissolved in love made me his own.
> Henceforth I'm no one's vassal; none I fear,
> We have reached the goal.

It is unlikely that Manikka Vasagar who did so much to reclaim the Christians to Hinduism even to the extent of persecuting them did not care to enquire into their religious beliefs. His intense theism was probably the result, at least in part, of a desire to give the reclaimed Christians the God of Love and Grace they were familiar with. He himself was a staunch theist with a strong sense of sin and the need for Divine Grace for salvation and was a contrast to Sankara, the exponent of the lofty theory of man's essential identity with God.

With their best efforts, the Shaiva theists could not completely disengage Shiva from his hoary past. The new aspect of Shiva discovered in the South remained confined to this part of India. In the north he was still the god of ascetics and power worshippers. Besides, the prevailing philosophy of Advaita (Monism) which under Sankara's campaign spread all over India gave Shiva an ephemeral character indistinguishable from Maya, the illusion that enveloped reality. Hence for a purely theistic movement it became necessary to discard Shiva altogether.

Such a movement now started, again from the South. Here along with Shaiva saints had appeared Alvars who sang the praises of Vishnu against those of Shiva. They too had strong theistic leanings but Vishnu at that time was a lesser god than Shiva. Then rose a teacher in the South who revolutionized Hinduism and gave it the much needed God of Love, Mercy and Grace. The god of the pantheon raised to this exalted position by Ramanuja, the new sage, was Vishnu as opposed to Shiva, the god of the then dominant sect.

Ramanuja first attacked the Absolute Monism of Sankara and cut God and souls asunder. He too like Sankara drew or professed to draw inspiration from the Upanishads. As a student he quarrelled with his Shaiva teacher Yadava and struck an independent line of his own. He maintained the reality of God, souls and matter. "These are not, however, independent reals but interdependent. The soul is the controlling factor of body or matter and God controls both. Without God neither soul nor matter has existence except as a conception. The three are in fact inseparable and form a complex whole and Ramanuja's Vishishat Advaita is neither dualism nor pluralism but monism with a qualification."

Whatever the philosophical background, the practical effect of Ramanuja's teaching was to give India a theism on the lines of Christian conceptions. The similarity is remarkable in the method of obtaining salvation. While the older school maintained that the goal of man was self-realisation through correct knowledge, Ramanuja maintained that the supreme bliss of man is in the soul's consciousness of the Divine Presence. This bliss is obtained through devotion and self-surrender. The Jnana Marga or the path of knowledge of the Advaitin is subordinate to Bhakti or devotion. Advaita was essentially aristocratic as true knowledge could be obtained only through the Veda and the lower castes were debarred from reading it; but the Vaishanavas maintain that the lowest creature on earth can obtain salvation through Bhakti and self surrender to Vishnu whose infinite grace extended to the high born and the lowly. Some of the greatest Vaishnava saints were of low birth.

The Shaivas persecuted the Vaishnavas as they did the Buddhists, Jains and Christians and efforts were even made to poison Ramanuja. But since Ramanuja professed to draw inspiration from the Veda, his doctrines had the stamp of orthodoxy and persecution proved ineffective. Within a short time the new doctrine spread all over India and successfully challenged Shaivism. The existing doctrine of incarnation in which Vishnu in his infinite mercy was believed to have taken human and animal forms to save suffering worlds gave the movement infinite variety and scope. The symbolism of sexual love, the nearest approach in ordinary human experience to the bliss of the mystic, was also introduced, and sensuous love cults sprang up in several parts of India. Rama, the seventh, and Krishna, the eighth incarnations of Vishnu became the particular deities of the Vaishnavas.

The soul-stirring theism of Ramanjua was carried by his disciple Ramananda to the north. His disciple Kabir, one of the greatest saints India has ever produced, preached the brotherhood of man and Hindu Muslim unity. Kabir's disciple Nanak founded Sikhism which attracted the virile races of the Punjab. Madhava, Chaitanya, Vallabha, Swami Narayana and a host of other saints and teachers hastened the spread of the new faith.

Poets sang in ecstatic devotion the praises of Vishnu and his incarnations. Those tiresome circumambulations of shrines, endless repetition of mystic syllables, weary pilgrimages to sacred waters, and careful performance of ablutions, and rigid observance of caste rules were rejected as meaningless; for Vishnu, who saw the hearts of men, was more impressed by a contrite heart than by a long list of correct actions. Vishnu was the tireless hunter after souls and his grace converted the most abandoned sinner into a saint in the twinkling of an eye. The Lord in the winning of one true devotee lost himself in rapture. He was not the Lord of the devotee, but Bhaktadasa (the slave of the devotee). Salvation by devotion became the watchword of the Vaishnava. The new doctrine spread all over India with lightning rapidity and filled the country with songs of the Lord. The greatest Vaishnava bards were Tulasi Das in the North, Tukaram in Maharashtra, Jayadeva in Bengal and Mira in Western India.

In Western India the worship of Krishna is more popular than that of Rama. There are many legends about Krishna which point to a Christian source. The comparatively late origin of the Krishna cult and its appearance in Western India which had constant commercial contact with the Christian communities of the ports of Persia make the hypothesis more than a probability.

The similarity in the name of Krishna and Christ is itself striking. Jesus was born in a cowshed, and Krishna's childhood days were spent among herdsmen, and one of his names is Gopalan meaning a herdsman. King Kansa, like Herod, wished to kill the divine child. Foiled in this attempt, Kansa ordered a general massacre of children. Krishna like Jesus suffered a violent death though the circumstances of his death differ from that of Jesus. In the *Bhagavat Gita* Krishna believed to have revealed, he appears as God who, out of love of man, descended to the earth to save the world from the catastrophe sin led it into. Some of the doctrines preached in the *Gita* have a definitely Christian note. A few passages of the *Gita* have been compared by a Western writer to extracts from the fourth Gospel, and the following will be of interest in this connection:

"The world was made by Him and the world knew him not! He came unto His own, and they that were His own received Him not!" St. John i 10-11.

"Men distraught know Me not in My highest nature; I take a human form and they honour Me not." Gita ix 11.

"I know whence I came . . . but ye know not." St. John viii 14.

"I have come through many births and thou also; I know them all; thou knowest them not!" Gita iv 5.

"He that loveth Me . . . I shall love him!" St. John xiv 21.

"I love them that are devoted to Me: even as they are to Me, so I to them." Gita iv 11.

"This is life eternal, that they should know Thee, the only true God, and Him whom Thou hast sent." St. John xvii 13.

"He who knows Me, the Lord of the World, is freed from sins." Gita x 3.

The similarity, however, ends here. For Krishna worship in practice differs widely from Christian worship and has very little in common with Christianity.

In the absence of positive evidence, the Christian influences on Hinduism so far mentioned remain mainly hypothetical. But with the rise of British power, Christian influence on Hinduism became more obvious. Of the many innovations Christian contact originated none is more important than the Brahmo Samaj founded by Rajah Ram Mohan Roy in 1828. Ram Mohan Roy was an ardent admirer of the Bible and was greatly influenced by the teachings of the missionaries. He was quite at home in the English society of Calcutta. It is typical of the man that when Alexander Duff during his first sermon distributed copies of the Bible to his students and some of these in true medieval spirit murmured that the book was a Christian Sastra the reading of which would lead them to apostasy, Ram Mohan Roy stepped forward and exclaimed: "Christians like Drs. Horace and Wilson have studied the Hindu Sastras and you know they have not become Hindus. I myself have read the Koran again and again, and has that made me a Mussalman? Nay, I have studied the whole Bible and you know that I am not a Christian. Why then do you fear to read it? Read and judge for yourselves."

The Brahmo Samaj was "open to all sorts and conditions of men for the worship and adoration of the Eternal, Unsearchable and Immortal Being who is the Author and Preserver of the Universe." Idolatry and caste were strictly forbidden. All the great religious leaders of the world like the Buddha, Jesus, Muhammad and Zoroaster were in principle treated with equal veneration. In Brahmo services "no sermon, preaching, discourse, prayer or hymn be delivered, made or used but such as have a tendency to the promotion of the contemplation of the Author and Preserver of the Universe, to the promotion of charity, morality, piety, benevolence, virtue and the strengthening of the bonds of union between men of all religions and creeds."

In Ram Mohan Roy's time, the disintegration of the old order had started and a section of Hindus were drifting to free thinking and rationalism. The missionaries naturally offered conversion to Christianity as the only means of saving India. Ram Mohan Roy, while publicly maintaining the greatness of Christianity and even regularly attending Christian services, still held that Hinduism was not so bad as was practised at the time. He professed to draw inspiration from the Upanishads, that inexhaustible source of all Hindu speculation and innovation, and interpreted the texts on the basis of his wide experience of Christianity, Islam and Hinduism. Ram Mohan Roy made no secret of the fact that he had benefited much by the study of Christianity but maintained that the Brahmo Samaj (Society of God) stood for pure Hinduism as distinguished from what he called the corrupt Hinduism practised in his time. The Samaj attracted a good many enlightened Hindus, young and old, although the orthodox pronounced it as heretical.

Ram Mohan Roy visited England several times and he was received here with much enthusiasm as a great Indian leader of enlightened views and as a possible convert to Christianity. But the latter hope was not realized. Though a staunch admirer of Christianity, Roy believed that the true Hindu way of life was as good as the Christian, and he died in England in the year 1833 as a Hindu. As for conversion, it may be mentioned that he converted his Christian tutor Mr. Adam to the Brahmo Samaj, and this missionary after the conversion was known in English social circles in Calcutta as the 'Fallen Adam'.

On Ram Mohan Roy's death, the leadership of the Samaj passed on to Devendranath Tagore, a man of independent means and endowed with a mystic bent of mind. Although he relinquished idolatry and was an ardent believer in the unity of Godhead, yet he was a staunch Hindu and a protagonist of Yoga and contemplation. It was under its third great leader, Keshub Chandra Sen, that the Samaj took a definitely Christian turn.

Keshub started life as a bank clerk. The boredom of quill driving became unbearable and looking for more congenial fields for the expression of his personality he joined the Brahmo Samaj in the year 1859. From the very start he showed his fiery spirit, and the creed and practice of the Samaj appeared too tame for the young zealot. The life and teachings of Christ had an irresistible attraction for him. Some of the young members of the Samaj viewed the reactionary leanings of Devendranath Tagore with disfavour, and under the leadership of Keshub they established the 'Brahmo Samaj of India' as an advanced section of the Brahmos; the older persuasion under Tagore came to be known as the 'Adi Samaj' (original Samaj). The personality of the venerable old patriarch who had ordained Keshub had a restraining influence on Keshub and the two sects worked in amity without coming into open conflict. After Tagore's death Keshub struck an independent line of his own.

Keshub's intellectual gifts and his power of eloquence won for him the admiration of all, and some of his followers began to imagine that he moved in a sphere different from theirs. The missionaries and the British generally viewed the activities of Keshub with favour because of his progressive views and Christian leanings, and the viceroy, Sir John Lawrence, befriended Keshub. This naturally enhanced the power and prestige of the Samaj and its leader. With this rise in popularity, a tendency began to rise among a section of the Samaj to venerate Keshub as a saint if not to worship him as a god. Though Keshub did not actively combat this tendency, in the beginning he was inclined to treat it with disfavour. But as time passed on and his popularity and prestige increased Keshub, like many another great man of his type, began to entertain and nourish a belief that he was born to achieve something unique and as such stood apart from the generality of men.

In the year 1870 Keshub visited Britain and received a great welcome in that country. His oratory, definite Christian leanings, and personality won for him the admiration of all, and the great ladies and noblemen of the realm vied with one another to befriend the Wise Man from the East. Keshub's impressions of the West as compared to the East are embodied in his farewell address delivered at Southampton, a passage from which is reproduced below:

"The true kingdom of God will not be realised, unless the East and West are joined together, for it has been said, and every day, through inspiration we hear the voice of God, that the East and West, the North and the South shall sit down in the kingdom of

God. The West with all its thought and culture, its social purity and domestic sweetness, is but half the circle of human civilisation and progress. The East is the other half. I admire the earnestness and firmness of purpose I have seen here; I admire those stupendous works of noble and disinterested works of charity in which thousands of pure and generous minded Englishmen and women are daily engaged. I admire the force of will and the strength of character which I see in your nation; I feel that you have nerves of adamant, with which you overcome any amount of opposition, and surmount obstacles that come in your path; but this is not all that God requires of us. When I turn to my country and the East, I find warmth of heart, solitary contemplation on her hills and mountains, deep communion with the indwelling and omniscient spirit of the One Supreme God; I see a voluntary and deliberate withdrawing of the heart from all anxieties and cares of the world for a time, in order to engage in uninterrupted contemplation of the attributes of God; I see the heart in all its fervour and sympathy in daily communion towards the one loving Father. I see there the heart of man, and in England the mind of man—there the soul, here the will; and as it is our duty to love God with all our heart and soul and mind and strength, it is necessary that all these four elements of character be united. I do not mean to say that there is no such thing as practical righteousness in the nations of the East but that each nation, so at least I believe, represents only one side of the truth, and represents it with peculiar fidelity. The truths which are represented in England and Western countries generally are those which refer to force of character, earnestness of purpose, conscientious strictness, noble charity, practical duty, while the truths which I find peculiarly developed in India—developed to a greater extent than anywhere else—and in Eastern countries generally are those which have reference to sweetness of communion, sweetness of temper, meekness and resignation to God. Is it not then our duty as brothers to unite England and India, the East and the West, that the East may receive some of the truths of the West, and the West some of the grand ideas of Eastern countries?"

The active virtues Keshub noticed in England fired him with a zeal to organize and popularize the Brahmo Samaj and for this purpose he generally adopted the methods used by the missionaries. Propaganda by means of cheap literature was the first step he took towards the spread of Brahmo ideals, and he started a newspaper with its price as one pice per copy. Schools for the education of women and a theological seminary for Brahmos were then established. Boarding schools, study circles, and other familiar institutions of Christian Missions were faithfully copied.

The most revolutionary activity of Keshub was the founding in 1880, of the New Dispensation Samaj; this was a Church, Christian in its main doctrines, but essentially Indian and altogether different from the churches of the West. He held that Europeans with their practical bent of mind could not adequately grasp the essentially mystic doctrines of an Asian Christ, and Indians, especially himself and his followers were better qualified to interpret the teachings of Christ. Keshub was now past middle age and inclined to the pantheistic view so deep rooted in Hinduism, and began to preach Christ in conformity with his views. His ambition now turned to the founding of a church of his own in which the teachings of Indian sages and the Hebrews were to be blended harmoniously in Christ to make a universal religion with himself as the prophet of the new church; and the New Dispensation Samaj was the result of this ambition. For the necessary authority for his mission he invoked Adesh or Revelation a factor hitherto unknown in Bramo Samaj which had always claimed to be a natural and rational religion.

Keshub thus proclaimed to the world the meaning of the New Dispensation: "It is the harmony of all scriptures and Prophets and Dispensations. It is not an isolated creed, but the science which binds and explains and harmonizes all religions. It gives to history a meaning, to the action of Providence a consistence, to quarrelling churches a common bond, and to successive dispensations a continuity. It shows by marvellous synthesis how the different rainbow colours are one in the light of heaven. The New Dispensation is the sweet music of diverse instruments. It is the precious necklace in which are strung together the rubies and the pearls of all ages and climes. It is the celestial court where around enthroned Divinity shine the lights of all heavenly saints and prophets. It is the wonderful solvent which fuses all dispensations into a new chemical compound. It is the mighty absorbent which absorbs all that is true and good and beautiful in the objective world."

In his admiration of Jesus, Keshub with a few followers decided to visit the Jordan where Jesus was baptized. The pilgrims, however, did not deem it necessary to travel all the way to Palestine for this purpose. Keshub and his disciples proceeded to a tank in Calcutta and here the Prophet of the New Dispensation converted the tank into the Jordan by a wave of his hand. He stood on the bank of the tank and exclaimed: "Beloved brethren, we have come to the land of the Jews, and are seated on the bank of the Jordan. Let them that have eyes see. Verily, verily here was the Lord Jesus baptized eighteen hundred years ago. Behold the holy waters wherein was the Son of God immersed." Then anointing himself with oil, Keshub immersed himself thrice in the water saying "Glory to the Father, Glory to the Son, Glory unto the Holy Ghost," and then took a fourth immersion to the glory of "Truth, Wisdom and Joy in One."

Keshub's original antagonism towards idolatry also underwent a change, and he began to view it in the manner of orthodox Hindus as a sincere attempt at finding God and as a stepping stone to higher religion.

In order to gain spiritual insight into the various cults Keshub performed the 'Hom' to the Hindu god Agni, danced mystic dances in honour of Krishna, and performed mysterious rites to hold communion with the shades of departed saints and prophets.

The result of this effort to please every one was universal displeasure. Except the blind followers of the new prophet none was impressed by these activities. Christians, of course, remained aloof. The orthodox Hindus would have nothing to do with the eccentric innovator. The Muslims were not at all interested. Even the Brahmos were not pleased; in fact a section of them had been viewing the activities of their leader with alarm from the very beginning of his career and had made several protests against Keshub's prophetic claims. The introduction of Adesh to explain away the irrational activities of the leader led to considerable misgivings, and when Keshub married his child daughter to the boy Rajah of Cooch Bihar in contravention of the accepted principles of the Samaj, the dissenting section passed a resolution in a meeting excommunicating Keshub. Keshub justified his action on the strength of a new revelation he had received from the Almighty. The dissenters were inclined to believe that revelation was effectively supplemented by a very human desire to get a ruling prince as son-in-law. They went so far as to seize the Brahmo Mandir and Keshub had to invoke the aid of the police.

This quarrel led to a schism in the Samaj and the dissenters under Pandit Sevanath Sastri founded the Saddharana Samaj. Their creed was the following: 1. Belief in the immortality of an infinite Creator; 2. Belief in the immortality of the soul; 3. Belief in the duty and necessity of spiritual worship of God; and 4. Disbelief in any infallible book of man as the means of salvation.

It is not necessary to go into the further history of the Samaj. Keshub died on the 8th January, 1884 and after his death the affairs of the New Dispensation Samaj fell into a bad way, and it now exists mainly on the charity of friends and well-wishers. The Brahmo Samaj has never been a popular religion. At best it supplied a refuge for those Hindus who under the impact of Christianity and Westernism wished to dissociate themselves with the popular Hinduism of the time. As for its grand ideal of uniting all peoples into one religion, it suffered the general fate of all such attempts, i.e.: it added one more sect to the number already existent.

An offshoot of the Brahmo Samaj, inspired mainly by Keshub, was the Prarthana Samaj of Bombay which had an uneventful history. At one time the Samaj had considerable following among the intellectuals of Bombay, and Mahadev Gobind Ranade, Sir Ramakrishna Bhandarkar, Sir Narayana Chandravarkar and other distinguished sons of Maharashtra were its members.

The spread of Christianity, especially the proselytizing activities of the missionaries, had its inevitable repercussions on Hinduism. A section of Hindus began to view with alarm the deflection of large numbers of their co-religionists to Christianity; with the spread of democratic ideals numerical strength began to count in politics and Hindus woke up to the need for stopping the constant flow of their members to Christianity by reforming Hinduism itself.

Swami Dayanand, the founder of the Arya Samaj, had probably this in view when he started his revolt against the old order. He was the Luther of Hindu Reformation. Dayanand was born in a village in Kathiawar and as a boy showed considerable religious precocity. He ran away from home and accepting the role of the Hindu Sanyasi wandered all over India visiting shrines and bathing in holy waters. In 1860 he accepted a blind old Brahmin as his Guru and this sage infused a new vigour in his young disciple.

Founding the Arya Samaj, Dayanand made a three pronged attack on Christianity, Islam and orthodox Hinduism. His horror of idolatry was almost Hebraic. He contemptuously dubbed the existing Hinduism as Pauranic or drawing its inspiration from the Puranas which according to Dayanand were no better than fairy tales. He abolished child marriage among his followers and encouraged widow marriage. His rejection of the Puranas made him extraordinarily loyal to the Vedas. He recognized no inspiration except that of the Veda and no knowledge outside this ancient text. His interpretation of the Veda is embodied in his work *Satyartha Prakash* which is the Bible of the Aryas. Dayanand's followers were called Aryas because they claimed to be the lineal descendants of the Vedic Aryans. He was a monotheist and his philosophy was based on the Vishishta Advaita of Ramanada. But he rejected the idol worship and mysticism of the Vaishnavas.

Unlike Ram Mohan Roy and Keshub Chandra Sen, Dayanand had no English education and he claimed inspiration solely from India and Sanskrit literature. The rising tide of nationalism of the early twentieth century gave an impetus to the Arya Samaj and its militant nationalism appealed to all Hindus especially to the martial races of the Punjab where the movement flourished with extraordinary vigour. In order to reclaim converts back to Hinduism, the Suddhi movement was started which by a religious rite reconverted to Hinduism Indians of other persuasions, an altogether new feature in Hinduism. By a wide interpretation of the word Arya even foreigners were taken into the Hindu fold. The Aryas not only started large scale reconversions to Hinduism, but vigorously combated the proselytizing activities of Christians and Muslims.

The Arya Samaj does not, at present, enjoy the same prestige and popularity it did in the first three decades of the twentieth century. With the rise of the Indian National Congress to power, religion was considerably disentangled from politics, and with the dawn of Indian independence the need for militant nationalism disappeared. Further, dissensions started in the Samaj itself which weakened its solidarity and one-time strength.

Another interesting development of the British period was the starting of missionary activities by the Hindus in Western countries. The Indian Buddhists, as we have seen, were the first missionaries in the world. But with the decay of Buddhism and the revival of Hinduism, the tendency in India had been to keep one's knowledge to oneself. By contact with the British and because of the new spirit of internationalism modern ideas engendered, many Hindus began to feel that India had a message for the world. It was to preach this message that Swami Vivekananda, an able exponent of Advaita, travelled westward and for the first time preached Hinduism to Christians. Both in America and England he had a good hearing. The Ramakrishna misssion continued the work of Vivekananda and established several centres in America and Europe for the dissemination of Hindu knowledge among Christians. These missionaries, being Sanatanists belonging to the old school, do not work for formal conversions but are content to propagate the Hindu view of life for its own sake. Mainly through their efforts and those of their Western sympathisers Hinduism is much better known in Europe and America now than ever before, and some of its doctrines like Yoga have ardent devotees in the West.

CHAPTER XIII

SOME CHRISTIAN COMMUNITIES OF THE WEST COAST

ALTHOUGH Christians form the third largest community in India, their distribution is so wide and allegiance so varied that there are few cohesive units with distinct characteristics. The only communities that have a continuous tradition and history are the Syrian Christians, and a few others on the West Coast who owe their origin to the Portuguese. There are a number of tribal Christian communities who are numerically considerable but politically and economically negligible. All over India and particularly in the South and in Bengal there are quite a number of Christians of the highest social standing but they have not formed into a numerically strong, cohesive community.

THE SYRIAN CHRISTIANS OF MALABAR

We have traced an outline of the history of this interesting Christian community from the time of St. Thomas to the historic revolt of Coonen Cross. This revolt marks an epoch in the history of the Syrians. The revolt was not so much against the authority of the Pope as against that of Goa and the Jesuits. The news of the revolt reaching Rome, Pope Alexander VII sent a mission of Carmelite monks to Cochin to win back the rebels to the Roman fold. They reached Malabar in 1657 and their mission proved eminently successful. They claimed back for Rome 84 churches. While they were actively working for bringing back the remaining 32 which owed allegiance to Mar Thoma I, the Dutch captured the port of Cochin and drove away all European missionaries from areas under their influence. The Syrian Catholics were then left to rule themselves as best as they could without any help from the missionaries.

The Dutch outburst against Catholic missionaries was, however, short-lived, and slowly one by one the missionaries returned. With the Carmelites the Jesuits also came back, and the old feud between the different orders started anew. The *Jus Patronable* by which the king of Portugal had the right to appoint Archbishop of Cranganoor and Bishop of Cochin was invoked by the Portuguese priests while others pointed out that the right ceased to exist since the Portuguese had no influence in Cochin or Cranganoor. The Carmelites established their first church at Chakiat near Ernakulam. A new see was created in Verapoly in 1698 and a Bishop appointed with jurisdiction over all Catholics, Syrian and Latin, in Cochin and Travancore. The Jesuits at Cranganoor and Cochin did not submit to the authority of Verapoly, and when the Papal Bull Multa Proceclare of 1838 virtually abolished the *Padroado* (Portuguese patronage) over Cochin, Cranganoor, Verapoly and Colombo, the Portuguese clergy contended that they were not bound by the Papal Bull. This trouble continued for some time till Pope Leo XIII by his concordat of 1886 finally gave the jurisdiction over Syrian Catholics to the Archbishop of Verapoly.

The Syrian Catholics lived under the See of Verapoly for some time when the old desire to have Bishops of their own began to agitate the Syrians and as a result of their repeated petitions, three Indian Bishops were consecrated. The Syrian Catholic community was divided into three dioceses in 1896 i.e.: Trichur, Ernakulam and Chenganassery. A further See of Kottayam was created shortly afterwards and an Indian Bishop appointed. The desire of the Syrian Catholics for independence did not, however, end here. They were still under the Archbishop of Verapoly. A further effort was made to establish an independent Syrian Catholic hierarchy, and Erankulam was raised to an Archdiocese and Mar Augustine Kandathil was consecrated the first Archbishop of the Syrian hierarchy in 1924. Thus an age old ambition of a section of Syrians was finally realized.

The history of those who, in spite of the efforts of the emissaries of the Pope, refused to recognize the supremacy of the Pope is more eventful and interesting. These under their first Metran (Bishop) who took the titular name of Mar Thoma, came to be known as Puthencoor (new sect) in distinction to the Syrian Catholics who were called Pazhayacoor (old sect). The division was somewhat unnatural as it conformed to no geographical distribution of population. It happened that several towns and villages with but one church each found the congregations divided into Puthencoor and Pazhayacoor, and interminable disputes started between the two sects for the possession of the church and its property. In some churches both parties held services indiscriminately and litigation ruined several Syrian Christian families. This dissension weakened both parties materially and spiritually, and in the bitter quarrels that ensued economic interests often dominated the religious issue.

A vigorous effort was made towards the unity of the Malabar church by well-meaning people and an able Malpan named Kariattil Joseph was selected to go to Rome and represent the facts about the Malabar Church before the Holy See. He took with him a Cattanar named Parammakkel Thoma, a literary genius who has left us an account of his travels.* The Malpan and the Cattanar with two young Malabar Christians who wished to prosecute higher studies in Rome set sail from Madras on the 14th October 1777. They travelled by way of the Cape of Good Hope but due to bad weather and the needs of the merchantman in which they sailed, the party had to go direct to Brazil and from here to Lisbon. From Lisbon they travelled to Genoa and Rome. After having been favourably received in Rome they started on their return journey by way of Portugal and Ceylon. In Portugal the Malpan was consecrated Archbishop of Cranganoor and he returned to India to take charge of his see. But reaching Goa in 1786, the worthy Archbishop died here and with him perished all hopes of a reunion of the Puthencoor and Pazhayacoor Syrians.

* This is probably the first work of its nature written by an Indian in an Indian language (Malayalam). But due to the indifference of Indians in general and of Indian Christians in particular to such matters, the work has not yet been published.

SOME CHRISTIAN COMMUNITIES

The political misfortunes of the House of Cochin added to the decline of the Syrians. The Syrians were traditionally attached to the Perumals and their lineal descendants the Maharajahs of Cochin, and most of them lived in the kingdom of Cochin. The benevolent rulers of this state had a high regard for the Syrians because of their traditional loyalty to their House.

Rajah Martanda Varma of Travancore now started the consolidation and expansion of the then little kingdom of Travancore and made successful inroads into Cochin, and many of the Syrian Christian centres were annexed by Travancore. The Rajahs of Travancore and their nobles looked upon the Syrians as undesirables, as most of them had fought on the side of Cochin in the local wars. Hence while there are no records of active persecution by the rulers themselves, the nobles and chieftains of Travancore treated the ancient privileges of Syrians with scant respect and they were subjected to harsh taxes, forced labour and other humiliations. Some petty chieftains even indulged in active persecution.

This was bad enough. But now suddenly descended on Cochin and northern Travancore with the quickness and violence of a cyclone the armies of Tippu Sultan. Tippu's hatred of the British extended to all Christians and thousands of them were carried away into captivity from Canara and the Tamil countries. Tippu was bent upon punishing the Rajah of Travancore for his alliance with the British and his hordes swept over the Serra which had for centuries enjoyed immunity from foreign invasion. The destruction Tippu carried before him has little to match in the history of Malabar or South India. His Vandals destroyed every temple and church that came in their way and forcibly converted Hindus and Christian alike. The people, terror sticken, fled to the hills and the country was laid waste. Old Christian centres like Palur, Cranganoor, Angamali and Alangad were all deserted. But fortunately before Tippu could complete his work of destruction he had to beat a hasty retreat from the bank of the river Alwaye in order to defend his own capital which the British had attacked in redemption of their promise of help to Travancore.

This no doubt saved Travancore, but the Syrian Christians were all but ruined. Those who came from the hills after the departure of Tippu had to start everything anew. Many fled to central and southern Travancore and founded new colonies there.

During these years of travail, the Puthencoor Syrians suffered worse than the Pazhayacoor. The Catholics because of the strength of their organization could still put up a united front to redress their grievances; they could always count upon the support of European missionaries and some of these came from families of the highest repute in Europe and the Dutch, though Protestant, could in many ways be influenced. During their supremacy in Malabar the Dutch did not actively interest themselves in the Syrians and were more amenable to social and political than religious influence.

If the Puthencoor Syrians had remained united under their chosen leaders they could have, no doubt, done something to have their influence felt. But dissensions broke out among them, and the old passion for Western Asian Bishops flared forth again. To meet their demand a Bishop was sent to the Puthencoor Syrians by the Jacobite Patriarch of Antioch. It is not clear how the Syrians came to accept a Bishop of the monophysite persuasion. They were not, as we have seen, so loyal to doctrines as to the ancient link with Western Asia and any Bishop from this part of the world was probably considered better than local Metrans (Bishops) or Europeans.

Anyway, the occasional arrival of foreign prelates only added to the troubles of Puthencoor Syrians. The Mar Thoma or Metran, the titular head of the Syrian Church, very often refused to submit to the authority of the foreigners whereas a good number of Cattanars and laity, especially those who had some grievance against the local head, readily accepted them. Some enterprising Cattanars even went to Antioch, and obtaining ordination from the Patriarch returned to Malabar and successfully disputed authority with foreign prelates and local Metrans. As long as the Dutch had supremacy over the coastal towns, they did not interest themselves in the internal affairs of the Syrians and were content to receive the passage money of the Bishops who travelled by their ships; even here there were disputes about overcharging which had to be settled by the Maharajah of Travancore.

With the arrival of the British a new element of discord was introduced into the affairs of the Puthencoor Syrians. The first two British Residents in Travancore and Cochin, Cols. Macaulay and Munro, took an active interest in the Syrians. They realized that the greatest need of the Syrians was their economic uplift. Col. Macaulay obtained for the Syrians considerable sums of money from the Travancore Durbar as compensation for certain injuries they had suffered, the exact nature of which is not known, for equal distribution between the Pazhayakoor and Puthencoor Syrians. The portion allotted to the latter proved but another source of trouble and the cost of litigation it had involved has by now mounted to more than ten times the original amount.

Col. Munro effectively helped the Syrians. He was a good administrator and a zealous Christian and he engaged large numbers of Christians in public service which, at that time, carried much prestige and power. In Cochin this innovation did not cause any trouble, as the Maharajah and his nobles had traditionally held the Christians in respect. But in Travancore upper class Hindus viewed this departure from tradition with suspicion and misgivings. Anyway the personality and power of Munro prevailed and the active support he received from the sovereign Rani silenced, for the time being at least, all opposition. It did, however, leave some ill-feeling between Christians and Hindus in Travancore which has come down to the present day. After giving considerable economic support to Christians and generally laying the foundation for their material prosperity, Munro turned his attention to their spiritual uplift. By now the missionary clause had been removed from the Charter of the East India Company, and the first band of Protestant missionaries came to Travancore at the express invitation of Munro. They were at first elated to find the Puthencoor Syrians not owing obedience to Rome and thought the work of making them good Protestants was easy. While the Syrians accepted with alacrity all the material benefits Col. Munro and the missionaries had conferred upon them, they were not equally eager to accept the doctrines and ways of the Anglican Church. Munro and the missionaries were much grieved to find Roman influence among the Puthencoor Syrians, who, from the Synod of Diamper till the Revolt of Coonen Cross, had been under the active leadership of the Catholic Church. While the local heads and Cattanars in their conferences with the missionaries admitted the need for removal of Catholic practices, they always pointed out the practical difficulties that had to be overcome. As the Portuguese had worked for the separation of the Cattanars from their wives, the C.M.S. Mission now tried to get the celibate Cattanars married. The Cattanars pleaded poverty as an excuse for celibacy. Munro decided to eliminate this excuse by promising allowances to married clergymen and even declared a prize of Rs.400 for the first Cattanar that would marry. The temptation was too much for the Cattanars and they started marrying.

Another Catholic practice that annoyed the missionaries was the prayers said for the dead. The Cattanars' main income was from Kurbanas (Masses) said for the souls of the dead, and if the practice were to be withdrawn, it would have ruined them completely as the laity then would not understand the need for clergymen. Here even the promise of allowances did not carry conviction to the Cattanars. These now told the missionaries that they were not so independent as they had imagined but had to abide by the decisions of the Patriarch of Antioch and his accredited representatives. The arrival of these dignitaries always caused trouble for the missionaries; the activities of the missionaries, on the other hand, were considered an interference by the foreign prelates. The Metrans and the Cattanars suffered much between the two. One Bishop went to the extent of flogging Cattanars into obedience and another, Mar Athanasius who arrived in Malabar in November 1825, threatened Mar Philoxenus, the local Metran, "that he would himself come, strip him of his robes and take by force his cross and staff and break them to pieces." Mar Philoxenus appealed to the British and they had the foreign Bishop deported. It appeared that the old procedure under the Portuguese was being repeated and there was considerable commotion among the Syrians who thought that the British interference was uncalled for.

The trouble between the Syrians and the missionaries came to a climax when Bishop Wilson visited Travancore and in an interview with Cheppat Mar Dionysius, the then head of the Puthencoor Syrians, pointed out that the time had come to introduce the much needed reforms in the Syrian Church along Protestant lines if not strictly Anglican lines. Mar Dionysius now decided that the time had come to settle once for all whether the Syrian Church should remain under Antioch or go Protestant. He convened a Synod of Puthencoor Syrians in January 1836 at Mavelikkara. The Synod acknowledged with gratitude all the help the Syrians had received from the British, but formally rejected all innovations on Anglican lines and reaffirmed the supremacy of Antioch. After this the missionaries left the Syrians to themselves in all matters concerning doctrine and practice, though they maintained cordial relations with them and were ever helpful.

The work of the missionaries did not, however, go in vain. Some of the Syrians were deeply affected by the simplicity of Protestant worship, and the Seminary founded and superintended by the missionaries had turned out many young Syrians with definite Protestant leanings. These founded under a Cattanar named Abraham, 'the Wickliffe of the Syrian Church', a new autonomous church; the service in the new church was conducted in Malayalam, prayers for the dead were given up and a Malayalam liturgy replaced the Syrian. The movement naturally found favour with the missionaries and the British, and under the influence of the Residents both the Travancore and Cochin Durbars recognized the new church and the Bishop. The members of this new autonomous church are known as Mar Thoma Syrians. Thus the Syrian church has, at present, three main divisions: The Catholics, the Jacobites and the Mar Thomaites.

Racially the Syrians are divided into Nordists and Sudists.

The Sudists are at present few in number and are fast getting absorbed into the powerful Nordists. The origin of the division is obscure and is lost in conflicting legends. One view is that the Sudists are later immigrants from Syria who settled near Quilon and retained their racial purity by not intermarrying with the Northerners of Cranganoor who had come under Canai Thoma. The Sudists retain the complexion and features of pure Syrians. Another account, current among the Nordists, is that Canai Thoma when he settled down in Mahadevarpatanam allotted the southern quarters of the colony to his dependants whereas he lived with his relatives and equals in the northern portion. The Malabar Christians treated the residents of the northern fashionable quarters as equals and intermarried with them whereas the southerners were not considered worthy of equality of treatment.

Whatever the origin, the feeling that existed between the two divisions during the middle ages was bitter. Intermarriage, interdining and even social intercourse between the two were taboo. Their disputes were even carried into religious congregations. An interesting legend which explains the origin of two churches close to one another in the town of Kaduthuruthi will illustrate the nature of the feelings that existed between the Sudists and Nordists. The older church known as Valia Palli or Big Church was built in the fourth century of the Christian era. In the ninth century when Cranganoor was deserted by Christians due to some civil commotion there, a large number of Syrians migrated to Kaduthuruthi, then as now a Syrian Christian stronghold. Some of these immigrants were Sudists and they were alloted a space behind the Nordists in the church; and so the Sudist congregation had to kneel behind the Nordists. The Sudists complained of this pointed humiliation to Bishop Mar John and the prelate ordered the parish priest and trustees of the church to remove the humiliating barrier. The men, it appears, agreed to remove the barrier, but not the women. They went on a deputation to the Bishop and demanded that he should cancel his orders; upon this the Bishop said that if the ladies did not like his orders they were free to build a church of their own. The women took the Bishop at his word and under the leadership of a wealthy lady named Elia (Elizabeth) built a church of their own where they could worship the Lord without suffering the presence of the Sudists.

With the modern tendency for fusion, intermarriages between the Sudists and Nordists are becoming common, and the time does not appear far when the Sudists will be absorbed by the Nordists.

At the beginning of the nineteenth century, as we have seen, the fortunes of the Syrians were at a low ebb. With the loss of prestige and power of the Rajah of Cochin, the indifference of the Rajahs of Travancore towards Christians, the oppression of petty chieftains, and finally with the invasion of the Serra by Tippu, the Syrians were on the verge of ruin and when the British came as the suzerain of Cochin and Travancore, they found everywhere signs of fallen glory. But with the active support of the first two British Residents, the community made a vigorous attempt at revival; although later Residents were not actively interested in the Syrians, the removal of their disabilities and the wary eye the British kept on any attempts at discrimination against Christians had a salutary effect on the progress of the community. The good work done by the missionaries in the matter of education was continued by the Syrians of all denominations and literacy and higher education spread rapidly throughout the community. In the matter of female education, the Syrians can be said to be pioneers in South India. The old occupations of trade and agriculture were actively pursued, and the twentieth century found the Syrians a flourishing community, in fact economically and politically the most important in the States of Cochin and Travancore.

The Syrian Church has been accused by Western writers of its want of missionary zeal. This has been true of the Syrians till the arrival of British and American missionaries. They were generally content to maintain their own entity in a country not familiar with Christian ways. This was the wisest course they could have possibly taken in India. Without any political influence anywhere except the comparatively small state of Cochin, if they had launched on any active proselytizing work especially among the lower classes and thereby engendered the hostility and contempt of caste Hindus among whom they lived, the community would have probably suffered extinction particularly after the commercial influence of the Syrians had waned and the Arabs had come into prominence. The main concern of the community in those days had been to keep themselves alive and for this they had to adopt many of the usages of the Hindus. Caste was one of these. Till recently, the Syrian Christians rigidly observed untouchability. Slaves and low castes were not allowed to enter a Syrian Christian household. Conversion from lower classes was discouraged and if it did occur, the convert remained an outcaste for all practical purposes. The respectable did not intermarry or interdine with him and the orthodox observed untouchability. Converts from higher castes were welcome though active work for proselytizing was not done by Syrians even among the higher classes. Only with the general breakdown of caste in India have the Syrians given up their old notions of caste.

Socially the Syrians have been following their ancient traditions inherited from Nambudiri ancestors. Purificatory ceremonies after death and childbirth were performed; under the Portuguese these were given a Christian significance. The marriage ceremony of the Syrians is still performed by the bridegroom tying the *thali* round the bride's neck like the Brahmins, the *thali* being blessed by a Christian priest before the ceremonial tying.

In the matter of dress, men followed the Nambudiri tradition, wearing but a loin cloth. Shirts were not used except by those affected by Syrian and European innovations. In the manner of hair dressing, the Syrians had given up the Nambudiri practice but shaved their heads clean like Syrians and Arabs. The dress of women, however, was different from those of Nambudiris. Unlike Nambudiri women they covered the upper part of the body by jackets. The lower garment was peculiar to Syrian women, nowhere else in the world the style being noticeable.

A piece of white cloth about four feet wide and ten long was wound round the waist leaving at the back a 'peacock tail' done into exquisite folds. The modern tendency is for wearing Saris but no Syrian Christian lady worth her name ever thinks of adopting the western frock. In the matter of wearing ornaments the older generation still adhere to the ear rings, necklaces, bangles and anklets of the Nambudiri tradition while younger ladies show a marked preference for modern styles. Syrian Christian women are modest and retiring, though not observing Purdah; they combine in themselves the reserve and modesty of Indians with the self reliance of the women of the West.

GOANS AND MANGALOREANS

In the West Coast due to the zeal of the early Portuguese missionaries there sprang up several communities of Christians. Mangalore and the adjoining regions have been strong centres of Christianity from the time of the Portuguese and many families of the higher classes of Hindus and Muslims had embraced Christianity during the Portuguese period. The origin of the Mangalore community of Christians may possibly be traced to the Apostles though positive proofs are wanting.

At the time of Tippu's invasion the Christians of South Canara were a powerful community. Tippu's soldiery all but annihilated the community. Over fifty thousand of them were deported to Mysore. "The daughters of many of them were beautiful girls, and Tippu Sultan was determined to have them for his seraglio, but this their parents refused; the parents were then seized and their hands were tied behind them. The Chamars or sandal makers were then sent for and the parents' noses, ears and upper lips were cut off. They were then mounted on asses, their faces towards the tail and led through the city."* A large number of Christians fled to Coorg the Chief of which brave independent kingdom gave them protection and asylum. Tippu's persecution was, however, short-lived and after his defeat and death, about 20,000

*James Scurry, quoted in *Captivity of Canara Christians* by S. N. Saldana.

captives who remained alive returned to Canara and rebuilt their churches. The Canarese Christians too, like their brethren farther south made a vigorous attempt at revival and under the British emerged as a well organized and respectable community.

The greatest gain of the Portuguese was in Goa, the capital of their once glorious Eastern Empire. Goa, as is well known, has remained under the Portuguese to this day, though the population and geographical position make it an integral part of India. The growth of this picturesque and historic city under the Portuguese is of particular interest to us.

Goa, situated on the north of the Malabar Coast, enjoys a hoary tradition reaching to the mythical Parasurama, the Brahmin warrior who is fabled to have miraculously reclaimed the Coast from the sea. The earliest name of the city was Gopakapuri or the City of Cowherds pointing to the building of the city by some pastoral tribe. The city had an eventful history and has changed hands many times. It was, however, the Portuguese who had brought fame to the city.

The Portuguese who commanded the Eastern Seas in the beginning of the sixteenth century, were on the look out for a suitable site in India for the capital of their Eastern possessions. Alfonso de Albuquerque, the great Portuguese admiral and Empire builder, decided that Goa should be the capital of the East. Several considerations influenced his decision. Its central position on the coast was favourable for a proper command of the Arabian Sea and its insular position made defence by a naval power easy. Further Goa was situated in the dominion of the Sultan of Bijapur and because of their bitter quarrels with the Arabs, the early Portuguese considered all Muslims as their natural enemies and no excuse was considered necessary for seizing a port belonging to a Muslim ruler. Besides, the Portuguese had an old score to pay off; when Vasco da Gama came to India in 1498, Adil Shah, king of Bijapur, sent the admiral of his fleet stationed at Goa, a Spanish Jew, to receive him but with secret instructions to destroy the Portuguese fleet. Vasco da Gama happened to discover the real intentions of the wily envoy and the Jew was captured and sent to Portugal where he was converted and given the name of Gaspar da Gama.

Goa at the time of Albuquerque was a goodly port with a fine harbour through which considerable volume of traffic passed to and from the Deccan. It was the main port of the Deccan for embarkation of Muslim pilgrims to Mecca and this itself gave the port considerable standing and importance at the time. The population of Goa was largely Hindu and the Muslim Governor with his 'two hundred Turks' tyrannised the population, imposed humiliating taxes on them and practised many exactions. The Hindus were on the look out for a deliverer, and Timoja, a Hindu Chief, lent active support to Albuquerque in his designs on the city. In February 1510, Albuquerque with a fleet of twenty sails of the line and a few small vessels surprised Goa and the port fell without a blow.

Albuquerque, having gained the city without loss of a single man, was extremely lenient to the population. He gave strict orders to his men not to interfere with the citizens and not to harm a man. He promised relaxation of the rigours of taxation and assured to all security of person and property.

Shortly after, the Portuguese left the city as suddenly as they took it. Adil Shah, coming to know of the fall of the port made extensive preparations to recapture Goa and in May 1510 laid siege to the city with a force of 60,000 men. The Portuguese were not prepared for such an attack and after an ineffectual resistance evacuated the city and moved their fleet off the harbour. The rainy season now set in and the Portuguese were forced to lie at anchor for better weather and supplies. As the rigour of the monsoon abated Albuquerque, reinforced with men and supplies from Cranganoor and Portugal, attacked the city. There was stiff and bitter fighting but the Portuguese won and they took the city in October 1510; and it has remained under them ever since.

Albuquerque, learning by the experience of his first occupation of the city, made all haste to put the city in a proper state of defence. He repaired the ramparts and turrets. A citadel was built in such a hurry that even the principal officers and Albuquerque himself had to work as common labourers day and night. When the construction was completed he congratulated his men and officers, and with a view to perpetuate their bravery in the battle ordered a slab to be put in a prominent place in the citadel with his own name and those of his officers inscribed on it. But the captains started quarrelling over precedence in inscribing the names and Albuquerque in sheer disgust ordered the following words to be inscribed on the stone: Lapideh Qem Reprobaverunt Edificantes: The stone the builders condemned.

Soon after the taking of the city by the Portuguese, the Franciscans aided by civil authorities started mission work in Goa. The Muslims were treated by Albuquerque and his successors with particular severity, but the Hindus were treated with much consideration. The Franciscans had started active mission work when the Jesuits arrived, and the citizens were induced to accept Christianity in many ways. Converts were treated with special favour and intermarriages between the Portuguese and Indians were actively encouraged. The Portuguese were singularly free from racial prejudices, and for them the needs of the soul were of greater importance than the pigmentations of skin.

Under the Jesuits Goa became the centre of Christianity in the East. In 1534 it was raised to an episcopal see. The Inquisition was established in 1560. In Goa at least there was no stigma attached to the Parangi and his religion and many Hindus of high standing embraced Christianity and shared with the Portuguese high positions in the state. The better class of present day Goans trace their descent from one or the other of high caste Hindu families that embraced Christianity during the heyday of Portuguese power in the East.

The Goans, though not so caste ridden as the Syrian Christians, have all along maintained the pride of race inherited from their ancestors. The higher classes still refuse to intermarry with lesser breeds even when these have risen to positions of economic equality or superiority. The modern tendency among the younger generation is, however, to set aside antiquated notions of social superiority and encourage intermarriage and interdining.

With the decline and fall of the Portuguese Empire in the East, Goa suffered severe losses and the once great city, known as the Lisbon of the East, fell into virtual ruin. The rise of the Maharatha power made considerable inroads into territories once dominated by Goa and the trade of Goa was lost to the rising ports of British India. The country surrounding the port could not support the large urban population of Goa, and the Goans started migrating in large numbers to the cities that were rapidly rising in British India.

By their unity and communal solidarity, no less by industry, the Goans have managed to get positions of influence in Indian cities. Bombay is the main centre of Goan immigration and they have contributed not a little to the building up of this great port and its prosperity. In the provincial services, in the Customs, in the Port Trust and in the Railways the number of Goan employees in Bombay are quite considerable; the learned professions have claimed the more intellectual and enterprising. The lower classes, drawn mainly from the farming classes of Goa, are employed in Bombay in occupations suitable to their ability and education. Goans have a particular genius for music and the culinary art. Above all they are staunch Christians, very peace loving. They offer a pleasing contrast to the Syrians noted for their thorough going individualism and excitability. The Goans are passionately attached to their beautiful but now poor country.

The mother tongue of the Goans is Konkani usually written in Roman script. The higher classes are familiar with Portuguese while those who live in India have more or less adopted English.

Unlike the Syrians whose long history has been marked by antagonism to the ways of the West, the Goans have been partial to European culture and manners. The better classes, both men and women, have adopted Western fashions in dress. The orthodox, especially women, still adhere to garments peculiar to Goa, while those who have emancipated themselves from the traditions of the past but not given up Indian ways have adopted the Sari.

CHAPTER XIV

CHRISTIANITY IN MODERN INDIA

WHILE, in the nineteenth century, mission work had been all important in India, in the twentieth century the emphasis has been on the Church as distinct from mission. As a result of the activities of the missionaries, indigenous congregations of considerable numerical strength had sprung up all over India. Most of the missions were under the control of foreign Boards or Churches and the missionaries were mostly paid employees. With the ever-growing numbers of Indian ministers and missionaries, the undesirability and in some cases the impracticability of continuing the old system became obvious. But the general poverty of Indian congregations and organizations made autonomy difficult and the problem is yet to be solved. The withdrawal of the British and the partition of India have made the problem more difficult but the solution imperative.

The identity of interests of different missions in India controlled from different centres of the world led to the formation of the National Christian Council in India in 1914. The Council has its headquarters at Nagpur with 18 Provincial Councils under it. While questions of doctrine and ecclesiastical policy remain outside the purview of the Council, its avowed objects are:

1. To stimulate thinking and investigation on missionary questions, to enlist in the solution of these questions the best knowledge and experience to be found in India and other countries; and to make the results available for all churches and missions in India.

2. To help to co-ordinate the activities of the Provincial Councils and to assist them to co-operate with each other where such co-operation is desirable.

CHRISTIANITY IN MODERN INDIA

3. Through common consultation to help to form Christian public opinion and bring to bear on the moral and social problems of the day.

4. To be in communication with the International Missionary Council regarding such matters as call for consideration or action from the point of view of the Indian Mission Field as a whole.

5. To make provisions for the convening of a National Christian Conference when such in the opinion of the Council is desirable.

Of greater importance than the Council, is the Church Union movement in India. The pioneers of this movement were the Presbyterians who held a general Conference in Allahabad in 1871 with a view to bring about some union between the different churches and missions in India. An All India Union was at that time considered impracticable, but it was suggested in the Conference that there should be periodical meetings of ministers and elders. As a result of these meetings the Indian Presbyterian Confederation was formed in 1873 and in 1875 the Presbyterian Alliance of India. For some time the idea of an organic union was dropped, but in 1900 the American Arcot Mission and two Scotch missions decided that union could no more be delayed at least in South India. Accordingly a scheme was drawn up which was approved by the Reformed Church in America and the Free Church of Scotland, and the consummation of the Union took place in Madras on September 25th, 1902, and the foundation of the United Church of South India was firmly laid. The Presbyterian Alliance of the North found the example stimulating and eight different sections of the Presbyterian church united into one General Assembly.

The union of Presbyters led other missions to reconsider their position, and the London Missionary Society and the Mission of the American Board, having everything in common but kept apart by the fact that one party came from one side of the Atlantic and the other from the other, united in the year 1905. The good work did not stop here, and negotiations were started with a view to a greater union with the South Indian Synod of the Presbyterian Church. The union of Presbyterian and Congregational churches was something new, but in India at least Christians felt that the innovation would be desirable and practicable. As negotiations progressed, the idea of a general union of all South Indian Churches began to gain ground. The difficulties were many, but these only stimulated the efforts of the unionists. While the idea was still under discussion the first world war broke out and the German Basel Mission of Malabar joined the Union. This gave an impetus to the movement. After protracted negotiations and determined efforts, the idea of Church Union was formally accepted by a large majority in the General Assembly of the South India United Church in 1946, and a practical scheme was drawn up. Accordingly, the Church of South India was inaugurated on 27th September 1947, when the South India Diocese of the Anglican Church, the South Indian Provincial of the Methodist Church and the South India United Church (with the exception of the North Tamil Council) became one Church. This bold measure is capable of wider expansion and the time is not far when other churches would fall into line and a Church of India will be established. In fact, the sponsors of the Union believe that the example of South India will soon be followed elsewhere and not at a very distant date all the Churches of the East and West will unite into a World Church, 'the body of Christ'. The exclusive organization and traditions of the Roman Catholic Church alone appear at present to offer serious difficulties for the realization of this ambitious ideal.

The Catholic Church in India has at present ten arch-dioceses including Ernakulam and Trivandrum of the Syrian Rite, and fifty Bishoprics with a papal internuncio. The *Padroado* has been finally abolished in India in 1950 and an Indian Archbishop was appointed to the important See of Bombay where before the abolition of the *Padroado* Portuguese and English Archbishops had to rule by turn. In 1952, the year in which India celebrated the nineteenth centenary of the advent of Apostle Thomas,

Valerian Gracias, the Archbishop of Bombay, was made a Cardinal, the first Indian to be elevated to this eminence.

The Anglican Church, known in India as the Church of India, Burma and Ceylon, has its metropolitan in Calcutta and thirteen diocesan Bishops. The Baptists have four Church Unions and Councils, each autonomous in its own sphere after the practice of the Baptists. The Lutherans have six churches. The Methodist Church of Southern Asia has four Resident and Presiding Bishops in India. And the Mar Thoma Syrian Church has a Bishop at Tiruvalla.

In the twentieth century peculiar problems have risen for the Churches and the Missions in India. The proselytizing activities of the missionaries are viewed with distinct disfavour. Real Christian work, by which was meant humanitarian work, is welcome but conversion is obnoxious. It is doubtful if a mere love of humanitarian work would produce zealots of the type of Francis Xavier, De Nobili, Henry Martyn, Carey, Gordon Hall and George Bowen. Anyway, Christians have accepted the challenge. Wherever there is human suffering, the missionary and the minister are there. The splendid work Christian organizations are doing to ameliorate the suffering of lepers in India is unique and too well known to be mentioned in detail here. Christians run about 700 dispensaries, four hundred hospitals and three hundred industrial schools. They conduct about 90 Colleges, 800 High Schools, 1,500 Middle Schools and thousands of primary and elementary schools all over the country.

Christian organizations are actively interested in welfare problems in India. The National Christian Council, the Y.M.C.A. and the American Marathi Mission are the pioneers in welfare movements in India.

★   ★   ★   ★

With the declaration of Indian Independence on 15th August 1947, a new era has begun for Indian Missions and Churches and what the future of Christianity in India will be only time can tell. The Constitution of India has been framed by able and conscientious men and women brought up in the liberal traditions of the British, and it guarantees equality of treatment to all castes and creeds, freedom of worship and the right to propagate religious ideas by peaceful methods. The first cabinet of free India was also formed in the spirit of the Constitution and it had members of all important communities in India. The first Cabinet Minister belonging to an Indian Christian community was Dr. John Matthai the well-known financier. Later Rajkumari Amrit Kaur, a staunch follower of Mahatma Gandhi and a devout Christian lady, was also taken in the cabinet.

All this augurs well for the future, and as long as the present leadership lasts Christians as a community have little to fear. But whether the same liberal traditions will be followed after the passing away of the present generation, the future alone will show.

BIBLIOGRAPHY

Anantakrishna Ayyar, L. K., *Anthropology of the Syrian Christians*
Banerji, Brajendranath, *Begum Samru*
Banerji, Gauranganath, *India as known to the Ancient World*
Cherian, P., *The Malabar Syrians and the Church Missionary Society*
Feroli, S. J., *Jesuits in Malabar*
Heras, Rev. Henry, S. J., *The Two Apostles of India*
Hewat, Elizabeth G. K., *Christ and Western India*
Kaye, Sir John, *Christianity in India*
Krishnaswami Aiyangar, S., *Ancient India*
Maclagan, Sir Edward, *The Jesuits and the Great Mogul*
Medlycot, Bishop A. E., *India and the Apostle Thomas*
Ogilvie, J. N., *The Apostles of India*
Panikkar, K. M., *Malabar and the Portuguese*
Rapson, E. J., *Ancient India*
Thomas, Dr. P. J., *Syrian Christian Literature* (Malayalam)

INDEX

Abbanes, 19
Abdiso of Geziresh, Patriarch, 79, 82, 83
Abdulla, 107
Abraham, Cattanar, 231
Abul Fazal, 111
Achaia, 19
Acts of Holy Apostle Thomas, 19
Adam, Mr., 215
Adelkhan, 117
Adesh, Revelation, 218, 220
Adil Shah, 236, 237
Adi Samaj, 216
Advaita philosophy, 210, 211, 222.
Advaitin, 211
Aethalstan, 23
Afghanistan, 20, 21
Africa, 2, 44, 49, 175
Agni, 219
Agra, 105, 106, 111, 112, 114-118, 122-125, 130
Ahimsa, 13
Ahtallah, Patriarch, 103
Akbar, 105-111, 114, 118, 121-124, 130
Alangad, 227
Alberuni, 204
Albuquerque, Admiral, 50, 236, 237, 238
Aleppo, 122
Alexander, 4
Alexander VI, Pope, 50
Alexander VII, Pope, 224
Alexandria, 5, 7, 13, 23, 24
Alexandrian library, 97
Alexio de Menezies, *see* Menezies
Alfred, King, 23
Aligarh, 129
Allahabad, 241
Alvars, 210
Alwaye, 227
Amboli Pass, 56
America, 6, 185, 186, 187, 196, 198, 222, 223, 241

American Arcot Mission, 241
American Board, 241
American Marathi Mission, 243
American Missionaries, 233
Americans, 187, 196
Amherst, Lord, 188
Amir Singh, 160
Amir-Ul-Umra, 131
Amouchi, 35
Amrit Kaur, Rajkumari, 244
Anabaptists, 180
Anantakrishna Ayyar, 35
Ananta Sastri, 195
Andhras, 2
Andrew, St., 19
Angamali, 83-89, 100-102, 206, 227
Anglican, 146, 230, 231
Anglican Church, 242, 243
Anglo-Indians, 177, 184
Anglo-Saxon Chronicle, 23
Anthropology of the Syrian Christians, 35
Antioch, 40, 228, 230, 231
Antoine, M., 145
Antonio da Porto, Father, 79
Antonio de Rozario, Don, 119, 120
Antonio, Don, 98
Antony and Cleopatra, 135
Antony Monserrate, 107
Anupshahr, 138
Apollo Bunder, 194
Apostles, 25, 157, 235
Apostles of India, 24
Apostle Thomas, *see* Thomas Apostle
Appa Khande Rao, 135
Appar, 208
Aquaviva, Rudolf, 107
Arabia, 5, 25, 105, 117, 174
Arabian Sea, 44, 54, 236
Arabic, 173, 174
Arabs, 7, 10, 38, 44, 45, 49, 51-54, 56, 58, 107, 234, 236
Arakkan Coast, 114, 115

246

INDEX

Archbishop of Canterbury, 147, 156
Archer, Maj., 144
Arishtakarman, 27
Armenians, 55, 87, 106, 119, 121, 122
Aryan Path, 13
Aryans, 7, 67, 221
Aryas, 221, 222
Arya Samaj, 221, 222
Aryavarta, 67
Ashram (de Nobile), 65
Asia, 2, 40, 44, 98, 174, 177, 198
Asia Minor, 5, 41
Asian Christians, 18
Asian culture, 122
Ashtamurti, 27
Asoka, 1, 9, 13
Assaye, 139
Astaruth, 26
Astreges, 27
Atesh, Fire-eater, 109
Athanasius, Mar, 230
Atlantic, 42, 45, 241
Augustine, Kandathil Mar, 225
Augustinians, 119, 120, 164
Augustus, Caesar, 7
Aurangazeb, 109, 118, 121, 124, 126, 127, 131
Avarian, 27
Avignon, 42
Ayahs, 136
Azan, 122

Babur, 103
Babylon, 87, 90, 91, 93, 94, 95, 97, 100, 101, 103
Bacon, —, 145
Baconian philosophy, 188
Bactria, 1
Bahadur Shah, 124
Banerji, 136
Banga Singh, 138
Baptist Missionary Society, 163, 164, 176
Baptists, 180, 243
Barsana, battle of, 129
Bartholomew, Apostle, 23-27

Barygaza, 6
Bassein, 79
Batuta, Ibn, 204
Baveru Jataka, 7
Bede, St., 26
Begum Samru, 136
Benares, 120
Benedict de Goes, 110
Bengal, 106, 113, 114, 115, 119, 124, 161, 166, 169, 185, 190, 192, 212, 224
Bengal, Bay of, 5, 115
Bengali, 162, 165, 167
Berhampore, 174
Bernice, 5, 7
Bernier, 109
Bhagavat, 207
Bhagavat Gita, 213
Bhaktadasa, 212
Bhakti, 211
Bhandarkar, Sir Ramakrishna, 221
Bharatars, 51
Bharatpur, 128, 142, 145
Bhopal, 124
Bhutan, 166
Bible, 155, 166, 173, 185, 190, 200, 214, 221
Bie, Col., 165
Bijapur, 117, 236
Black Sea, 5
Blanshard, Chaplain, 170
Bolan, 1
Bombay, 26, 168, 170, 182, 187, 188, 191, 194, 196, 202, 220, 221, 239, 242, 243
Book of Hymns, 155
Botelho, Father, 117
Bourbons, 124
Bowen, George, 191, 243
Brahminism, 14
Brahmins, 4, 8, 10, 13-16, 25, 28, 36, 49, 64-68, 71, 106, 117, 154, 181, 182, 191, 192, 221, 234, 236
Brahmo Mandir, 220
Brahmo Samaj, 213, 215, 216, 218, 220
Brazil, 226

British, 49, 112, 121, 126, 127, 128, 135, 136, 138-146, 148, 156, 159, 160, 165, 175, 177, 182, 183, 185, 188-190, 192, 193, 197-199, 202, 203, 204, 205, 214, 216, 222, 227, 229, 230, 231, 233, 236, 239, 240, 244
Britto, Don Esteben de, 102-103
Broach, 6, 42
Brown, David, 171
Brunsdon, 165
Buchanan, Claudius, 171, 179, 180
Buddha, 13, 198, 206, 214
Buddhism, 1, 2, 9, 206, 207, 208, 222
Buddhists, 2, 11, 13, 204, 207, 211, 222
Burma, 166
Burmese, 69, 166
Burn, Col., 142
Busi, Father, 118
Buxar, 128

Cabinet of Free India, 244
Cafres, 46
Caius, 6
Calcutta, 147, 161, 162, 163, 164, 165, 167, 168, 169, 170, 171, 173, 174, 180, 187, 188, 191, 214, 215, 219, 243
Calicut, 38, 44, 45, 46, 48, 50, 52
Cambridge, 171
Campbell, Capt., 148
Canai Thoma, 30, 31, 32, 33, 232
Canara, 227, 236
Canarese, 166
Canarese Christians, 236
Canning, Paul, 112
Canton, 59
Cape Comorin, 8, 53
Cape of Good Hope, 44, 83, 226
Captivity of Canara Christians, 235
Cardinal Valerian Gracias, See Valerian Gracias
Carey, William, 151, 162-167, 197, 243
Carmelite monks, 224, 225
Carneyro, Father, 81

Carthusians, 80
Castanheda, Ferna Lopez de, 46
Catherine, Queen (of Portugal), 81
Catholics, 39, 40, 80, 146, 150, 161, 169, 185, 225, 230, 231, 242
Cattanars, 77, 88, 90, 93, 95, 96, 97, 99, 101, 104, 226, 228, 230, 231
Celestial Empire (of China), 59
Central Asia, 2, 3, 25
Central Asian hordes, 1
Central India, 2
Ceylon, 26, 29, 32, 45, 72, 187, 226
Chaitanya, 212
Chakiat, 225
Chaldean Bishop, 81
Chamars, 235
Chanda Sahib, 75
Chandragupta, 1
Chandranagar, 127
Chandravarkar, Sir Narayana, 221
Charnock, Job, 168
Chayil, 16
Chenganassery, 225
Chengiz Khan, 105
Cheppat Dionysius, Mar, 231
Chera, 3, 6, 8, 9, 14, 16, 29, 37
Cheraman Loka Perum Chetty, 34
China, 16, 42, 59, 151
Chinese, 10, 59, 166
Chista Seva Sangh Ashram, 201
Chittagong, 114
Chola, 3, 6, 16, 29, 37
Chowghat, 14, 15
Christ, 2, 14, 18, 19, 24, 25, 30, 39, 55, 57, 59, 69, 70, 71, 93, 94, 96, 109, 155, 163, 172, 186, 190, 200, 201, 204, 212, 215, 218, 242
Christ, Asian, 218
Christ, European, 49, 50
Christ and Satyagraha, 201
Christendom, 23, 39, 49, 59, 71, 72, 202
Christian Emir, 37
Christian Faquirs, 119
Christian Knowledge Society, 182
Christian Medical College Hospital, 198

INDEX

Christian Sastra, 214
Christians, St. Thomas, 48, 96, 209
Chrysopolis, Bishop of, 117
Church Missionary Society, 176, 178
Church of England, 200
Church of India, 242
Church of India, Burma and Ceylon, 243
Church of South India, 242
Church Union Movement, 241, 242
Chuttanutty, 168, 169
Citerior India, 25
Civil Disobedience Movement, 200, 201, 202
Clement VIII, Pope, 86, 87, 93
Clive, 152, 161, 184, 185
C.M.S. Mission, 230
Cochin, 18, 30, 35, 37, 38, 44, 45, 48, 50, 51, 52, 53, 54, 58, 61, 68, 69, 71, 81, 84, 88-93, 96, 98, 101-103, 124, 150, 187, 224, 225, 227, 229, 231, 233, 234
Cochinites, 99
Colombo, 225
Columbus, 5, 6, 44
Congregational Churches, 242
Congress, 202, 203
Constantinople, 174
Constantius, 26
Constitution of India, 244
Cooch Bihar, 220
Coonen Cross revolt, 15, 104, 224, 230
Coorg, 235
Copenhagen, 156
Cornwallis, Lord, 142, 170, 175
Coromandel Coast, 27
Corrie, 173, 190
Corsi, Father, 109, 112
Coryate, 122, 123
Cosmas, Indian Voyager, 25, 26
Cossys, 168
Costa, Dona Juliana Diaz, 119, 124-125
Counter Reformation, 64, 105
Covilham, Dom Pedro de, 50

Cranganoor, 6, 16, 33, 37, 38, 45, 48, 50, 51, 61, 69, 71, 78, 81, 91, 95, 101, 102, 150, 225, 226, 227, 232, 237
Crete, 19
Crusade on the Naboabs, 168
Cruz, Joao, 52-53
Cuddalore, 157, 158, 162

Dacca, 115, 120
Danes, 23, 165
Danish Liturgy, 155
Dara, Prince, 118, 124
Dauphine, 41
Dayanand, Swami, 221, 222
Dean, Mrs., 143
Deccan, 2, 237
Delhi, 105, 114, 118, 120, 121, 124, 125, 128-133, 135, 136, 138, 139, 142
Demetrius, Bishop of Alexandria, 24, 25
Demetrius, Georgian, 42
Denmark, 153, 156
De Silva, astronomer, 120
Devaram, 207
Devas, 208
Diamper, 37, 93, 96, 97, 100, 101, 103
Diaz, Bartholomew, 44
Dinapore, 173, 174
Divus, 26
Doab, 129, 141, 142
Dollar Land, 186
Dominicans, 50, 102
Dravidian liturgy, 30
Dravidians, 7
Duarte Leito, Father, 110
Dubois, Abbe, 75
Duff, Alexander, 160, 167, 188, 190, 191, 214
Dutch, 117, 124, 150, 153, 154, 224, 225, 228

Eastern Church, 21
East India Company, 124, 151, 152, 156, 158, 162, 164, 167, 169, 170, 171, 175, 176, 177, 178, 179, 180, 181, 182, 183, 185, 187, 229

Ebrahim Lodi, 105
Edessa, 21, 22, 23, 30
Edinburgh Review, 178
Egyptians, 5, 7, 10
Elementary Compendium of Theology, 155
Elia, Lady, 233
Elizabeth I, Queen, 144
Ellis, British Factor at Patna, 127
Elwin, Father Verrier, 201
England, 23, 147, 156, 157, 159, 162, 165, 170, 174, 175, 177, 178, 179, 183, 184, 185, 187, 188, 192, 196, 198, 200, 201, 215, 217, 218, 222
English, 49, 111, 112, 114, 117, 124, 127, 140, 150, 152, 153, 156, 157, 158, 159, 160, 161, 163, 164, 167, 168, 169, 170, 173, 176, 188, 190, 194, 198, 214, 215, 222, 239
Englishmen, 127, 128, 145, 167, 168, 176, 177, 179, 180, 186, 188, 192, 199, 217
Ephraem, 21
Epicureans, 151
Eranadu, 34
Ernakulam, 225, 242
Ethiopia, 25, 117
Euergetes, 7
Europe, 41, 42, 43, 44, 49, 54, 55, 60, 70, 71, 81, 82, 83, 118, 156, 169, 186, 189, 197, 222, 223, 228
Eugene IV, Pope, 37
Euphrates, 21
European Adventurers, 126, 128
Europeans, 44, 45, 50, 56, 59, 63, 64, 70, 72, 111, 114, 117, 121, 122, 123, 127, 129, 130, 141, 144, 150, 152, 153, 154, 158, 159, 166, 170, 192, 195, 197, 218, 228
Eusebius of Caesarea, 23

Fa Hian, 204
'Fallen Adam', 215
Far East, 10
Farman, 107, 112, 130, 131
Farzana, 128, 129

Fatehpuri Sikri, 108
Ferangi, 66
Fernandez, Father, 68, 69
Feroli, S. J., 47
Fifth Veda (de Nobile), 67
Figueredo, Emmanuel de, 120
Finch, Sir Heneage, 168
Fire Ordeal, 109
Fishery Coast, 51, 53, 54, 56
Flaxman, sculptor, 160
Forbes, 180
France, 41
Franciscans, 27, 42, 43, 50, 67, 78, 116, 117, 121, 164, 238
Francks, Pietist leader, 156
Frederick IV, King, 153
Free Church of Scotland, 241
French, 127, 128
Fuller, Mr., 163

Gad, 20
Galilean, 13
Gama, Gaoparda, 237
Gama, Vasco da, 6, 37, 44-47, 50, 236
Gamaliel, 13
Ganapathy, 33
Gandhara, 2, 4
Gandhi, Mahatma, 199, 200, 201, 202, 203, 244
Ganesh, 182
Gangamula, 195
Ganges, 180
Genealogy of the Deities of Malabar, 155
Genoa, 226
Gentiles, 71
George I, King, 156
George, Archdeacon, 87-93, 98, 99, 101-103
Gerhard, John, 151
German Basel Mission, 242
Germany, 156
Ghats, 16, 209
Gita, 207, 213

INDEX

Goa, 48, 50, 51, 55-59, 61, 68, 69, 71, 77, 80-88, 90, 91, 92, 93, 97, 98, 100-104, 106, 107, 108, 110, 111, 115, 117, 120, 152, 224, 226, 236, 237, 238, 239
Goans, 117, 235, 238, 239
Golconda, 117
Gopakapuri, 236
Gopalan, 213
Gorakhpur, 123
Gore, Father, 196
Gospels, The, 12, 14, 20, 25, 107, 150, 151, 155, 156, 162, 163, 175, 176, 177, 178, 186, 187, 192, 197, 213
Goths, 12
Gouldsborough, Sir John, 169
Grant, —, 165
Grant, Charles, 162, 183
Great Britain, 187, 193, 199, 203, 219
Greece, 12
Greek, 4, 12, 13, 25, 64, 197
Gregorio, Father, 130, 134
Gregory, Bishop of Tours, 22
Gregory XIII, Pope, 71
Gregory XV, Pope, 71
Gregory XVI, Pope, 146
Guericke, 160
Gujerati, 166
Gundaphoros, 2, 19, 20, 21, 192
Gurgin Khan, 127
Guru, 68, 205, 221
Guthrie, G. D., 142
Gwalior, 131

Hall, Gordon, 187-188, 243
Hamilton, 148
Hari, 33
Hastings, Lord, 184
Hastings, Warren, 152, 170, 184
Hawkins, Captain William, 111-112
Heber, 181
Hebrew, 24

Hebrew Prophets, 171
Hebrews, 218
Henriquez, Francis, 107, 108
Henry, Cardinal, 81, 82
Heras, Father, 25, 26
Herod, 213
Herodotus, 4
High Caste Hindu Woman, 196
Hindi, 166
Hinduism, 2, 9, 11, 13, 49, 65, 70, 74, 120, 161, 179, 181, 185, 196, 204, 206-209, 210, 214, 215, 218, 220-223, 227
Hindu Kush, 21, 119
Hindu Reformation, 221
Hindus, 7, 42, 46, 48, 55, 56, 63-68, 70, 74, 78, 99, 105, 106, 118, 119, 121, 122, 152, 155, 158, 165, 172, 173, 175, 176, 179, 182, 189, 190, 191, 192, 195, 196, 197, 200, 202, 204-206, 214, 219, 220-222, 229, 234, 235, 237, 238
Hindustan, 3, 20, 127, 128, 133, 139, 140, 143, 166, 178, 185
Hindustani, 123, 172-174
Hindu women, 195
Hippaulus, 5
Holkar, Jaswant Rao, 140, 142
Hom, 219
Home of Salvation, 196
Hoogly, 165
Horace, Dr., 214
Hugli, 114, 115, 124
Huien Tsang, 204
Humayun, 105
Hyder, Ali, 159

Iberians, 66, 150
Iberian Wars, 49
Illyria, 19
Indian Elizabeth, 144
Indian independence, 203, 222, 243
Indian missionaries, 41-42
Indian Missions, 243

Indian National Congress, 222
Indian Ocean, 5, 47, 49, 55
Indian Seas, 26, 30, 33, 38, 40, 41, 75, 87, 168
Indian Union, 203
'Indian Voyager', *see* Cosmas
Indian Witness, 201
Indonesia, 6
Indo-Scythians, 20
Innocent IV, Pope, 42
Inquisition, 50, 238
Iravi Kortan, 31, 33, 34
Isa, Hazarat, 122
Islam, 9, 38, 40, 49, 75, 105, 106, 108-111, 113, 114, 116, 119, 121, 123, 168, 215, 221
Islam, Prophet of, 43, 109, 122
Isle of Dioscroris, 26
Israel, 12, 20
Isvara, 207
Italian City States, 44
Italians, 49, 66, 69
Italy, 41

Jacob Abuna, Mar, *see* Mar Jacob Abuna
Jacobite Patriarch, 228
Jacobites, 40, 228, 231
Jaffna, 57, 58
Jagannath, 180
Jainism, 2
Jains, 11, 106, 211
Jaipur, 120
Jaisingh Sawai, Rajah, 120
James, I, 111, 112
James II, 168
James of Padua, 42
Japan, 58, 59
Japanese, 59
Jats, 129, 132
Jawahar Singh, 128, 129
Jayadeva, 212
Jehangir, 109, 111, 112, 113, 114, 121, 122, 123, 130
Jerome, 19, 24, 25

Jerome, Xavier, Father, 110, 111
Jerusalem, 19
Jesuits, 21, 58, 64, 75, 79, 81, 82, 86, 102, 103, 105, 106-114, 116-124, 157, 164, 197, 224, 225, 238
Jesuits and the Great Mogul, 118
Jesuits in Malabar, 47
Jesus, 12, 14, 19, 24, 70, 93, 94, 113, 122, 151, 172, 190, 201, 203, 213, 214, 219
Jews, 11, 12, 20, 21, 69, 219
Jeziah, 119
Jhujjar, 135
Jnana Marga, 211
Joanna (Begum Samru), 130, 133, 135, 136, 137, 138, 141, 149
John, Bishop of Persia and Great India, 39
John de Britto, 73, 74
John, Friar, 42
John, King of Portugal, 53, 55
John, Mar, Bishop, 232
Johnson, Chaplain, 170
John, St., 213
Jordan, 217
Jordanus, 27, 42, 43
Joseph Beschi, Father, 74, 75, 155
Joseph, Bishop, 31
Joseph, Kariattil, 226
Joseph, Mar, *see* Mar Joseph
Judsons, 187
Julius Scotti, 146, 147
Juma Musjid, 114
Jumna, 131, 132, 139
Jupiter, 34
Jus Patronable, 225

Kabir, 212
Kaduthurithi, 90, 232
Kalady, 206
Kali, 17, 18, 47
Kaliankavu, 15
Kalli, 15
Kalliana, 26
Kalma, 119

Kalyan, 26
Kalyana, 6
Kanabadi Vathiar, poet, 155
Kanpur, 174
Kansa, King, 213
Kashmir, 1
Kassim, Mir, 127, 128
Kathiawar, 221
Kaveri, river, 6
Kaveripatanam, 6
Kerala, 3, 8, 18
Keralaputra, 9
Keshub Chandra Sen, 215, 216, 218, 219, 220, 222
Khirwa, 135
Khorasan, 205
Khyber, 1, 5
Kidderpore, 165
Kiernander, 161, 170
Kodungalloor, 34
Konkan, 6, 25, 26
Konkani, 239
Koran, 214
Kottayam, 225
Kotwal, 46, 47
Kozhikkod, 38
Krishna Chandra Pal, 166
Krishna, Hindu God, 212, 213, 219
Krishna Mohan Banerjee, Babu, 190, 191
Krishna, river, 3
Kshatriyas, 8
Kudumi, 65, 68, 70, 71
Kulins, 192
Kumarappa, J. C., 201
Kurbana, Mass, 230
Kushans, 1

Labour Government, 202
Lahore, 110, 111, 122
Lake, Lord, 142, 145, 146
Land of the Five Rivers, 2
Land of the Perumals, 14
Land of the Rising Sun, 57, 58
Latin, 80, 91, 197

Latin rite, 43, 78, 80
Lavassoult, 133-135, 137, 138
Lawrence, Sir John, 216
Lazarus, Dr. H. M., 198
Legend of the Sagacious Ape, 113-114
Legios, 135
Leo Grimon, 110
Leo X, Pope, 50
Leo XIII, Pope, 225
Life of Christ, 155
Linhares, Count, 103
Lisbon, 52, 79, 81, 82, 83, 86, 89, 226, 239
L.M.S. Mission, 73
Lollia Paulina, 6
London, 23
London Mission, 176
London Missionary Society, 241
London Times, 194
Loyola, Ignatius, 55
Lucknow, 201, 202
Lutaf Ali Khan, 128
Luther, 150-151
Lutherans, 243
Luther of Hinduism, 221

Ma'bar, 27
Macaulay, Col. 229
Macaulay, Lord, 188
Maclagan, 118
Madhava, 212
Madras, 157, 158, 159, 160, 162, 179, 226, 241
Madura, 3, 7, 52, 65, 66, 67, 68, 70
Madura Mission, 63, 71-75
Magadha, 1
Mahabharata, 205
Mahadevar Patanam, 31, 34, 232
Maharashtra, 196, 212, 221
Maharathas, 121, 126, 133, 139, 140, 141, 142, 193
Mahatma Gandhi, *see* Gandhi
Mahmud of Ghazni, 3

INDEX

Malabar, 5-10, 12, 14, 16, 17, 18, 20, 24, 25, 30, 31, 32, 33, 35, 37, 38, 41, 42, 44, 45, 46, 47, 51, 73, 75, 76, 78-84, 87, 88, 89, 97, 98, 99, 100, 103, 155, 209, 224, 226, 227, 228, 230, 236, 242
Malabar Christians, 14-16, 18, 20, 29, 31, 32, 33, 40, 41
Malabar Church, 29, 30, 33, 39, 40, 41, 77, 81, 82, 83, 84, 85, 96, 100, 226
Malabarik Dictionary, 155
Malabathrum, 6
Malacca, 50
Malayalm, 6, 17, 31, 40, 46, 91, 93, 166, 226, 231
Malayalam liturgy, 231
Malayattoor, 18
Malda, 162, 164, 165
Maldive Islands, 26, 41
Male, 26
Maliakkel Thomas, *see* Thomas Maliakkel
Malpan, 226
Mammon, 168
Manar, 57, 58
Mangalore, 6, 235
Mangaloreans, 235
Manichees, 206
Manigramakkar, 209
Manigramam, 33, 34
Manikka Vasagar, 209, 210
Man of Sorrows, 202
Manucci, 113
Manzur Ali, 131, 132
Mar Abraham, 82-88, 90, 92, 94, 103
Marathi, 166
Marchand, M., 130
Mariamma, 47
Mar Iso, 31
Mar Jacob Abuna, 78, 79
Mar Joseph, Bishop, 79-84, 88, 90
Marsh, 179, 180
Marshman, Joshua, 165
Martanda Varma, 227
Mar Thoma, 17, 18, 31

Mar Thoma I, 104, 224
Mar Thoma, Bishop, 226, 228
Mar Thomaites, 231
Mar Thoma Syrian Church, 243
Mar Thoma Syrians, 231
Martinus, Kwaja, 123
Martyn, Henry, 171-176, 197, 243
Maruvan Sapor Iso, 35
Massachusetts, 186
Matheus de Castro Melo, Dom, 117, 123
Mattanchery, 104
Matthai, Dr. John, 244
Matthew, St., 24, 25
Mauritius, 187
Mauryan, 1
Mavelikkara, 231
Maya, 210
Mecca, 9, 55, 237
Medical Missions, 198
Mediterranean, 2, 4, 5, 12, 30, 41, 45
Medlycot, 22
Meerut, 145, 147
Memoir of Lake, 145
Menezies, 40, 43, 86-93, 96, 98-103
Messiah, 12, 20
Methodist Church, 242, 243
Metran, 226, 228, 230
Middleton, Bishop, 181, 183
Mihiragula, 3
Mills, Manuel, 186
Mira, 212
Miriam, 124
Mlecchhas, 7
Mogor Mission, 107, 108, 110, 116, 117, 118, 120, 121
Mogul, 21, 87, 105, 107, 108, 110, 114, 115, 116, 118, 121, 122, 124, 126, 127, 129, 130, 131, 150, 193
Moluccas, 58
Mongols, 105
Monism, 210, 211, 222
Monophysites, 39, 40
Monte Corvino, 42
Montgomery, Sir Henry, 179, 183
Moors, 49, 80, 168
Moravian brotherhood, 167

INDEX

Muezzin, 122
Muhammad, Prophet, 117, 176, 214
Mukti, 207
Mullahs, 106, 109
Multan, 122
Mumtaz, Empress, 115
Munro, Col. 229, 230
Musiri, 6, 7
Musiris, 6, 7, 10, 11, 12, 20, 29, 31, 32, 33
Muslim League, 203
Muslims, 9, 28, 33, 38, 40, 44, 45, 48, 51-56, 73, 98, 106, 107, 116, 120, 121, 122, 158, 173, 174, 175, 176, 182, 190, 192, 195, 197, 200, 202, 219, 235, 236, 237, 238
Mutiny, Indian, 192, 198, 199
Mutiny of Paravars, 52
Muttra, 120
Muyiri Kotta, 6
Muzzaffarnagar, 129
Mylapore, 9, 17, 18, 21, 23, 42, 45, 51, 72, 103
Mysore, 126, 159

Naboab, 168, 169, 177, 179, 180, 182, 192
Nadir Shah, 121
Nagpur, 119, 240
Najaf Khan, 129
Nakshatra, 34
Nalikas, 18
Nambudiris, 8-10, 14, 207, 234, 235
Nanak, 212
Napean, Sir Evans, 187, 188
Narayan Sheshadari, 191
Narbadda, 6
Nasik, 188
National Christian Conference, 241
National Christian Council, 240, 243
National Movement, 202
Nautch, 183, 184
Navarre, 54
Nawab of Carnatic, 158
Nayacker, 52
Nayars, 8, 9, 35, 36, 37

Nazrani, 30, 33
Necho, Pharaoh, 44
Negapatam, 154, 158
Nelcynda, 6
Nepal, 119
Nestorians, 39, 40, 77, 78, 86, 93, 95
New Dispensation Samaj, 218, 219, 220
Newells, 187
New Testament, 155, 162, 174
Newton, John, 168
Nicene Council, 39
Nicolas IV, Pope, 42
Niranam, 16
Nirguna Brahmam, 207
Nirkunram, 6
Nobili, Robert de, 63-69, 70, 71, 72, 73, 74, 192, 197, 243
Nordists, 231-233
Norman, Lt., 194
Northamptonshire, 163
North India, 2, 4
North Tamil Council, 242
Notts, Mr. & Mrs., 187
Nurjehan, Empress, 114

Ochterlony, Lt. Col., 139, 142
Odunadu, authorities of, 34
Okla, 124
Omar, 97
Ooriya, 166
Order of Redemption of Captives, 50
Order of St. Basil, 80
Order of St. Paul, 107
Orient, 187
Orissa, 166
Ormuz, 42, 87
Owen, Chaplain, 170

Pacific, 49
Padroado, 50, 79, 225, 242
Pagans, 155
Pakalomattam family, 15, 39, 78, 88

INDEX

Pakistan, 203
Palestine, 219
Palur, 14, 15, 16, 99, 227
Panam, 52
Panchamas, 9
Pandyan, 3, 6, 7, 16, 29, 37, 51, 54, 56
Panipat, 105
Panniyur, 34
Pantaenus, 23, 34, 25
Parangi, 46, 48, 49, 63, 64, 66, 68, 69, 71, 77, 99, 192, 238
Parasurama, 8, 10, 236
Paravars, 51-54, 56, 57, 58, 63, 64, 68, 69
Pariah, 157
Paris, 57
Paris University, 55
Parsi, 191, 192, 195
Parsiman, 97
Parthia, 2, 12, 20, 25
Parthians, 12, 20
Parur, 16, 36
Pauli, 130
Paul, St. 13, 19
Pauranic, 221
Pazhayacoor Syrians, 226, 228, 229
Peacock Throne, 114
Pearse, 145
Pegu, 45
Peking, 13, 42
Pereira, Iago, 59
Pereira, Father Julian, 106
Persia, 20, 26, 38, 40, 41, 105, 121, 122, 174, 205, 213
Persian, 113, 122, 173, 174
Persian Gulf, 5, 30, 38
Persians, 7, 10
Perumal, 8, 10, 11, 14, 16, 29, 30, 31, 32, 33, 35, 37, 38, 227
Perum Chetty, 31
Perumalil, Father, 25, 26, 27
Peter of Siena, 42
Peter, St., 19, 92, 94, 99
Peton, 144
Petronius, 6
Pharisees, 14

Phillip III, King, 112
Philostorgius, 26
Philoxenus, Mar, 230
Pinheiro, Emmanuel, 110
Pires, Dominic, 107
Pisces, 34
Plassey, battle of, 185
Pliny, 5, 6, 25
Plutschau, Heinrich, 153
Polo, Marco, 27, 28, 204
Polymius, 26, 27
Ponnani Taluk, 14
Poona, 196
Port Trust, Bombay, 239
Portugal, 37, 44, 52, 53, 54, 74, 75, 78, 79, 88, 90, 98, 100, 117, 120, 225, 226, 237
Portuguese, 15, 23, 27, 28, 31, 35, 38, 39, 41, 44-54, 56, 57, 58, 63, 64, 68, 69, 75-92, 95, 96, 98, 99, 101, 102, 103, 104, 106, 107, 111, 113, 114, 115, 117, 150, 152, 168, 170, 176, 182, 224, 225, 230, 231, 234, 235, 236, 237, 238, 239, 242
Poulose, Bishop Mar, 18
Prarthana Samaj, 220-221
Presbyterian Alliance, 241
Presbyterian Confederation, 241
Presbyterians, 241, 242
Prestor John, 45
Prince of Peace, 201
Protestant Missions, 150, 153, 157, 229
Protestants, 151, 152, 154, 155, 156, 157, 161, 169, 185, 228, 229, 231
Puhar, 6
Pulomavi, 27
Punjab, 1, 3, 21, 185, 212, 222
Puranas, 27, 221
Purdah, 144, 235
Puthencoor Syrians, 226, 228, 229, 230, 231

Qadir, Ghulam, 131, 132
Quilon, 16, 35, 43, 150, 187, 232

INDEX

Rajahs, 69, 154
Rajputs, 106, 131, 144
Rama, 212
Ramabai, Pandita, 195, 196
Ramakrishna Mission, 222
Ramananda, 212, 221
Ramanuja, 212
Ramayana, 205
Ram Mohan Roy, Rajah, 188, 214, 215, 222
Ramnad, 3, 74
Ranade, Mahadev Gobind, 221
Rani of Travancore, 229
Ranjit Singh, 141, 142, 145
Ravi Kartan, Lord Sun, 31, 33
Red Sea, 5, 7
Rebeiro, Estevao, 110
Reinhardt, Louis Balthazaar, 130
Reinhardt, Walter, 127, 128, 129, 130
Restoration, 176
Resurrection, 14
Revelation, 218
Revolt of Coonen Cross, 104
Rice, Mr., 187
Rishi, 68
Robinson, William, 73
Roe, Sir Thomas, 112, 113
Rohilas, 130, 131, 132
Rohini, 34
Roman Brahmin, 63, 66, 67, 68, 74, 155, 157
Roman Martyrology, 41
Romans, 4, 7, 11, 12, 13, 25
Roman script, 239
Rome, 5, 7, 12, 19, 23, 39, 40, 41, 65, 69, 71, 79, 81, 82, 83, 84, 85, 86, 87, 93, 94, 102, 117, 118, 120, 123, 150, 224, 226, 229
Round Table Conference, 203
Royal James and Mary, 168
Roz, Francis, 85, 88, 100, 101, 102
Rufinus, 25
Rumbold, Sir Thomas, 159
Ryland, Mr., 151, 163

Saa, Joao de, 47
Sabat, 173, 174
Saddharana Samaj, 220
Sadhu, 15, 16, 26, 65, 71, 72
Saharanpur, 131, 142
Saka era, 2
Sakas, 1, 2
Saldana, 235
Salim Prince, 111
Salsette, 42
Salur, M., 136, 138
Salvation Army, 194
Sambhar, 123
Samoothiri, 38
Samru, Begum, 126, 130–148, see Joanna
Samru, Dyce, 138, 146, 147, 148, 149
Samru, Reinhardt, 127-129
Sanatanists, 222
Sancian, 59
Sancta Maria, 47
Sankara, 206, 207, 208, 210, 211
Sankarapuri, 15
Sanskrit, 65, 166, 188, 189, 197
Santos Chapel, 123
Sanyasi, 65, 69, 74, 209, 221
Sapakkad, 15
Saracens, 27
Sarda Sadan, 196
Sardhana, 126, 129, 130, 132-137, 139, 140, 142-143, 145-149
Sari, 235, 239
Sastras, 208, 214
Sastri, Pandit, Sevanath, 220
Satgaon, 115
Sati, 180, 196
Satyartha Prakash, 221
Saugar, 116, 180
Saviour, 15, 30, 72, 155, 172
Schwartz, 158-162, 165, 197
Scindia, 131, 132, 133, 137, 139
Scotch mission, 241
Scotland, 186, 192, 241
Scribes, 14
Scurry, James, 235
Scudder, Dr. Miss, 198
Scythian nomads, 1

INDEX

Serampore, 165, 166, 167, 174, 187
Serampore Mission, 162, 166, 167
Serfojee, 160, 161
Seringapatam, 159
Sermon on the Mount, 151-152, 190, 200
Serra, 83, 84, 86, 88, 89, 90, 92, 102, 206, 227, 233
Seven Seas, 44
Severus, S., 41
Shah Alam, 129, 131
Shah Jehan, 114, 115, 116, 118, 123, 127, 130
Shah Nizamuddin, 131
Shaivism, 208, 209, 210, 211, 212
Shakir Shah, Saint, 147
Shanars, 36
Shiva, 27, 208
Shivaji, 121
Shripat, 191
Sighlem, Bishop of Shireburn, 23
Sikander, Mirza, 122, 123
Sikhism, 212
Sikhs, 126, 132, 133, 134, 138, 141, 142, 185, 192, 203
Simhala, Ceylon, 32
Sind, 21
Singhalese, 69
Skinner, Col., 133
Smith, Rev. Sydney, 178
Smith, William, 180
Society of Jesus, 55, 62, 64, 155
Society of Wayfarers for Christ, 42
Socotra, 26
Soigram, 34
Sombre, Begum, 149
Son of Man, 172
Southampton, 216
South Canara, 235
Southern Ocean, 3
South India, 2, 3, 7, 13, 16, 18, 20, 24, 51, 66, 71-74, 79, 155, 209, 227, 233, 241, 242
South Indian Synod, 242
South Indian United Church, 242
Spain, 44, 112, 114
Spaniards, 50, 150

S.P.C.K., 156
Srinivas, 196
Statement of Christian, Jewish, and Pagan Religions, 155
Sthanu Ravi Gupta, 35
St. John's College, 171
Stoics, 24
St. Thomas Christians, *see* Christians, St. Thomas
Stuart, Col., 138
Suddhi, 222
Sudists, 232, 233
Sudras, 8, 63
'Sultan of Mecca', 106
Sunderbans, 164
Surat, 42, 111, 108, 168
Swami Narayana, 212
Synod of Diamper, 97, 230
Syria, 2, 5, 33, 38, 232
Syriac, 91
Syriac, St. 99, 100
Syrian Catholics, 97, 224, 225, 226
Syrian Christians, 33, 36-39, 45, 49, 57, 63, 76, 77, 82, 84, 99, 206, 224, 226, 228, 234, 235, 238
Syrian liturgy, 30, 33
Syrian rite, 30, 47, 77, 97, 242
Syrians, 10, 30, 31, 33, 37, 40, 43, 45, 48, 75, 76, 77, 78, 79, 81-91, 96-98, 100-104, 209, 224, 225, 227, 228, 230-234, 239
Syro-Chaldean liturgy, 39

Tagore, Devendranath, 215, 216
Taj Mahal, 114, 118
Tamil, 6, 7, 16, 18, 47, 65, 66, 72, 73, 74, 75, 153, 155, 158, 209, 227
Tamil-German Dictionary, 155
Tandolini, sculptor, 149
Tanjore, 158, 159
Taprobane, 26
Tavares, 115
Telegu, 166
Terry, Chaplain, 113
Thali, 234
Thana, 42, 43

INDEX

Theism, 207, 210
Theodore Beza, 151
Theophilus, the Indian, 26, 41
Thoma, Parammakkel, 226
Thomas, Apostle, 2, 8, 9, 11-25, 27-30, 42, 72, 73, 78, 92, 94, 95, 96, 99, 103, 224, 242
Thomas, Archdeacon, 104
Thomas de Campos, 103
Thomas, Dr. John, 162-166
Thomas, Emperor of the Indies, 38
Thomas, George, Irish Adventurer, 130, 133, 134, 135, 136, 137, 138
Thomas, Maliakkel, 17
Thomas of Canaan, see Canai Thoma
Thomas of Tolentino, 42
Tibet, 124
Tibetan Mission, 147
Timoja, 237
Timur, 105
Tindis, 6
Tinnevelly, 162
Tippu, 3, 72, 73, 75, 179, 227, 228, 233, 235
Tiru Mular, 208
Tiruvalla, 243
Tiruvanchikkulam, 6, 31
Titus, 19
Tokat, 174
Tranquebar, 153-158, 161, 162, 171
Travancore, 18, 30, 38, 56, 57, 225, 227, 228, 229, 231, 233
Trichinopoly, 75, 158, 162
Trichur, 225
Trivandrum, 242
Tucker, Maj., 194
Tukaram, 212
Tulasi Das, 212
Turkey, 122
Turks, 42, 44, 237
Tuticorin, 51
Twining, Mr., 177, 178
Two Apostles of India, 25

Udayamperoor, 93
Udney, 164, 165

Ujjain, 2, 108, 120
Ulterior India, 25
Umboor, 168
Unapproachables, 9, 10
Union, 171
United Church of South India, 241
United Kingdom, 176, 200
United Missions of India, 166
Unlookables, 9, 10
Upanishads, 211, 215
Uraha, 30
Urfah, 21

Vaipicotta Seminary, 85, 88, 91
Vaishnavas, 211, 212, 221
Valerian Gracias, Cardinal, 243
Valiar Vattam, 37, 38, 45
Valignani, Father, 86
Vallabha, 212
Valluavanadu, 34
Vedalai, 51, 54
Vedas, 10, 68, 208, 211, 221
Vega, Christovel de, 110
Vellore Mutiny, 179
Vellore, Nawab of, 75, 198
Venadu, 34
Verapoly, 225
Victoria, Queen, 193, 194
Vico, Father, 65
Vienne, 41
Vindhyas, 3
Vira Kerala Chakravartin, 34
Vira Raghava Perumal, 33, 34
Virgin Mary, 46
Vishishta Advaita, 211, 221
Vishnu, 181, 210, 211, 212
Vivekananda, Swami, 222

Wantage Sisters, 196
Ward, William, 65
War of Jenkin's Ear, 51
Wellesly, Lord, 138, 139, 142, 165, 167

Wendt, 157
Western Asia, 38, 39, 40, 48, 87, 228
Western Ghats, 8
Western India, 2, 212
Whitbread, 180
White Country, 205
Wilberforce, 180
Wilson, Bishop, 231
Wilson, Dr., 214
Wilson, John, 191
Women and Marriage in India, 195
World Church, 242

Xavier, St. Francis, 44, 54-63, 78, 110, 164, 197, 243

Yadava, a teacher, 211
Y.M.C.A., 243
Yoga, 215, 223
Yogi, 66, 209

Zafar Yab Khan, 130, 135, 136, 137, 138
Zamindar family, 119
Zamorin, 38, 44-46, 52, 54, 99
Zanzalow, Jacobus, 40
Zebunissa, 126, 132, 149
Zenana, 132
Ziegenbalg, 153-158, 161, 164
Zophanay, painter, 144
Zoroaster, 214
Zoroastrians, 106
Zulqarnain, Mirza, 116, 118, 122, 123